picture wsu

picture wsu

Images from Washington State University

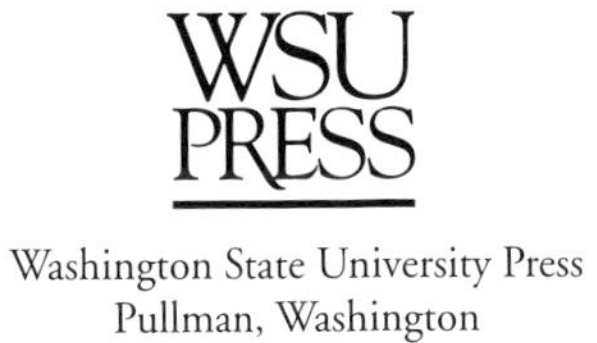

Washington State University Press
Pullman, Washington

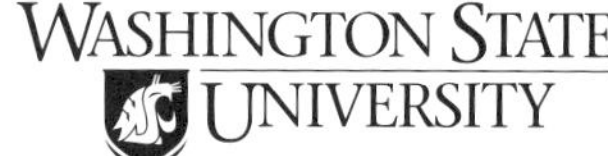

Washington State University Press
PO Box 645910
Pullman, Washington 99164-5910
Phone: 800-354-7360
Fax: 509-335-8568
E-mail: wsupress@wsu.edu
Web site: wsupress.wsu.edu

Library of Congress Cataloging-in-Publication Data

Picture WSU : Images from Washington State University.
   p. cm.
  ISBN 0-87422-287-7 (alk. paper)
  1. Washington State University--Pictorial works. I. Washington State University. Press.
LD5731.W633P53 2006
378.797'39--dc22
2006006557

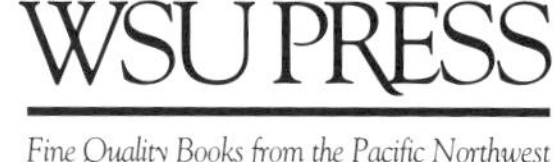

Fine Quality Books from the Pacific Northwest

To Cougars—

Past, present, and future

Foreword

ashington State University is a place known to engender lifelong connections with those who study, live, and work here. The main campus, nestled in the Palouse Hills of Pullman, Washington, reflects the tranquil farmland and natural beauty of the area, while three regional campuses embrace more urban settings in Spokane, the Tri-Cities, and Vancouver. The blending of a strong liberal arts tradition within a nationally recognized research university provides a unique balance of science, culture, and quality of life.

WSU alumni, faculty, and staff consistently recall the values that surround their experience on campus—values they carry with them into successful careers, relationships, and community service. In return, these same individuals have left their mark on Washington State University. The caliber of their character has helped WSU become a highly regarded institution—embodying the University's innovation

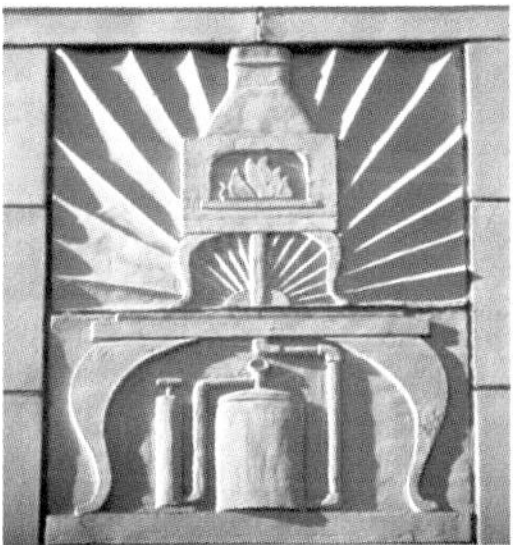

and discovery, and educating the leaders of tomorrow.

As you travel through the images within this volume, I hope you will discover these values. Those of you who have been here will immediately feel you are home. Others will experience a desire to come, to learn—and to feel the distinct significance of this place, where you learn as much about yourself as your field of study. Whether a student, educator, worker, or visitor, you will find engagement, application, leadership, diversity, stewardship, and teamwork. You will experience the dynamic environment of a nationally renowned faculty and staff engaged with today's students.

You will experience Washington State University. *World Class. Face to Face.*

Sally Savage
Vice President for University Relations
Washington State University

Fulmer Hall decorative detail.

Acknowledgments

Friends of WSU have long requested an affordable color pictorial of today's University. *Picture WSU* fulfills this wish.

It was a natural decision to develop the book in-house. WSU Press employs four alumni and enjoys a close association with the University's photographers. Because our publishing mandate focuses on the history, society, and culture of the greater Pacific Northwest region, *Picture WSU* is an especially appropriate addition to the catalog.

The Director and Editor-in-Chief selected photos with the invaluable assistance of proof editor Kerry Darnall. The Editor-in-Chief penned the captions, and together with the Director made final editorial decisions.

University photographers Shelly Hanks and Robert Hubner proved essential to the success of this volume. These extraordinary professionals constantly compile a treasure trove of images for University purposes. Bob and Shelly shot the greater majority of scenes chosen for *Picture WSU*—as clearly evident in the credits at the end of the volume.

Henry Moore, Jr., at the College of Veterinary Medicine, Jeff T. Green, Dean Hare, Chris Mather, John Snyder, and Yost Grube Hall Architecture framed other shots included here. Jeff Lawton loaned a quality image of Kamiak Butte in Whitman County.

Fine contributions from additional collections were graciously provided by the following—Rod Commons of the WSU Sports Information Office, Kathleen Hatch and Theresa MacNaughton Lehman at the Student Recreation Center, Terry Maurer of WSU Tri-Cities, Judith Van Dongen at WSU Spokane, and Joe Winton of WSU Vancouver.

Nancy Grunewald artfully designed the interior of *Picture WSU*. Other Press members due recognition include publications coordinator Jean Taylor, marketing coordinator Caryn Lawton, and Jenni Lynn of sales and order fulfillment. Staff from WSU Press's parent organization—University Publishing—likewise provided able assistance, including printing services director Steve Rigby, production manager Denise Pressnall, and cover designer Diana Whaley.

And finally, special appreciation goes to Dick Fry, author of *The Crimson and the Gray* (WSU Press, 1989), for reviewing the Introduction.

Thank you, good readers everywhere!

Mary Read, Director
University Publishing & WSU Press

Glen Lindeman, Editor-in-Chief
WSU Press

The Founding of WSU, 1890–1893

By Glen Lindeman

Washington State University's origin dates to an era when the Pacific Northwest had barely passed beyond the frontier stage. In 1890, the automobile, paved roadways, and radio lay decades in the future, though train service, telephones, and the print media were well established. Many communities were but a decade or two old. It was a time when cowboys and ranch hands, miners with pack mules, farmers in buckboard wagons, and Native American families on horseback still traveled Pullman's dusty streets.

> *A college of science and technology, shot through and through with the spirit of the liberal arts.*
> —President Enoch A. Bryan (1893–1916).

The vast majority of Washington's citizens had no more than an eighth-grade education, and few accredited high schools existed across the Northwest. A baccalaureate degree was a rarity—and almost invariably held by someone who had attended college in the East or Midwest.

Aware of their region's educational shortcomings, astute Washingtonians saw the coming of statehood as the supreme moment for rectification. Sparks of contention also arose, however, with the federal government's generous financial incentives to help build a solid infrastructure in the new state.

As Washington joined the Union on November 11, 1889, representatives from communities throughout the region raised a clamor in Olympia over which towns and cities should get state hospitals, normal schools for educating teachers, the penitentiary, and other facilities, including a new "land-grant" college.

This host of brazen advocates—including a capable Pullman contingent—buttonholed, arm-twisted, and bartered with politicians and officials in public and private meetings.[1] The institution known today as Washington State University emerged from these provocative circumstances.

The Organic Act (March 28, 1890)

As with many significant human endeavors, the new college's founding exhibited both great inspiration and colorful partisanship. On March 28, 1890, Washington's first state legislature passed a bill authorizing "a State Agricultural College and School of Science," but did not select a location for

> *No discrimination shall be made in respect to race, sex, political opinion or religious belief.*
> —The college's 1890 charter.

it. This singular prize would be a desirable plum for any community.

The proposed institution was an innovative "land-grant" college, one of a number being established with federal and state cooperation in this period, particularly in the West and Midwest. It would be a radical departure from the small, traditional, denominational colleges—then particularly common in the East—wherein the "professional" classes received a rather narrow classical education focusing on literature, philosophy, Latin, Greek, and mathematics, with a smattering of social studies, natural history, and modern subjects.

Technological research and the study of science, being new, advanced concepts in higher education, were the main focus of the college's charter. The institution would be dedicated to educating the common citizenry, eventually utilizing elective course work and a broad, modern curriculum—a prototype of the great, state-supported universities that are so familiar to Americans today.

The southeast Washington citizens who authored the enabling act originally wished to identify the college as a "School of Science," since that best described the institution's aims. Statewide agricultural interests, however, insisted on including the designation "Agricultural" in the title. This was perfectly understandable in an era when so many Washingtonians depended on farming for their livelihood. Agricultural production, of course, would especially benefit from scientific research.

The act allowed the state to acquire federal land endowments, plus annual monetary assistance, to support the proposed college. In this farsighted national program, the state received a 90,000 acre "land-grant" under the terms of the 1862 Morrill Act—i.e., 30,000 acres for each of Washington's two senators and one representative then serving in the U.S. Congress. Another 100,000 acres were granted for establishing a "school of science."

Thus the new college qualified overall for 190,000 acres (nearly 300 square miles) of U.S. government land in the state.[2] In addition, generous federal funding for "experiment stations" and scientific research would be provided by the Hatch Act (1887) and the second Morrill Act (1890).

The state legislature had adopted the legal and financial groundwork for a land-grant college, and now it was time for the school's newly appointed governing body, the Commission of Technical Instruction, to select a site for the institution—a task bound to heat up competition between communities.

Locations both east and west of the Cascade Range were eligible. Seattle already had the University of Washington (founded 1861) and essentially was out of the running, but the Elliot Bay city's chief commercial rival, Tacoma, was especially anxious to see a college located in Pierce County. Most people, however, expected an eastern Washington site to be chosen.

Governor Elisha P. Ferry appointed as commissioners E.C. Ferguson (from Snohomish), Edward Whitson (from North Yakima), and Senator Thomas Smith (from Penawawa, in the Colfax vicinity). Shortly, this Commission of Technical Instruction set out to choose a home for the college. They visited sites offered by various aspiring eastern Washington candidates—Walla Walla, North Yakima (now Yakima), Sprague, Spokane Falls (now Spokane), Pullman, Colfax, and other communities.

When sitting down to vote, however, inflexible partisanship and high stakes deadlocked the commissioners—Whitson voted for his hometown of North Yakima, while Smith selected Colfax in his political district. Snohomish's Ferguson chose Spokane, perhaps with conviction that it was the best selection. On the other hand, Ferguson might have hoped a stalemate would send the locating issue back to the legislature and reactivate chances for a western Washington site.

At loggerheads, the commission ignominiously "adjourned indefinitely" in July 1890, failing in its initial mission. Efforts to create the college ground to a halt, and could only be revived when the legislature met again eight months later.

When they reconvened, the legislators remained determined to forge ahead. In March 1891, they passed a modified act abolishing the Commission of Technical Instruction, replacing it with a five-member Board of Regents to govern the institution.

Also authorized was a three-person Board of Commissioners to select a location. The governor's appointees to the locating body—all three had to be from western Washington to avoid partisanship—included George A. Black of Fairhaven, and two of the new regents, Andrew H. Smith from Tacoma and Dr. Simon B. Conover of Port Townsend.

The amended 1891 charter—much influenced by the maneuvering of Pullman supporters in Olympia—also stipulated that communities west of the Cascades now were ineligible for consideration, as were towns in eastern Washington counties already possessing state institutions. This eliminated Spokane County with its normal school (Cheney) and mental hospital (Medical Lake), Walla Walla County with the penitentiary (Walla Walla), and Kittitas County with a normal school (Ellensburg).[3]

Competition essentially narrowed to North Yakima in Yakima County; and to Pullman and Whitman County, which was a fairly well populated area for the times. Other communities did not give up, however, and put in bids, including Pasco, Sprague, Davenport, Tekoa, Farmington,

> *WSU retains a majority of its original 190,000-acre federal land grant—these properties are spread across the state and continue to generate income for operating budgets.*

Oakesdale, Garfield, Palouse City, Colfax, and Dayton.

Selection of Pullman (April 25, 1891)

After investigating the proposed sites in early-to-mid April, the committee returned to the state capital, convening at the Olympia Hotel at 4 P.M. on April 25, 1891, to settle the issue. Pullman's offer of artesian water and the especially eligible 200-acre William Vedder property was chosen over North Yakima's bid. An abundant and dependable source of water, of course, was critical for the college's future growth into a large campus.

Thus Pullman, in Washington's richest agricultural county and with excellent rail connections to Spokane, 75 miles north, had won out over North Yakima, a newborn railroad town whose great promise of irrigation and extensive settlement lay in the future. In this era before good highways, too, the Yakima Valley community stood rather isolated from much of the state due to high ridges and mountain spurs.

Inevitably, advocates in North Yakima and other thwarted communities felt resentment over their dashed hopes. Some angry politicians, newspaper editors, and civic leaders protested vigorously, charging irregularities in the selection process and claiming that Pullman was an unfit site. North Yakima interests filed an injunction in Pierce County, which, before denial in late 1891, seriously hampered the Board of Regents in establishing the college.

Even two of the five regents disapproved—one from nearby disgruntled Colfax, J.H. Bellinger, refused to attend board meetings for more than a year, leaving business entirely in the hands of the other regents.

The College Opens (January 13, 1892)

A majority of the five-member Board of Regents quickly pushed ahead to open the campus, hoping to head off opposition attempts to have the legislature consider relocation. A small brick building—soon commonly called the "Crib," literally in regard to the institution's infancy—was hastily built with state and local community assistance on a hill overlooking Pullman. On a wintry January 13, 1892, the Agricultural College, Experiment Station and School of Science of the State of Washington opened its doors.

Forty-seven students initially appeared before the new faculty of five men and one woman. Enrollment eventually stood at 84 for the first abbreviated academic year of two terms. Most attendees were local

> *The first faculty selected in late 1891 were all from South Dakota and the Midwest—*
> *Nancy L. Van Doren (English; salary $1,500)*
> *George G. Hitchcock (Chemistry; salary $2,000)*
> *Edward R. Lake (Botany, Forestry, Horticulture; salary $2,000)*
> *Charles E. Munn (Veterinary Science; salary $2,000)*
> *John O'Brien Scobey (Agriculture; salary $2,000)*
> *President George W. Lilley (Mathematics, Physics; salary $4,000)*

residents, but some came from considerable distances in Washington to attend the state's new college.

The applicants ranged greatly in age, from 11-year-old Lula Alma Henry, to 36-year-old Levi P. Farr, a farmer. Most were in their mid to late teens. They were the daughters and sons of farmers and stockmen, and of laborers and businessmen. Two were sons of college professors. Some were life-long Washingtonians, but the majority had been born in the Midwest (and several in the East), having come to the Pacific Northwest as youths with their parents by wagon train or railroad in the late-19th-century Western Migration.

Most had attended small, rustic, public schools, which hardly could have provided them with sufficient skills required for college work. In 1892, in fact, Washington had few academies and only a trio of four-year high schools (in Seattle, Tacoma, and Spokane) to prepare youths for collegiate studies.

Consequently, most of the enrollees were relegated to a Preparatory Department, offering a curriculum somewhat equivalent to senior-year high school work. Following completion of these courses, students then could enter the college's freshman class. In

fact, the school's first graduation ceremonies were held for students completing preparatory work.[4]

The college's first years proved tumultuous, as opponents across the state retained hopes of seeing the institution fail and having it relocated. Of course, the tough tasks of providing for more facilities, organizing a growing curriculum, and maintaining legislative and political support continued after classes started.

But more serious difficulties were endemic—some regents and Olympia politicians ill-advisedly interfered with purchasing and operations, including staff and faculty hiring; personality conflicts factionalized the faculty, regents, and Pullman's citizens; the administration kept inadequate records and practiced poor fiscal management; and an unrealistic facilities construction plan was adopted.

The early college's most scandalous episode occurred in late 1892, shortly after the regents' firing of the college's first president, George W. Lilley, over competency and integrity issues. On December 21,

as Regent Andrew H. Smith guided a new president-elect, John W. Heston, to the campus for the first time, the two men were met by jeering students still loyal to their former mentor, President Lilley. Shortly, Smith and the unfortunate Heston went reeling toward downtown Pullman under a barrage of snowballs, vegetables, and eggs. This shocking incident provided fodder to the opponents' propaganda machine.

As debt spiraled and enrollment faltered, the quick letting-go of the first two presidents (December 1892 and August 1893),[5] and Governor John C. McGraw's firing of the first Board of Regents (spring 1893), were evidence of the college's early pains.[6] Nancy L. Van Doren would be the only instructor of the original six-member faculty not to resign or be fired.[7]

Enoch A. Bryan and the College's Renewal (July 22, 1893)

Washington's governor, most legislators, and many people across the state, however, remained determined to see the college succeed. Though some bitter opposition continued for several years, the prognosis turned for the better when the governor

appointed a second Board of Regents. Even more eventful, 38-year-old Enoch A. Bryan, the former head of Vincennes University in Indiana, became the college's third president on July 22, 1893.

Bryan arrived in Pullman on August 28, 1893, fully committed to the task at hand. His first impressions on that sweltering summer day, though, were far from favorable. Standing downtown, Bryan glanced up at the college to see a "gaunt" five-story brick dormitory (which would burn down in 1897) and wood-framed College Hall, sitting "very distant, very isolated, very lonesome" on a barren hill east of Pullman. Bryan little realized at the time that he was to be the true founder of Washington State University.

With his excellent administrative experience, Bryan provided the stability and sense of direction that the college had lacked. He oversaw the adoption of a semester system in the fall of 1894, and continually broadened and improved the curriculum. Through his honest and forthright dealings, Bryan developed a statewide consensus of goodwill for the college, while at the same time becoming a nationally recognized proponent and spokesman for land-grant ideals.

Though many battles lay ahead for the young college, the grandly attended dedication of the new, turreted Administration Building (now Thompson Hall) in June 1895 symbolized a vigorous new beginning for the institution. ∎

The first graduating collegiate class, 1897—
Carl Estby (Snohomish; Civil Engineering)
Emma Jane Hardwick (Pullman; Botany)
Jessie Eugenia Hungate (Pullman; English)
Mary Corinne Johnson (Pullman; English)
Edward Kimmel (Waitsburg; Economic Science and History)
George Nixon (Harrisburg, Oregon; Electrical Engineering)
Orin Hector Stratton (Pullman; Civil Engineering)

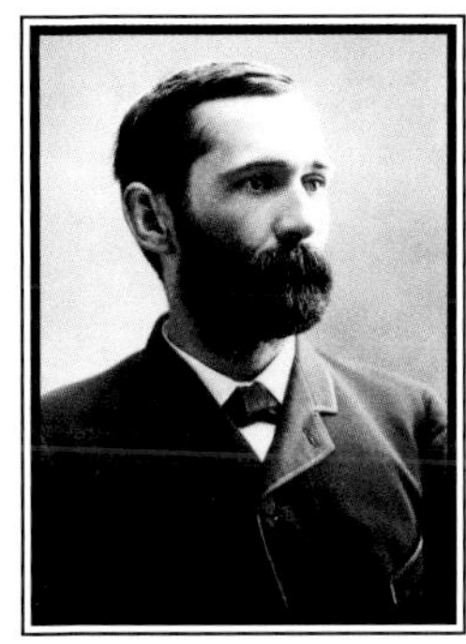

Enoch A. Bryan in 1893.

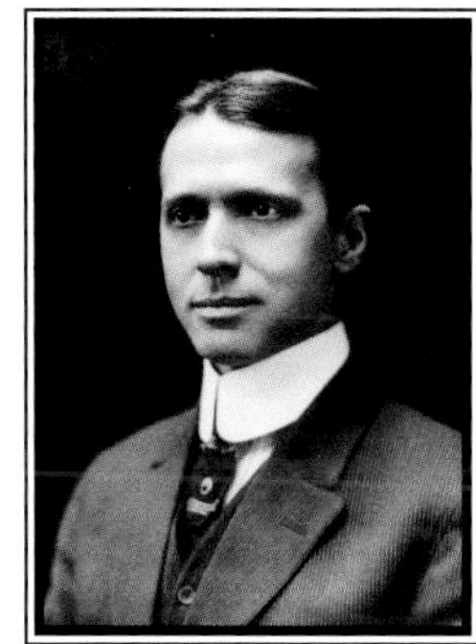

Ernest O. Holland in 1916.

Notes

1. Similar vibrant outbursts, of course, were common all across the West when other states entered the Union.

2. A college in each state was eligible to receive a federal "land-grant" under the terms of the Morrill Act. WSU, however, was not the first college in Washington to receive a public land endowment. The University of Washington, founded in 1861, had accepted a federal grant of 46,000 acres under the terms of the eminent Ordinance of 1787. This property had to be quickly sold and traded to get the Seattle institution established, which almost served for naught—the University of Washington mostly floundered in bankruptcy and disinterest for three decades, and had remained quite small in size, until moved to a new site in 1895 when a revitalized second beginning was instituted after Washington statehood.

3. In this period, the Washington legislature also granted 100,000 acres of "state" land to the University of Washington, and provided the normal colleges at Cheney and Ellensburg (both founded in 1890) and Bellingham (established 1893) with other state acreage.

4. Across the West and Midwest in this era, preparatory departments were common in most collegiate curriculums. Normally, enrollees had to be at least fourteen years of age. As Washington's four-year high schools increased in number, incoming students at WSC no longer needed preparatory work by the early 1910s.

5. George W. Lilley remained in Pullman for a time, which fomented discourse in the community. Soon, he and a fired faculty member bought an Olympia newspaper to challenge their critics. Lilley eventually taught mathematics at the University of Oregon, until his death in 1904. John W. Heston, a Seattle high school principal before coming to Pullman, would later serve as president of the South Dakota Agricultural College (1896–1903) and the Eastern State Normal School at Madison, South Dakota (1905–1920).

6. Such difficulties were common at other new state-supported colleges as well, including the nearby University of Idaho in Moscow.

7. Her tenure proved long and distinguished, and the naming of Van Doren Hall (1908) acknowledged her successful career at the college.

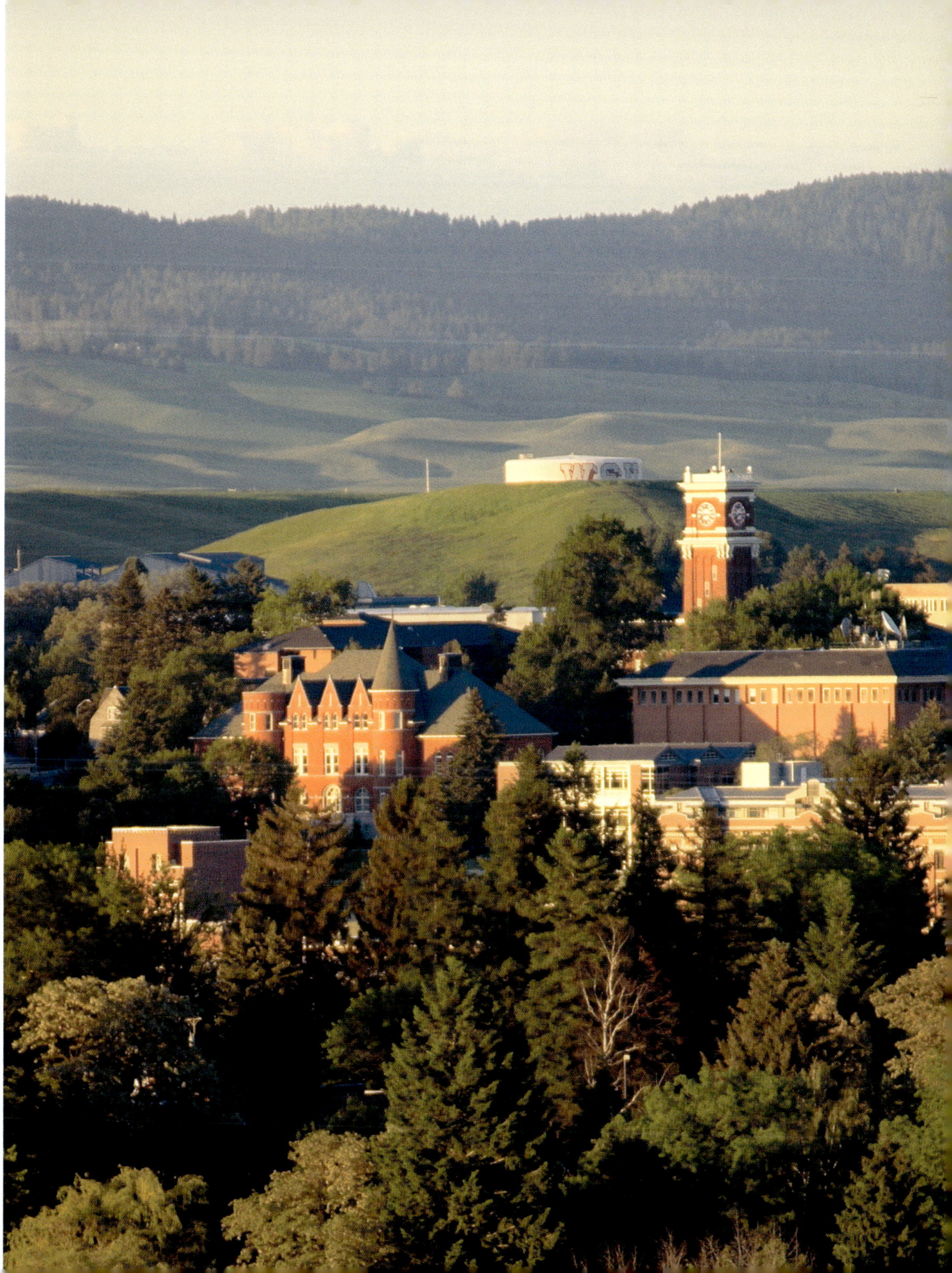

Early summer view of the Pullman campus with Idaho's Palouse Range on the horizon.

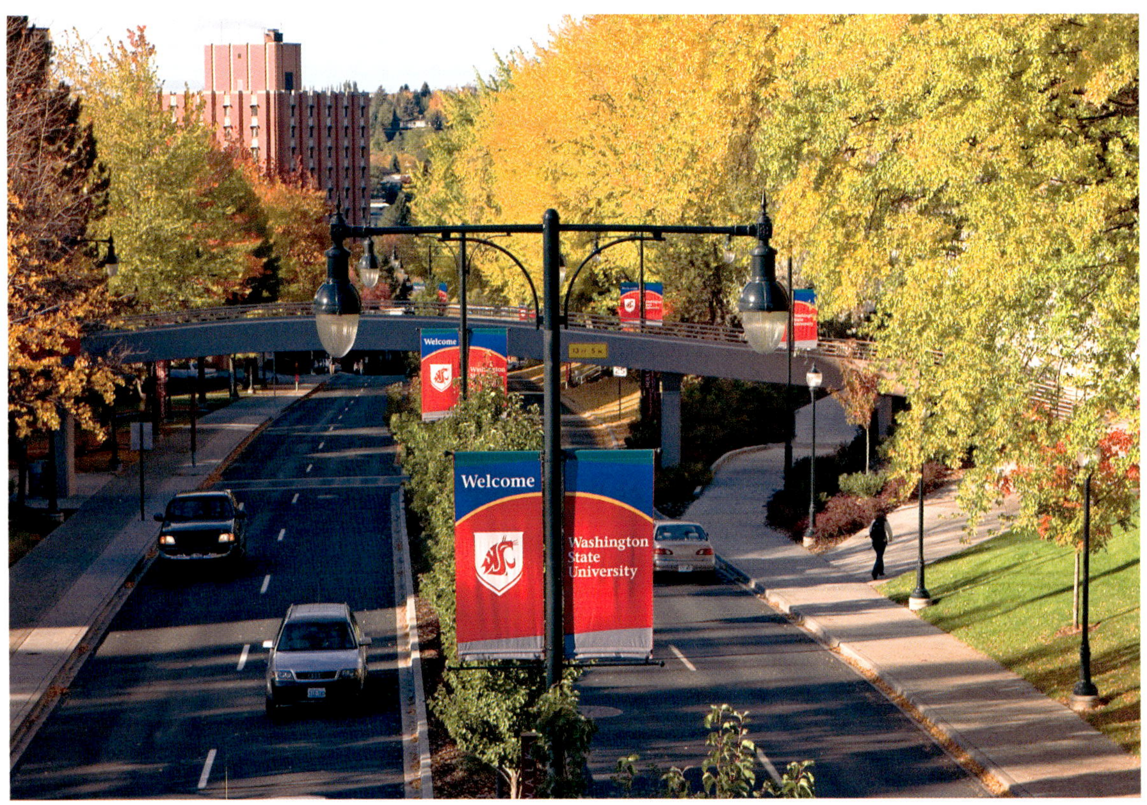

Welcoming banners line Stadium Way,
the two-mile-long campus thoroughfare.

Bryan Tower is the beacon
of the campus community
and the Palouse.

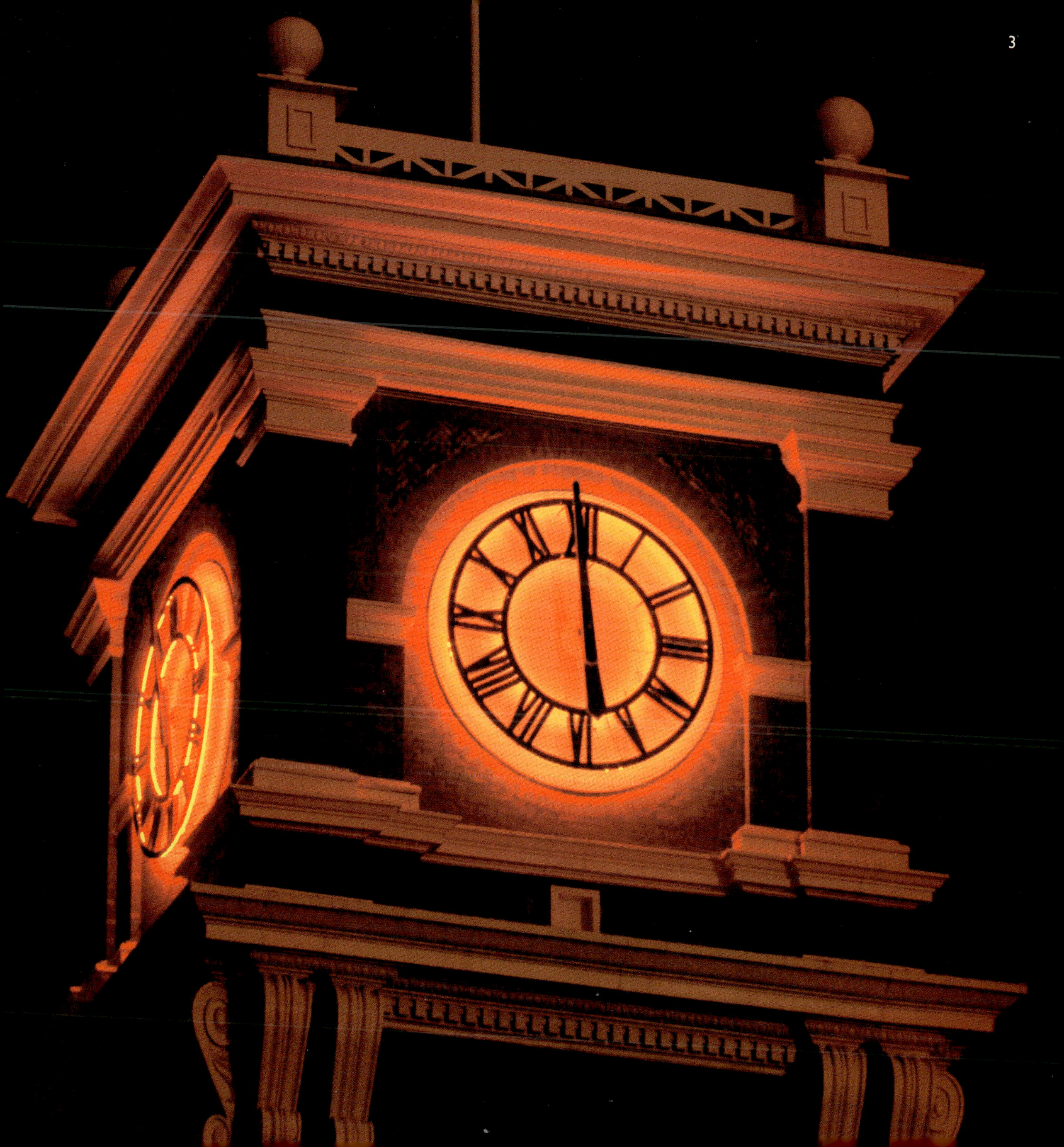

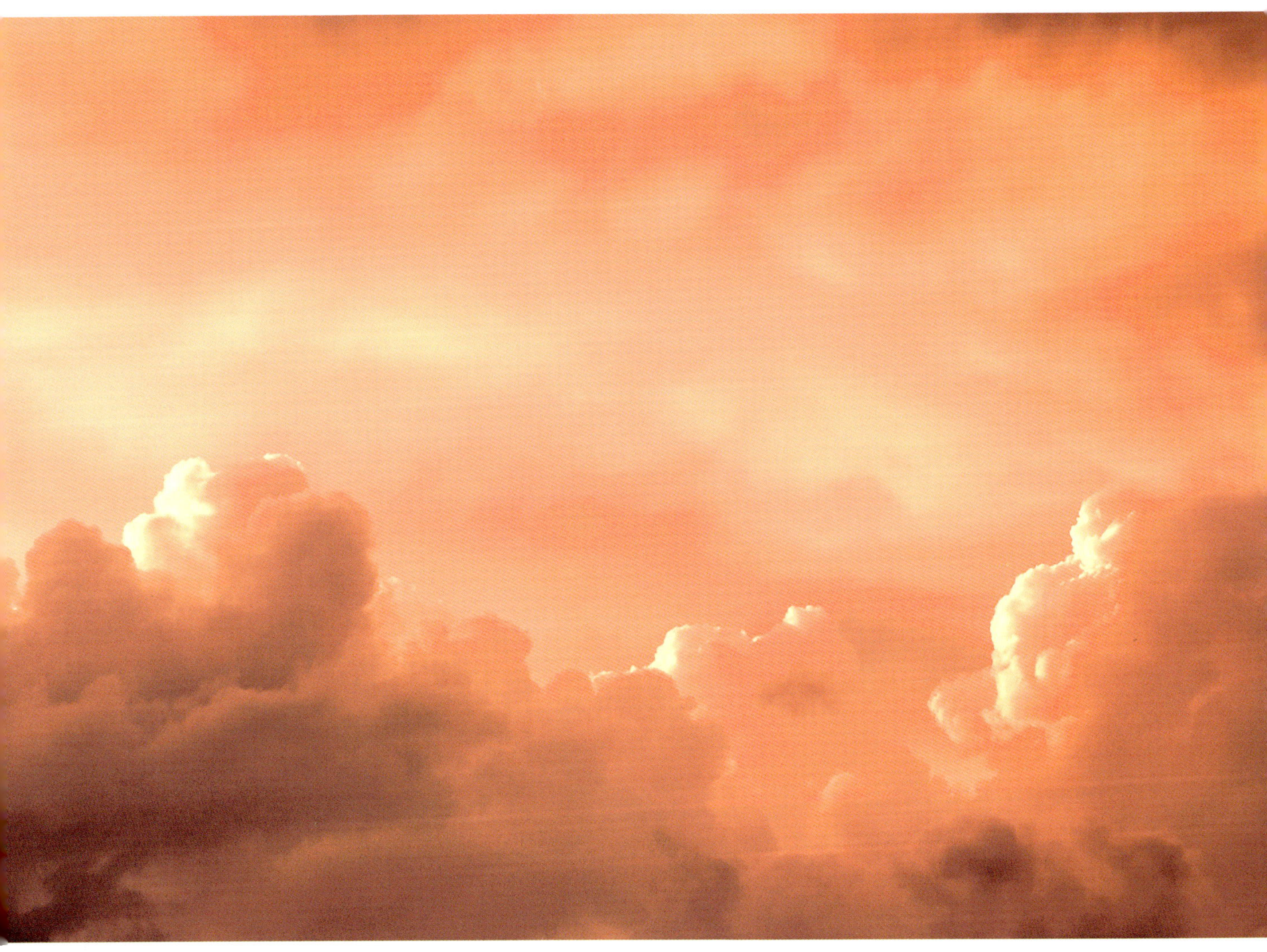

Spectacular sunsets are
frequent during long stretches
of sunny weather.

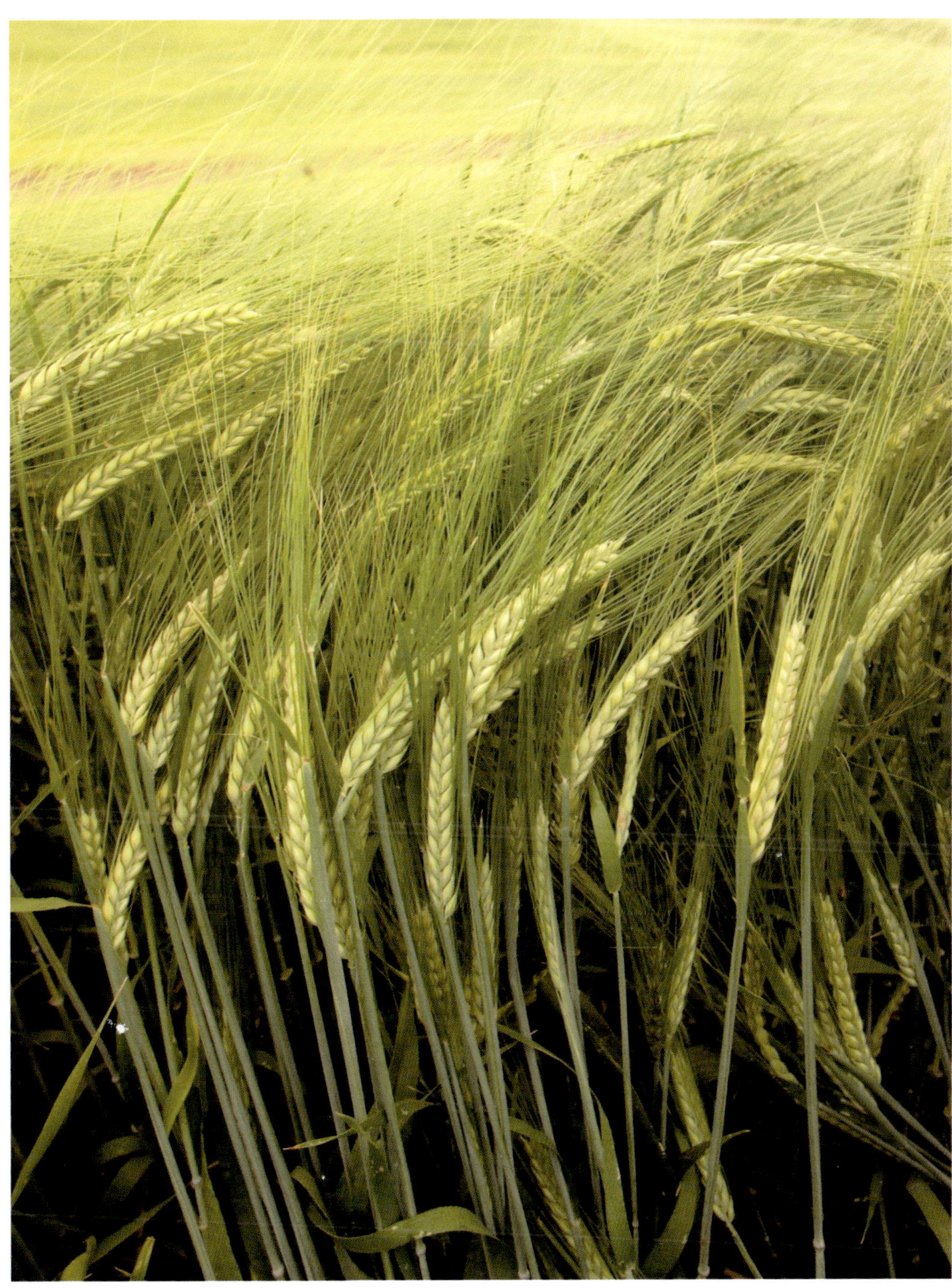

Wheat stalks bend rhythmically in the wind—waves across a sea of grain.

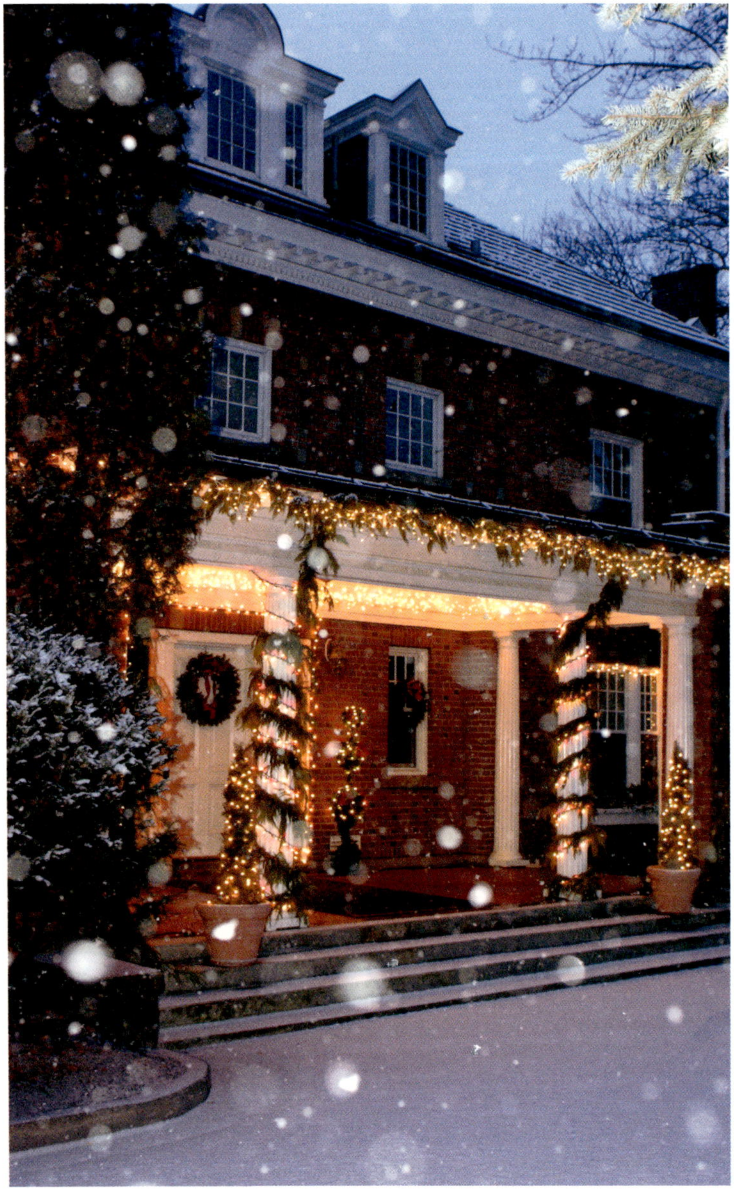

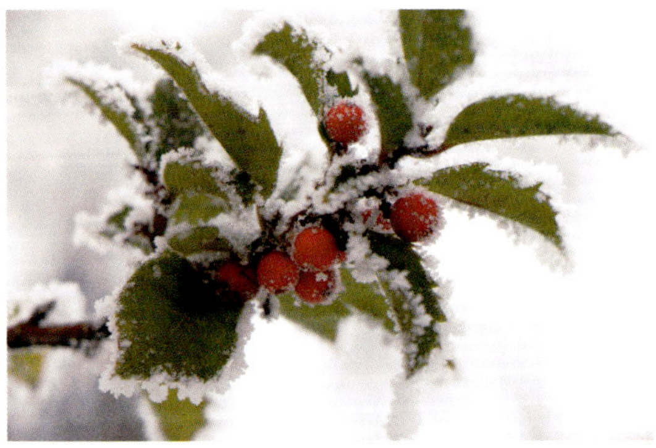

Winter holiday season at the
President's Residence.

Walkways in front of the French Administration Building are busy all hours of the day. The name of the University's administrative center commemorates C. Clement French, WSU's sixth president (1952–66).

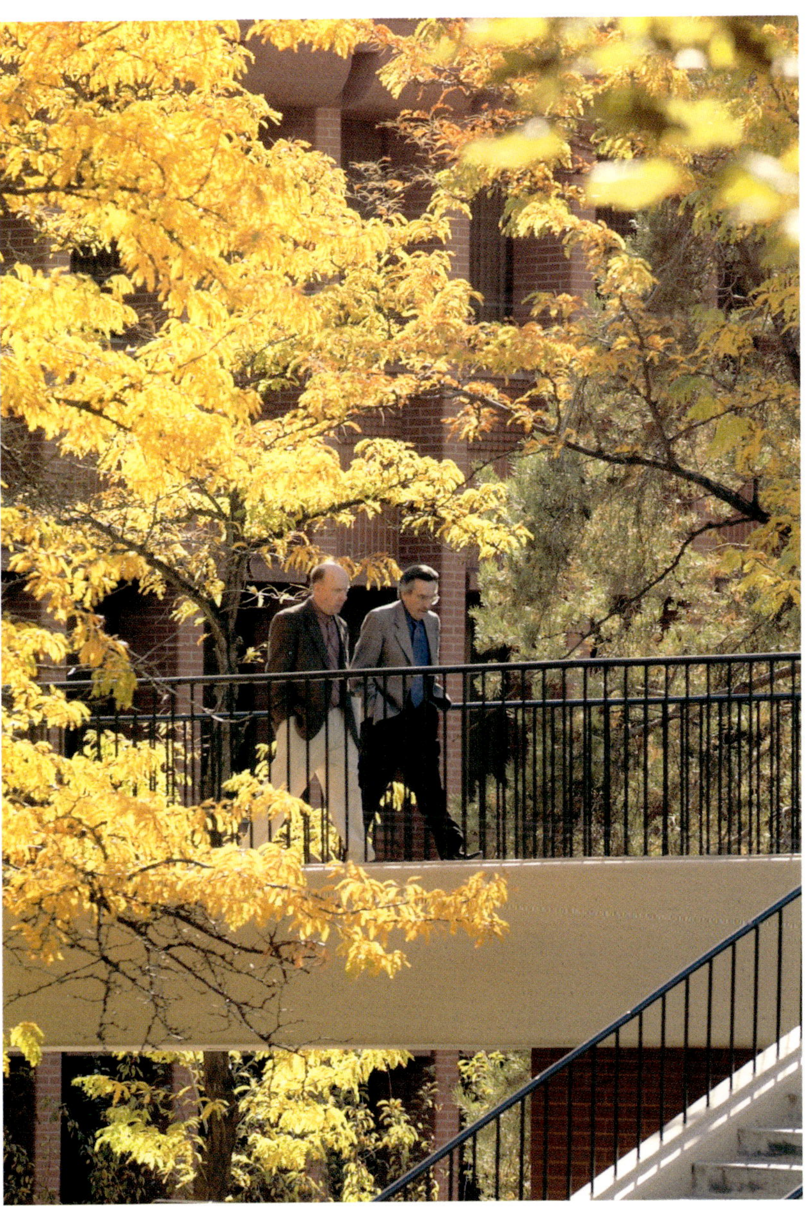

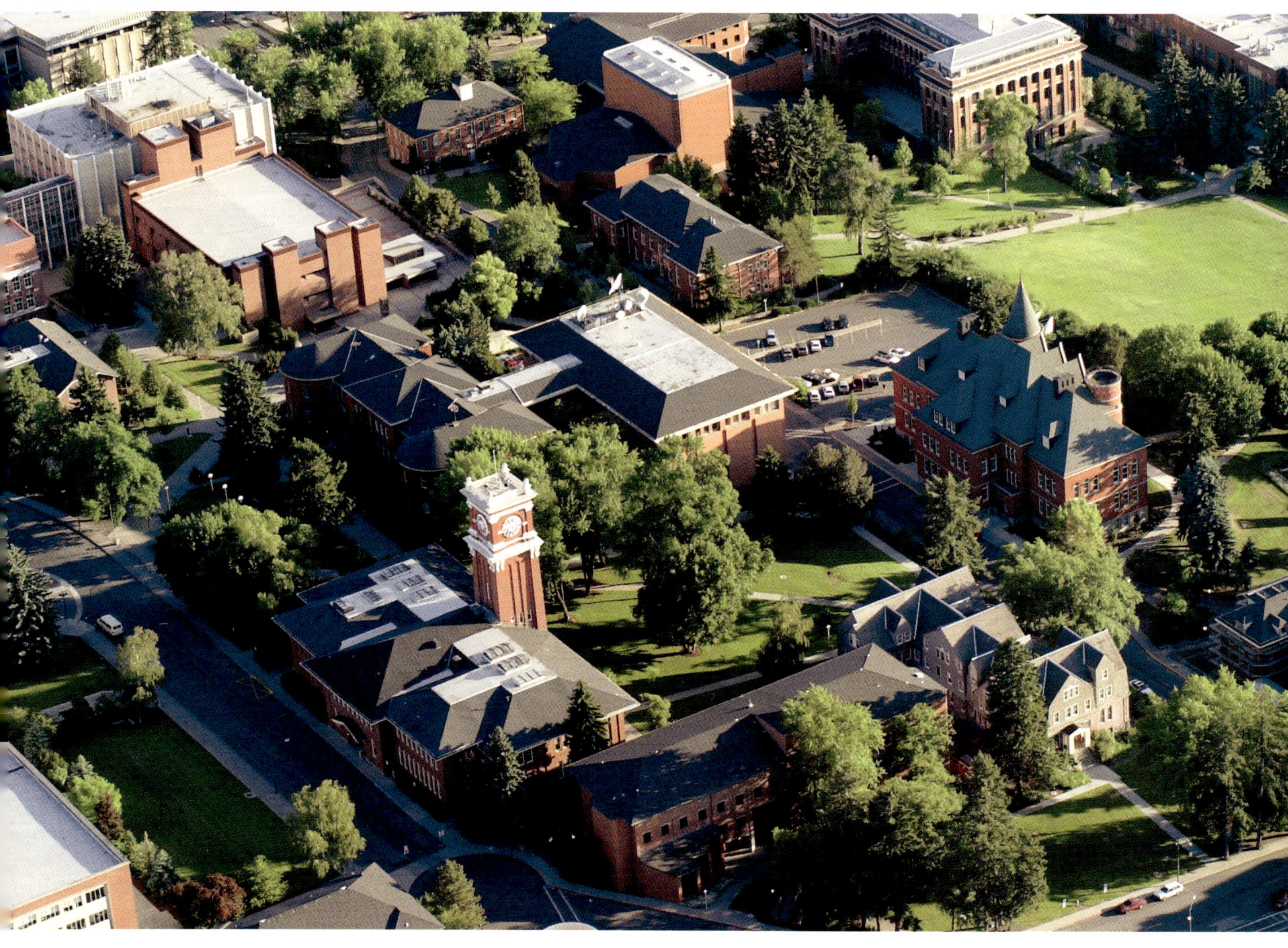

View of the early campus core, with Bryan Hall (1909) facing turreted Thompson Hall (1895) across a grassy quad area. In 1893, Harriet Bryan (wife of the college's third president) planted an elm seedling here that she had brought from the Massachusetts estate of writer and poet James Russell Lowell. The Lowell elm thrives today, though aging.

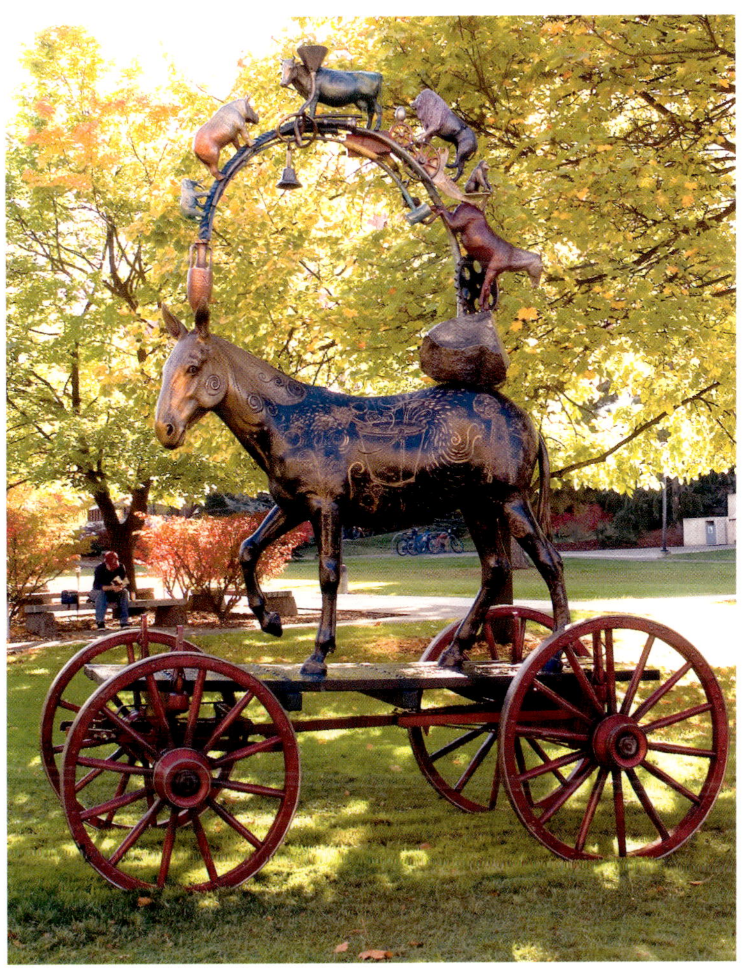

A World Beyond, by Brad Rude of Walla Walla, is in the permanent WSU collection of outdoor sculpture.

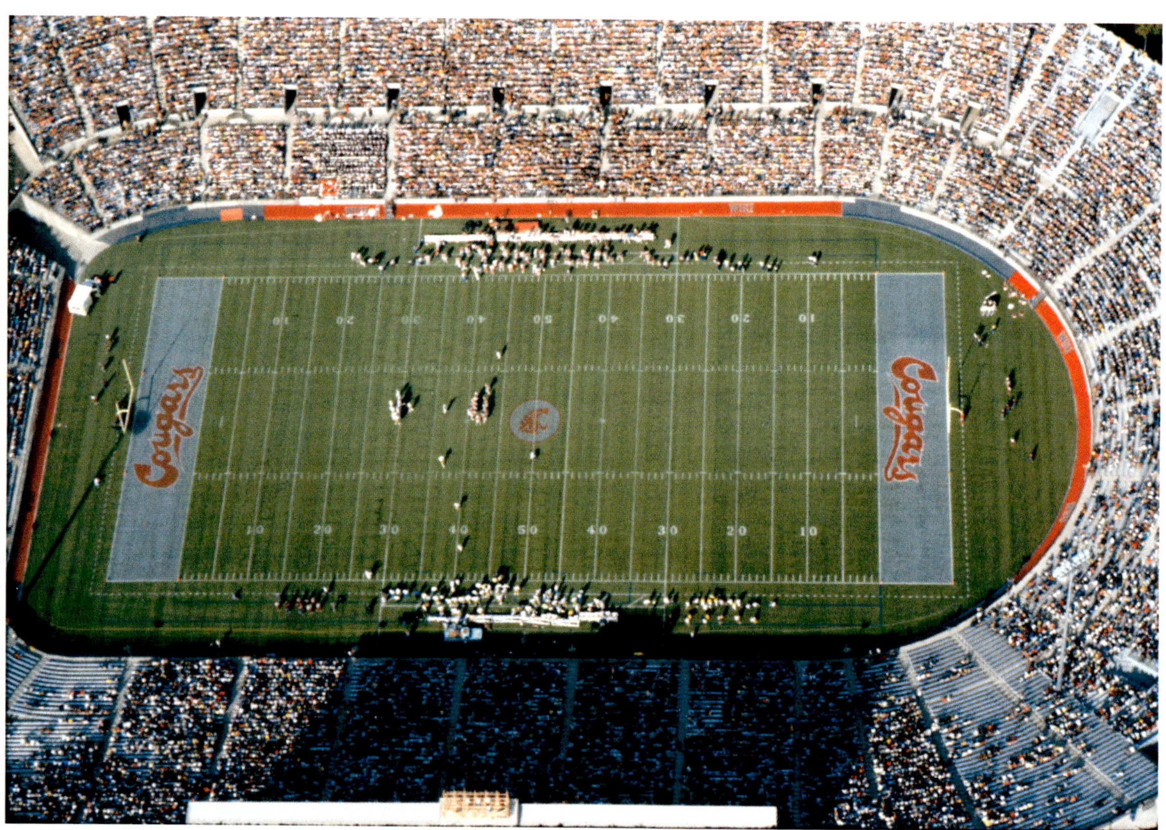

Game day at Martin Stadium. The 40,000-seat facility is named for Clarence D. Martin, a Cheney resident who served as Governor of the State of Washington from 1933 to 1940.

Footsteps lead to the west entrance of the Lewis Alumni Centre, where open doors and a warm welcome greet students, faculty, alumni, and visitors alike.

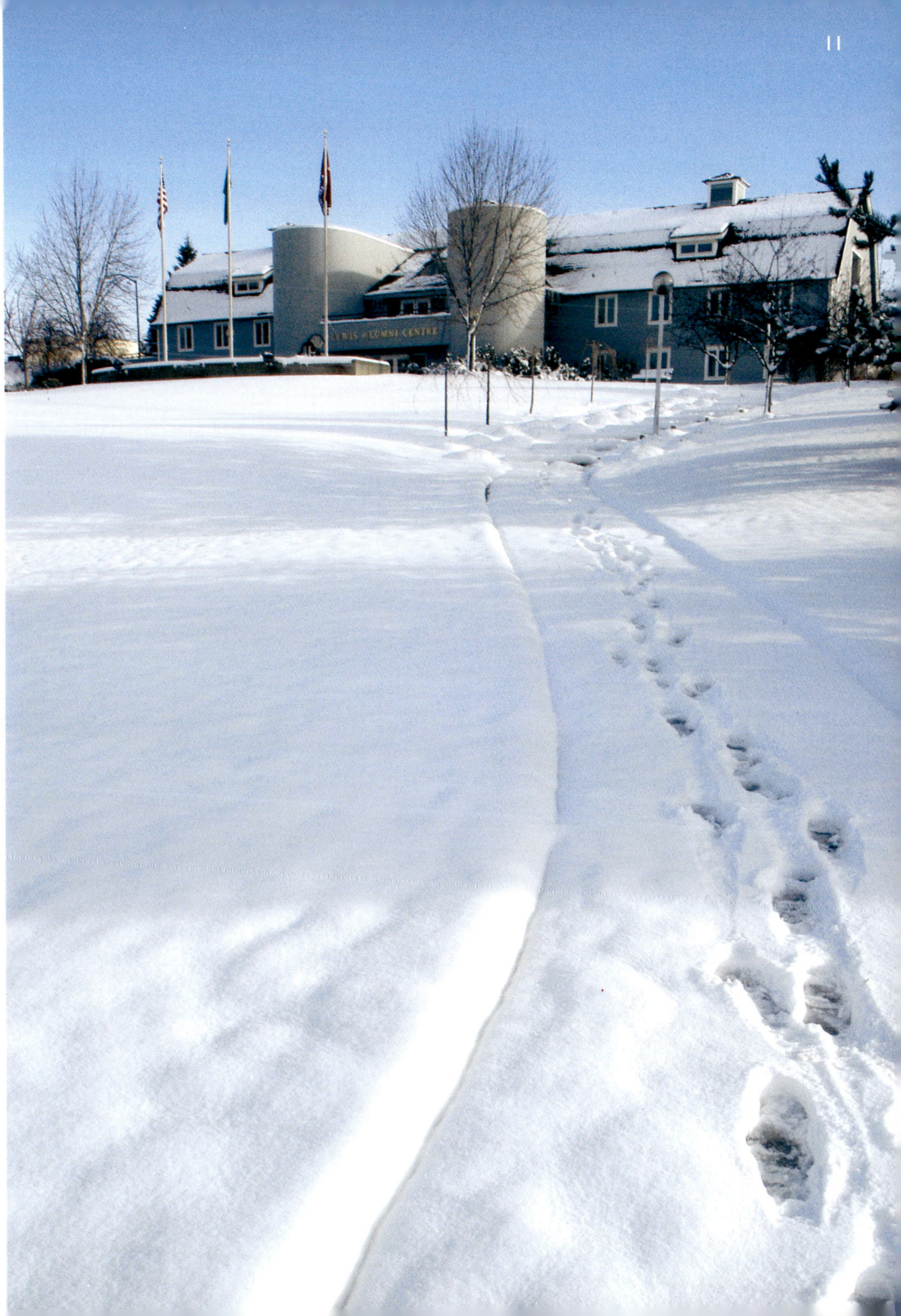

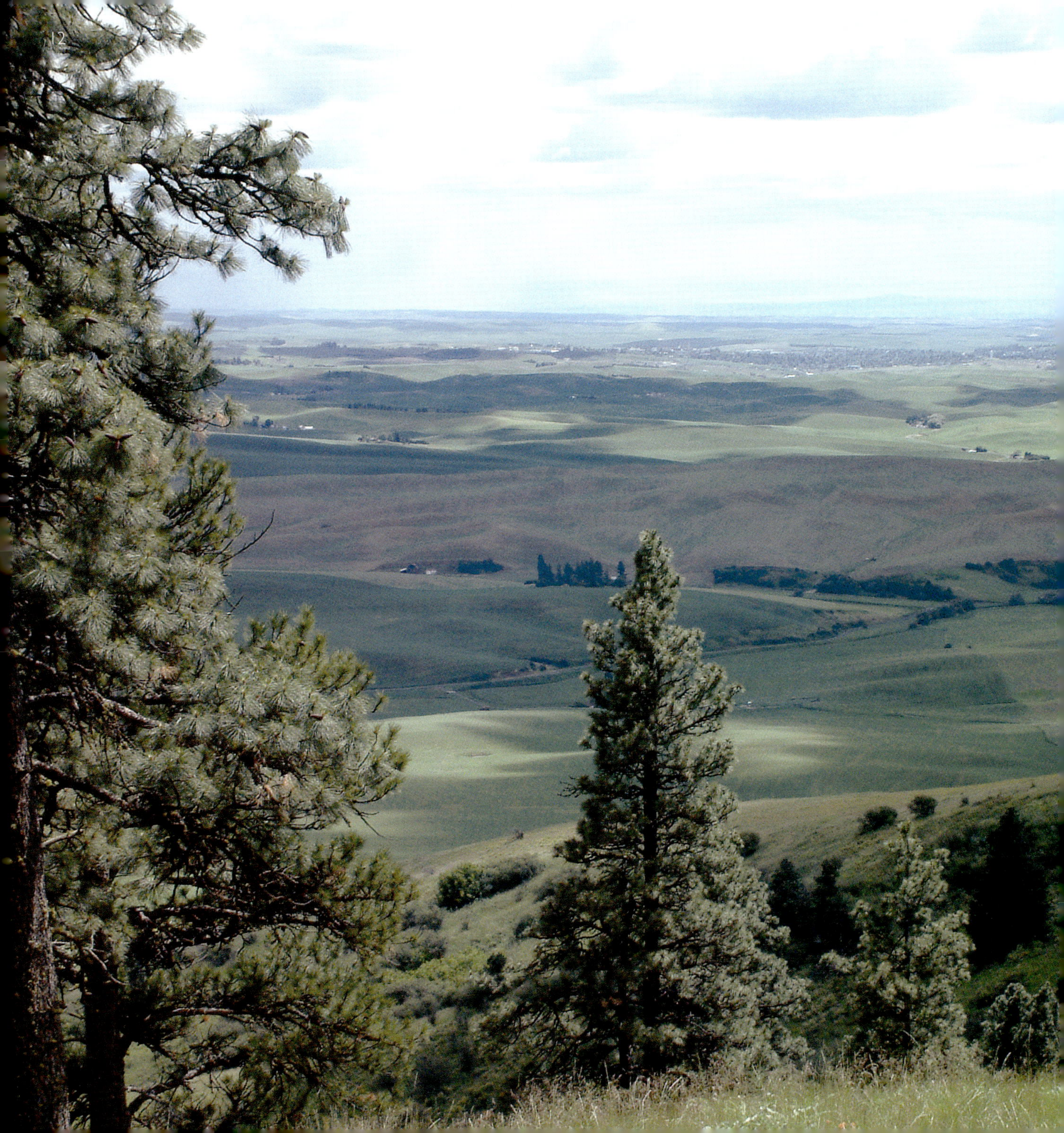

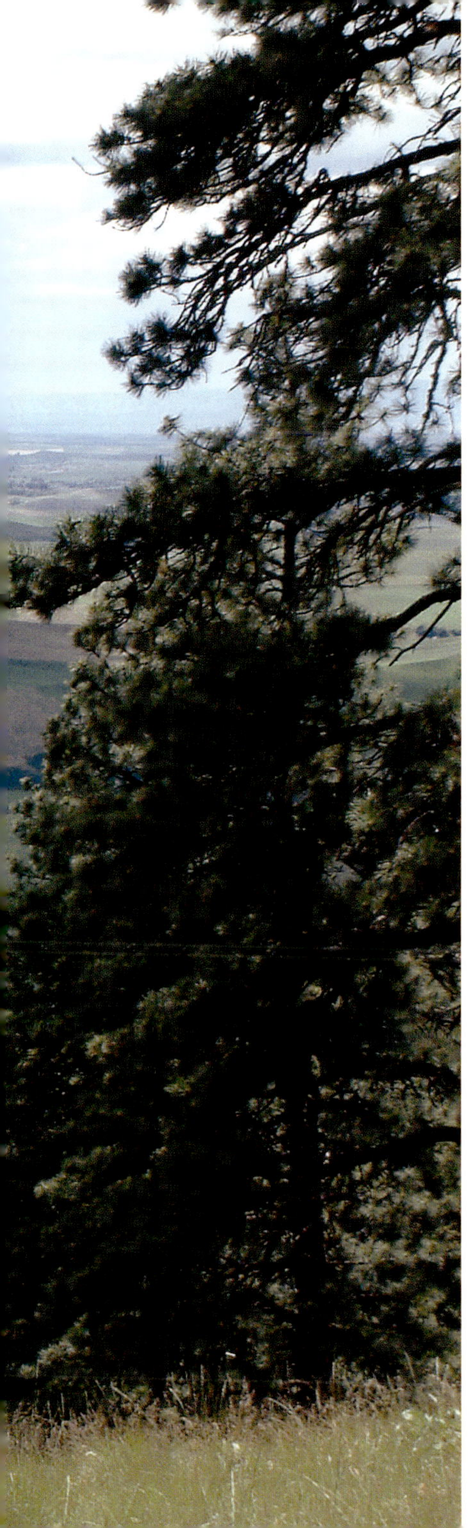

Pullman can be seen tucked in the Palouse Hills of southeast Washington in this distant view from Kamiak Butte (3,641 ft.). Located nine miles north of the WSU campus, the county park here is popular with hikers, campers, and nature enthusiasts.

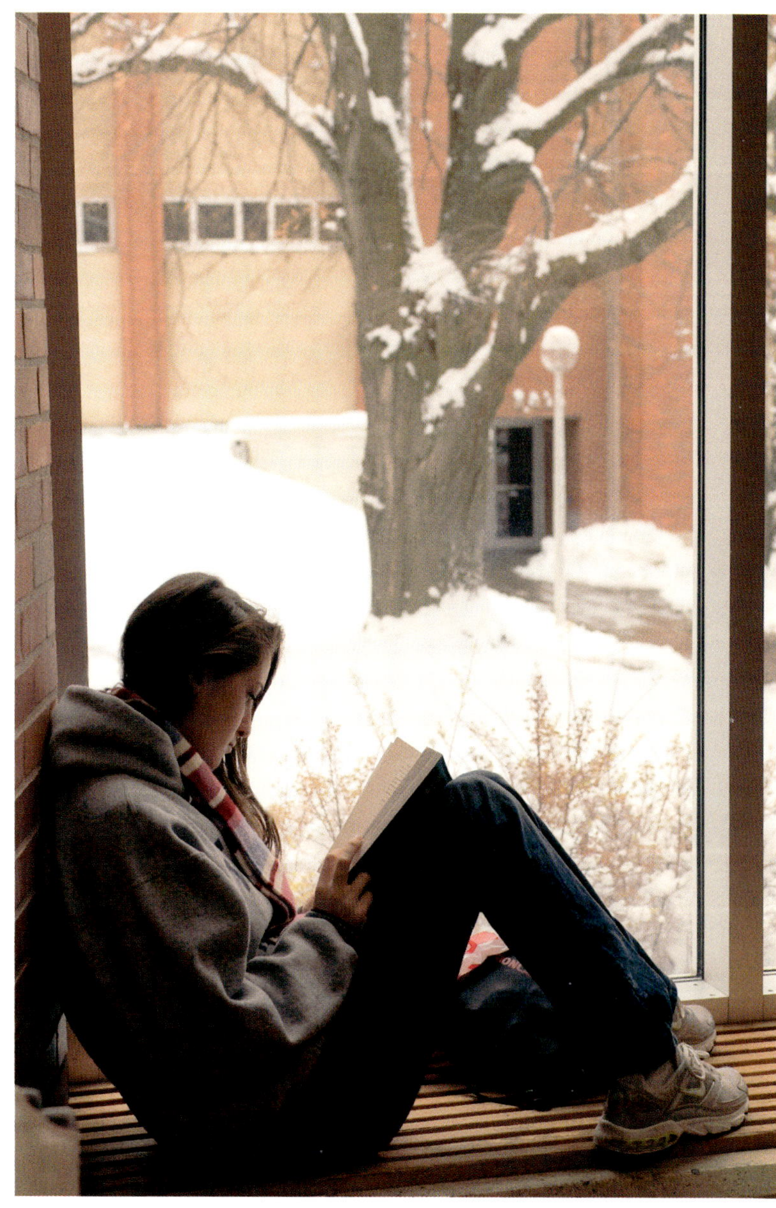

Heated seats in the Todd Hall atrium are popular places to study between classes. Fulmer Hall stands in the background, home of the Chemistry Department and the School of Molecular Biosciences.

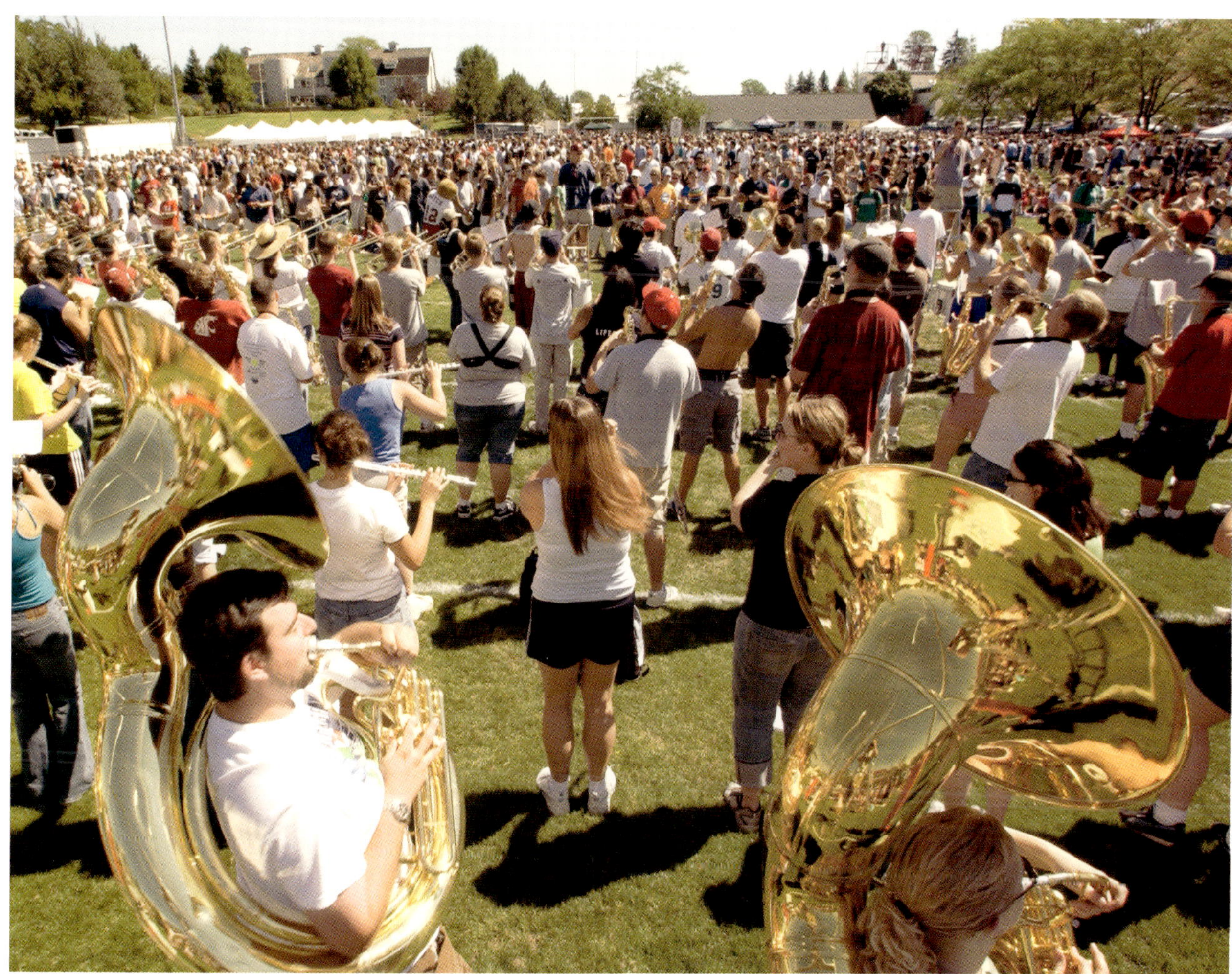

The WSU Marching Band welcomes
students, faculty, and staff at the
annual All Campus Picnic, kicking
off the fall semester.

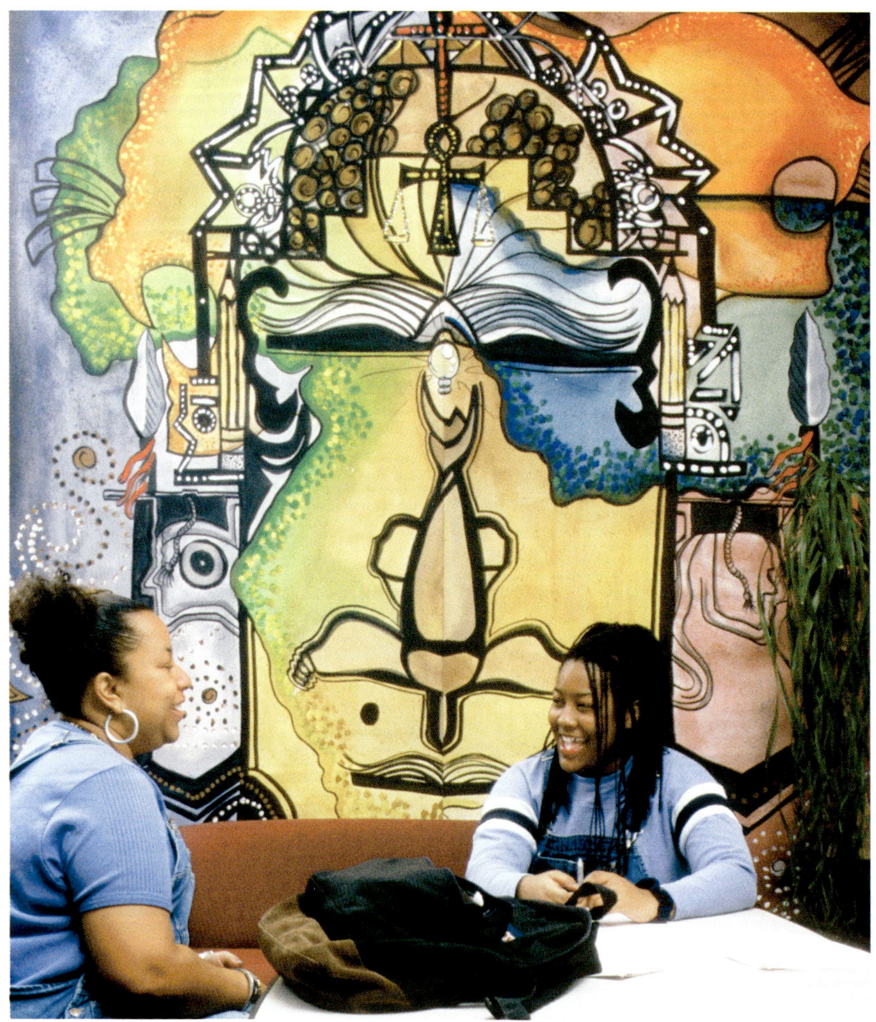

Friends at the
Multicultural Center.

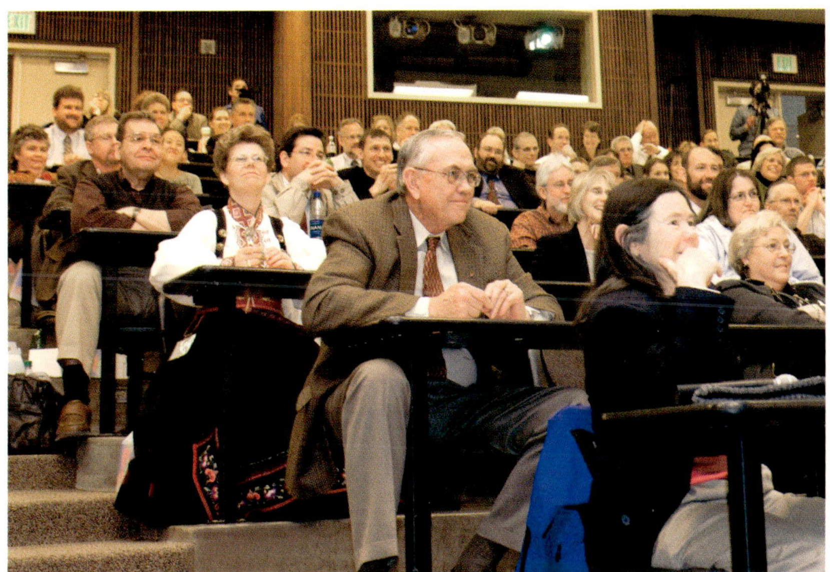

President V. Lane Rawlins (center) and professors attending Showcase—WSU's annual day long celebration focusing on outstanding faculty and staff achievements. Since the early 1890s, WSU has benefited from having long serving presidents. Rawlins took office in 2000, only the ninth in succession.

Dean of the College of Business discusses market research at a large Pullman food store.

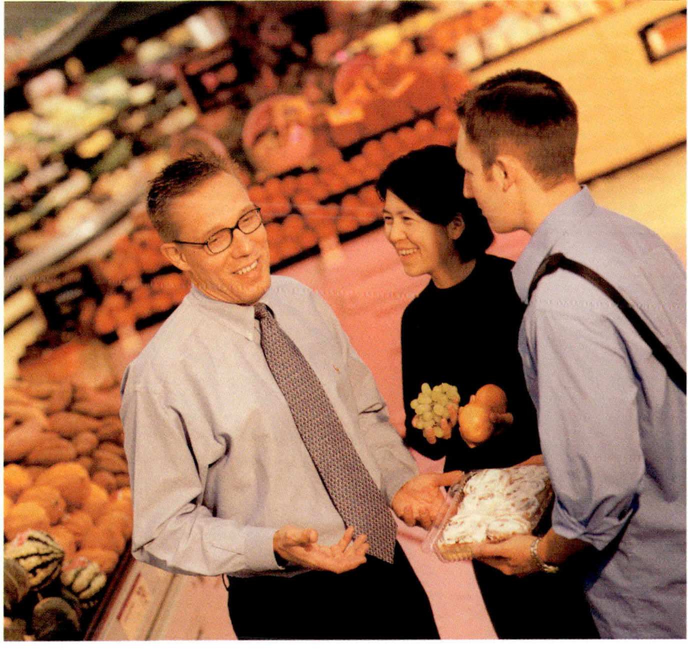

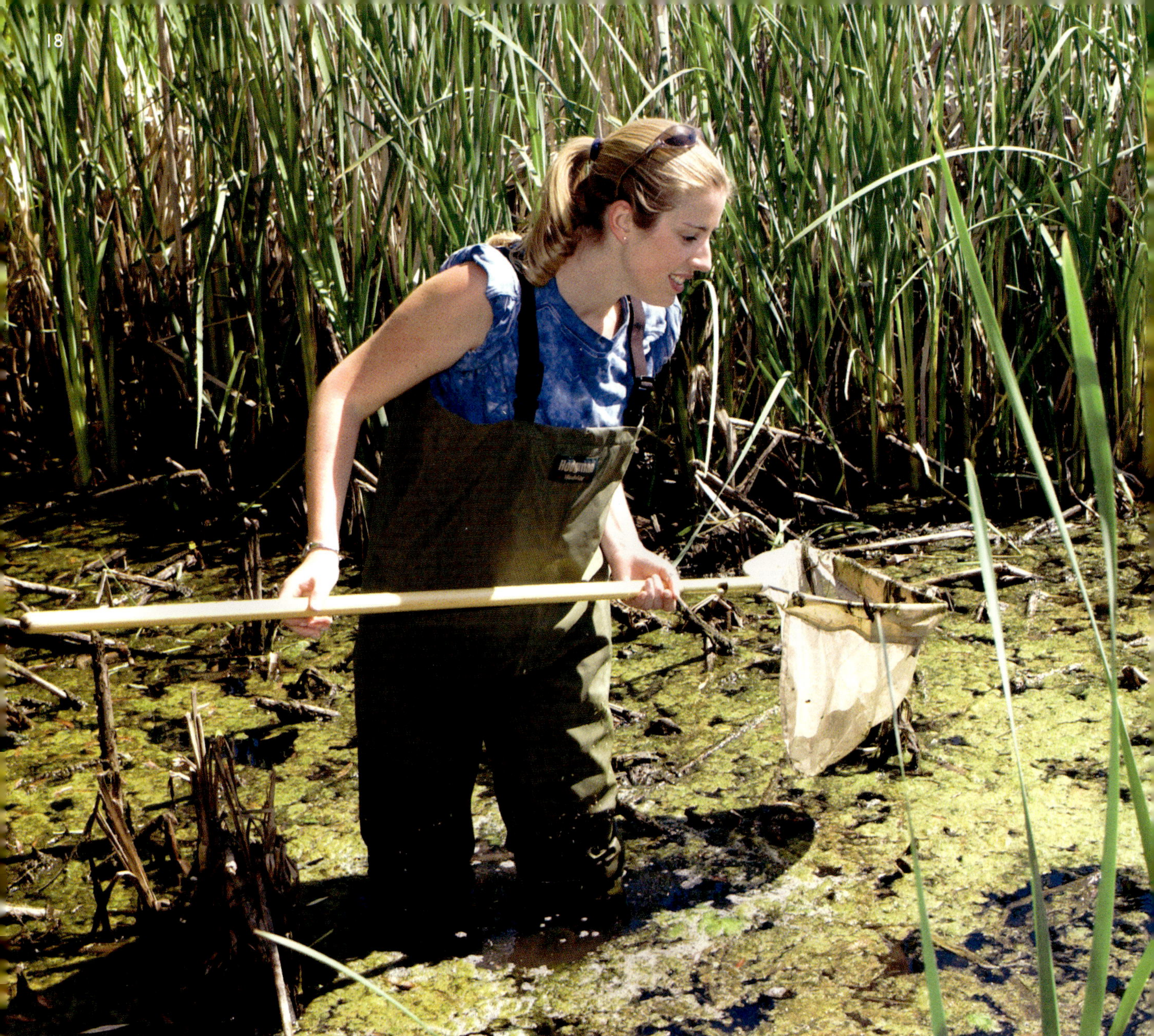

A student investigates pond life.

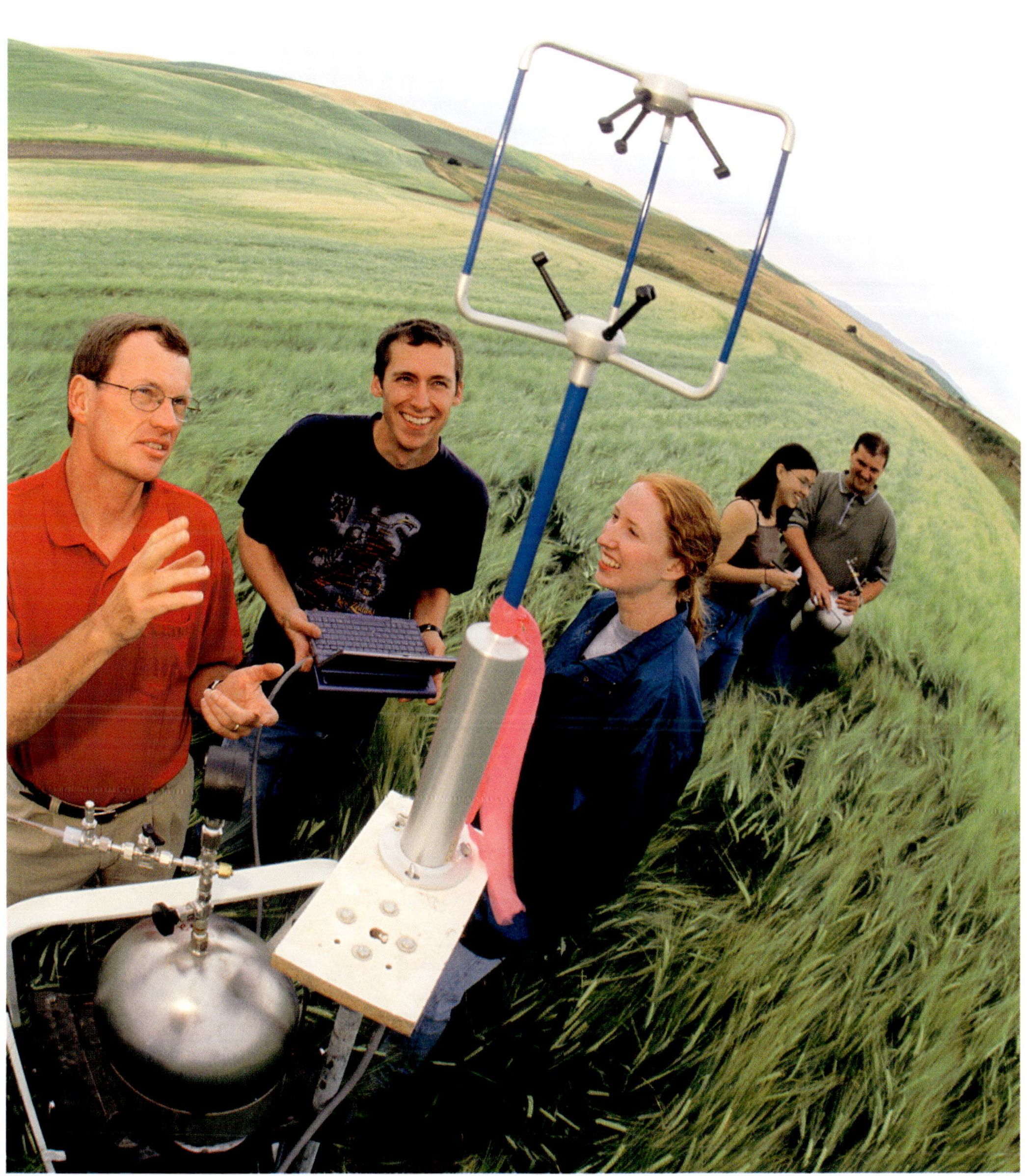

Air quality monitoring by a team from the Department of Civil and Environmental Engineering. WSU has conducted air emissions research in North America, Europe, and Antarctica.

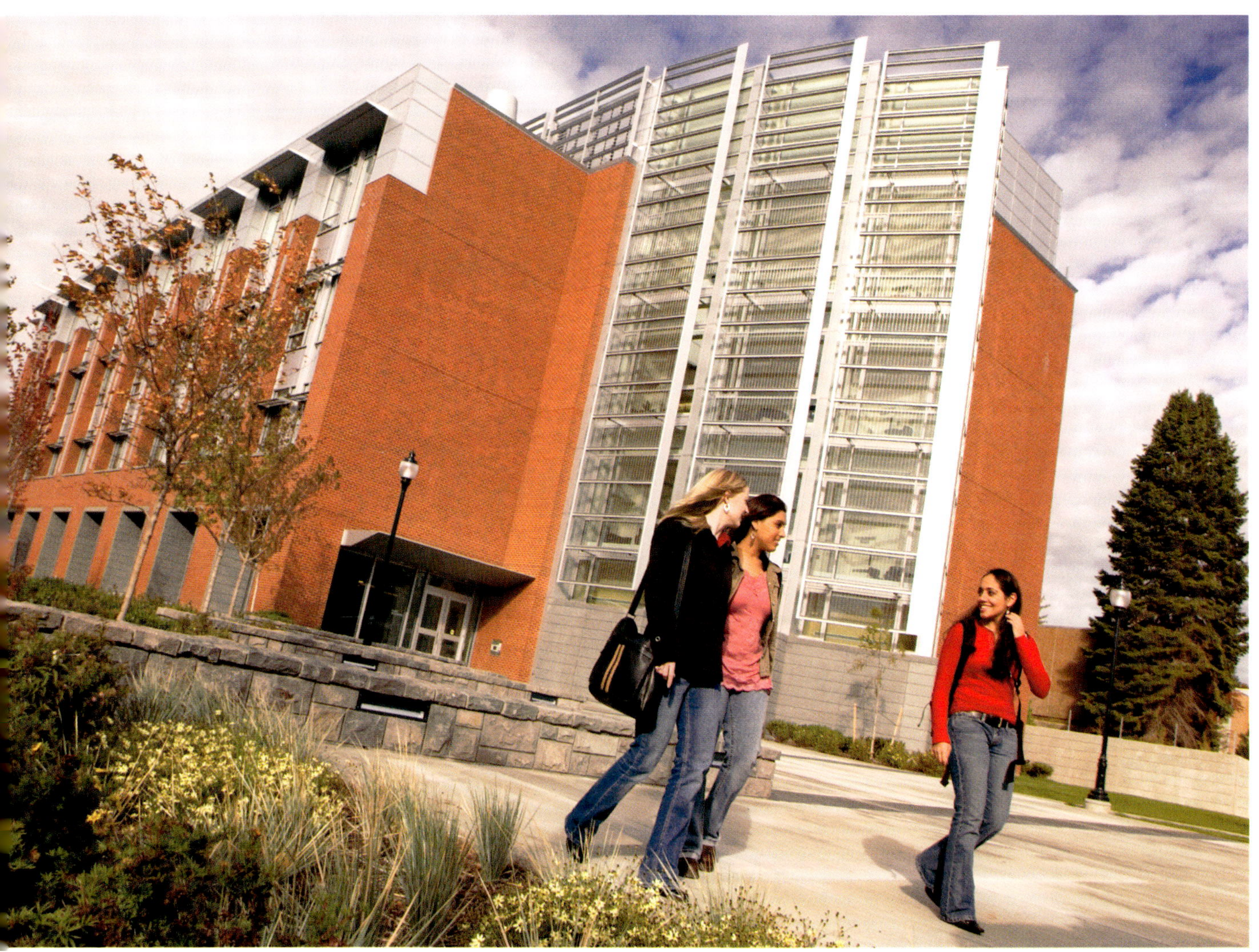

The state-of-the-art Plant
Biosciences Building opened its
doors in the autumn of 2005.

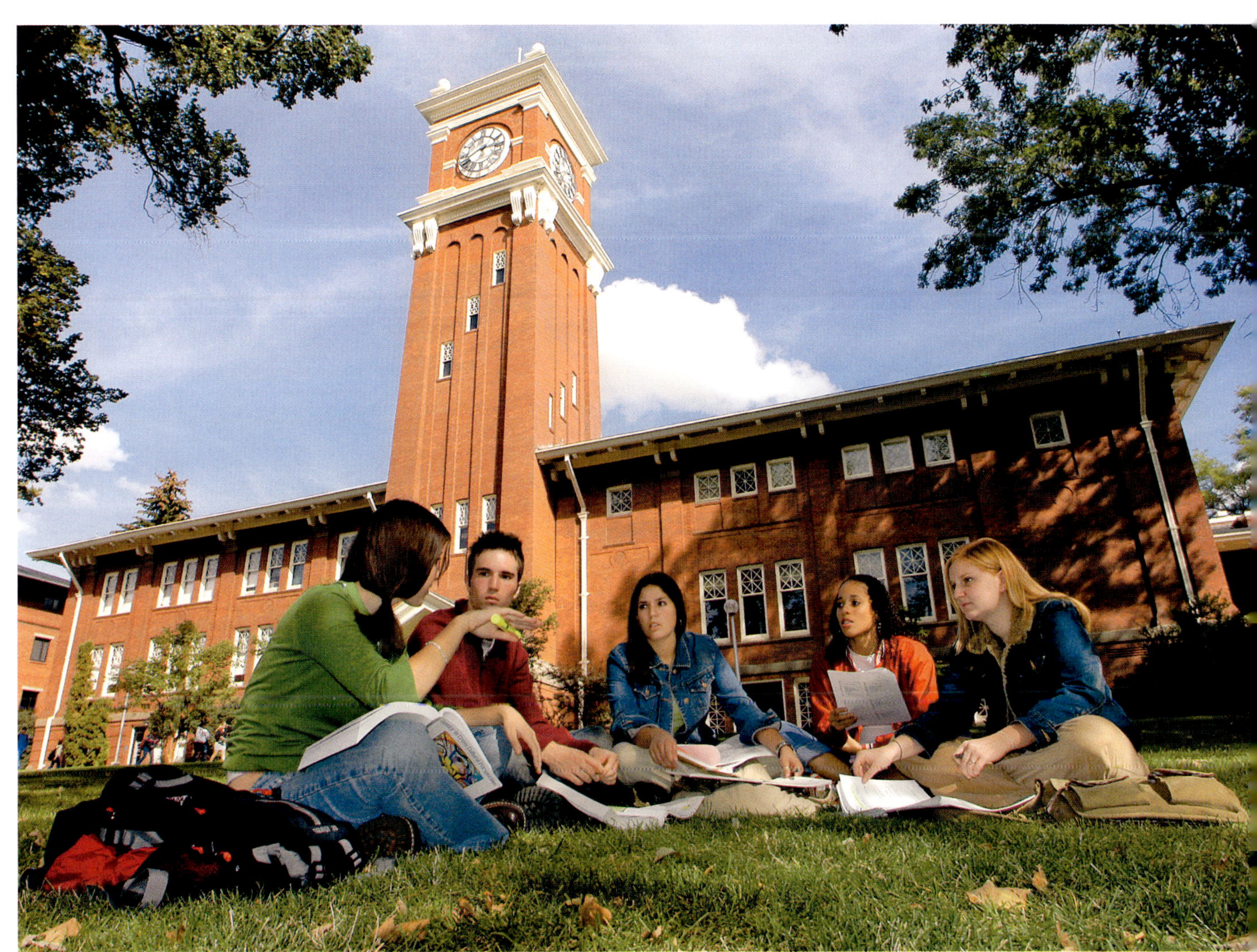

Study group in front of Bryan Hall.

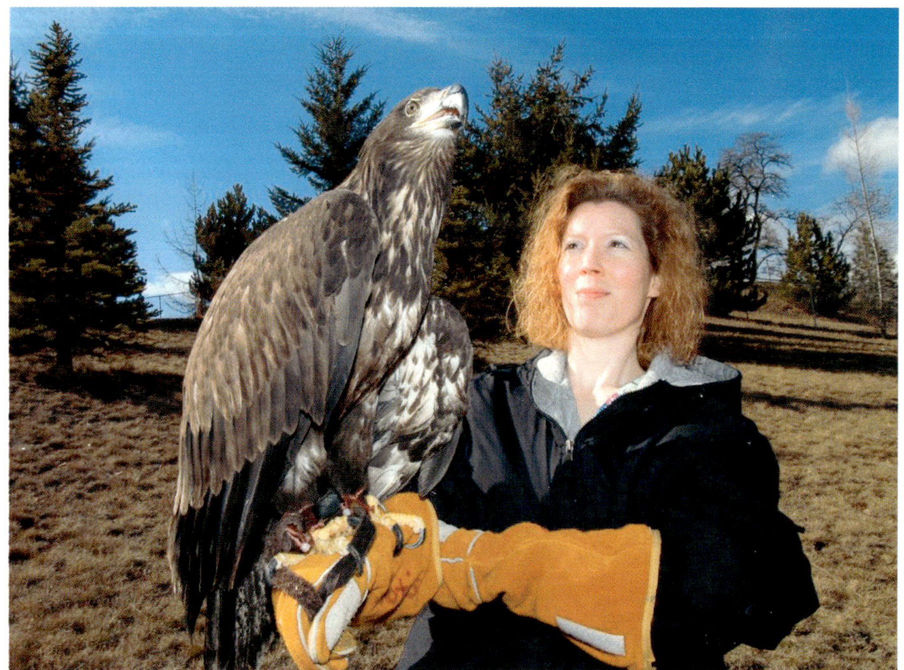

The College of Veterinary Medicine treats injured or ill animals, releasing them into the wild again whenever possible. Otherwise, they are presented to wildlife sanctuaries. After this young bald eagle was found with a fractured wing near McCall, Idaho, it was restored to health and later given to a special zoo in California.

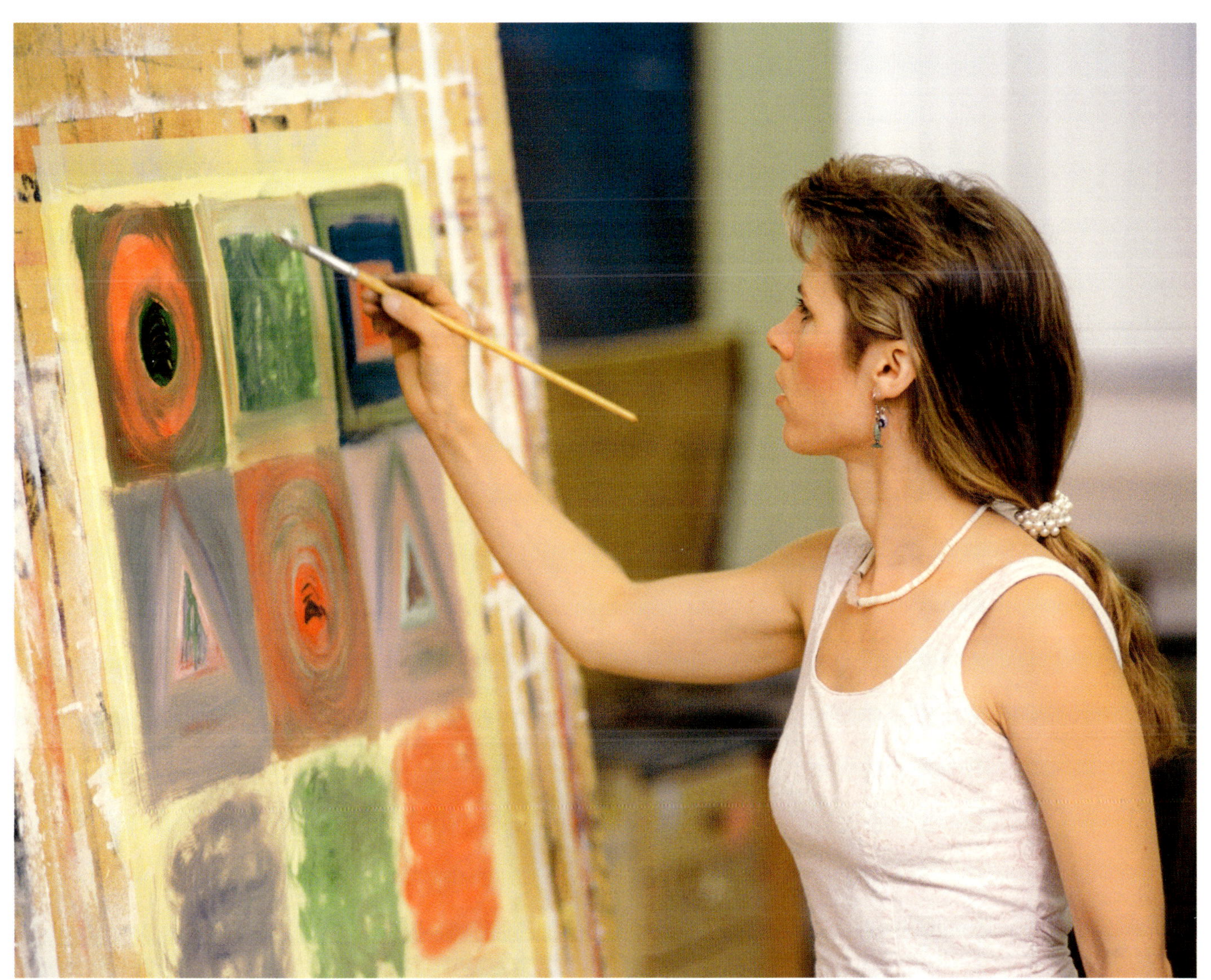

Painting in an art class.

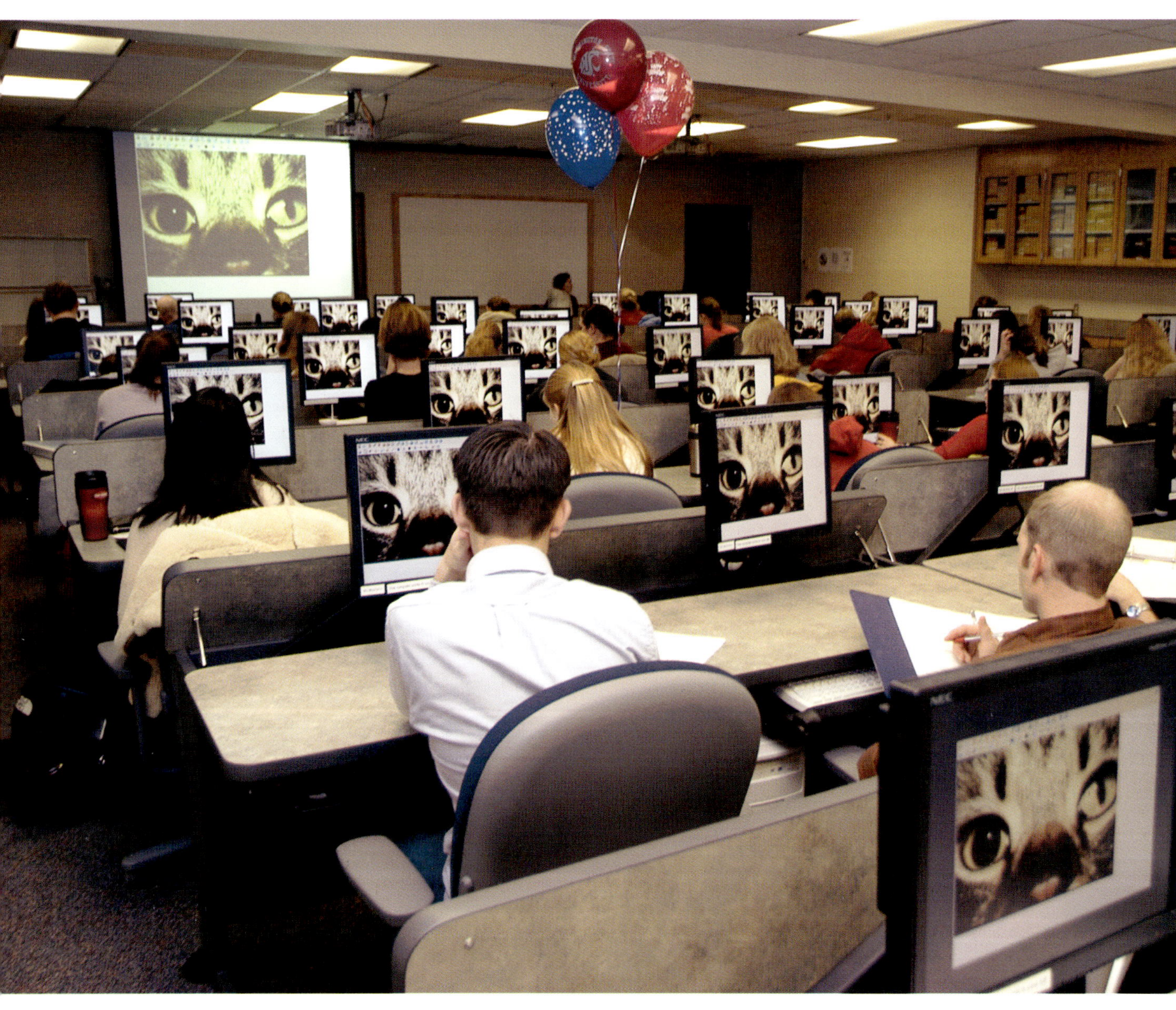

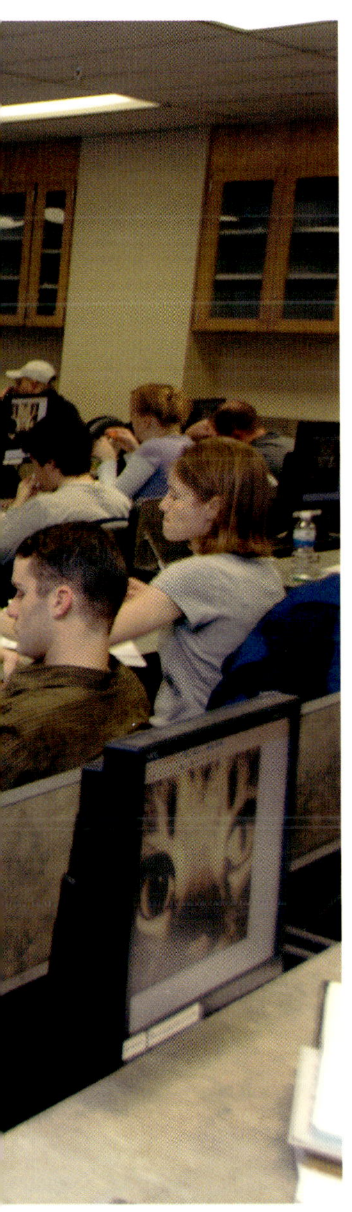

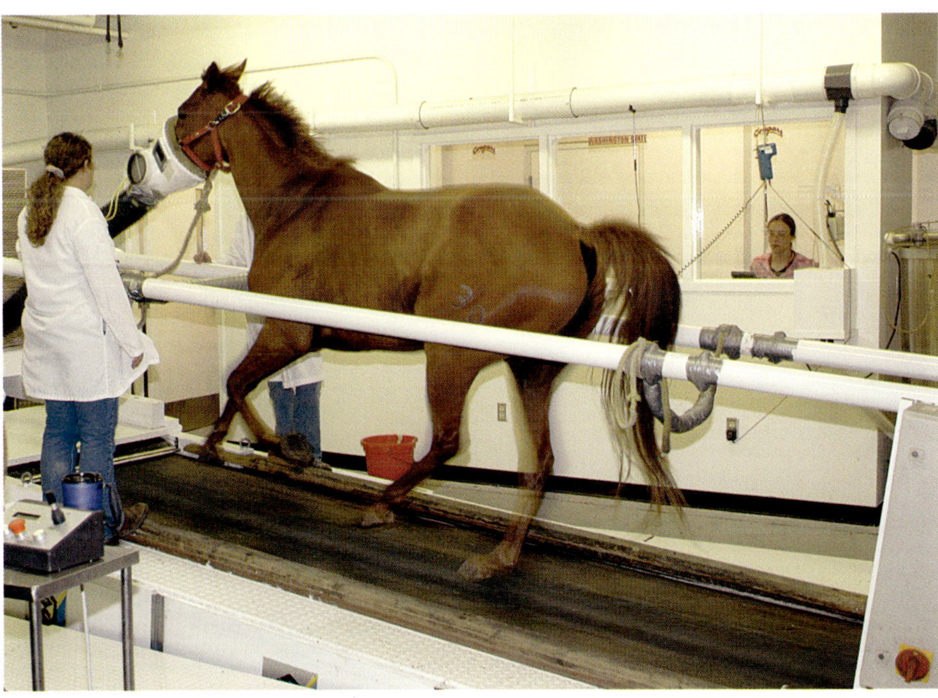

In conjunction with a major teaching hospital and clinical services, WSU's nationally acclaimed College of Veterinary Medicine provides instruction and research in comparative anatomy, pharmacology, physiology, microbiology, and pathology.

Research and education at the bear facility focuses on grizzlies and other bears, and is dedicated to conserving bear populations around the world.

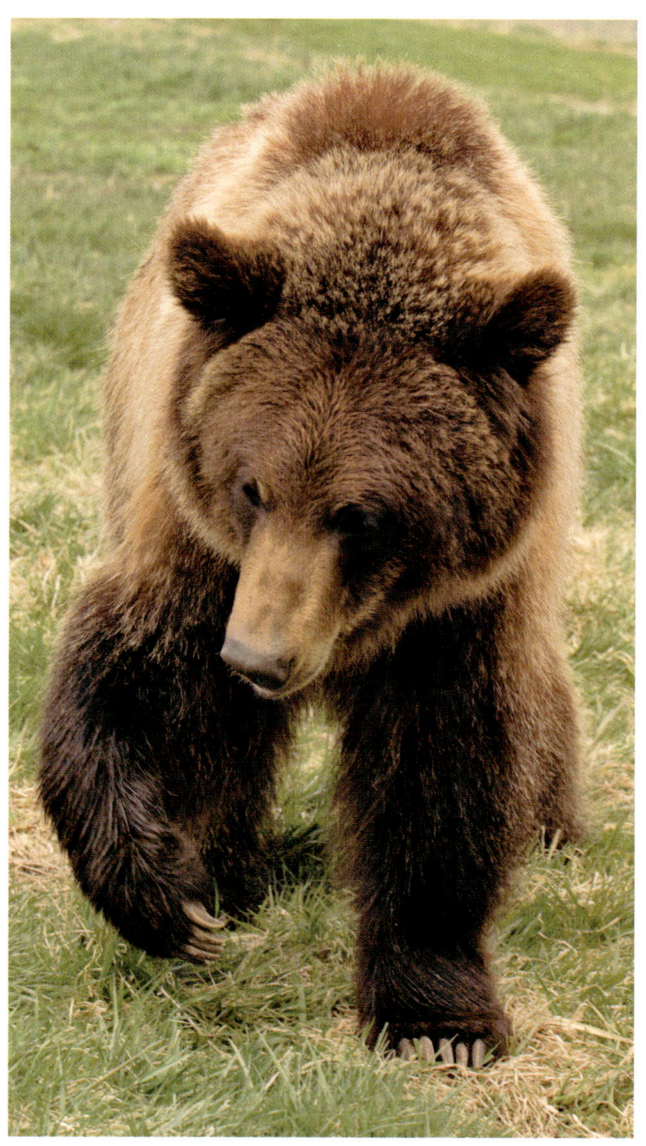

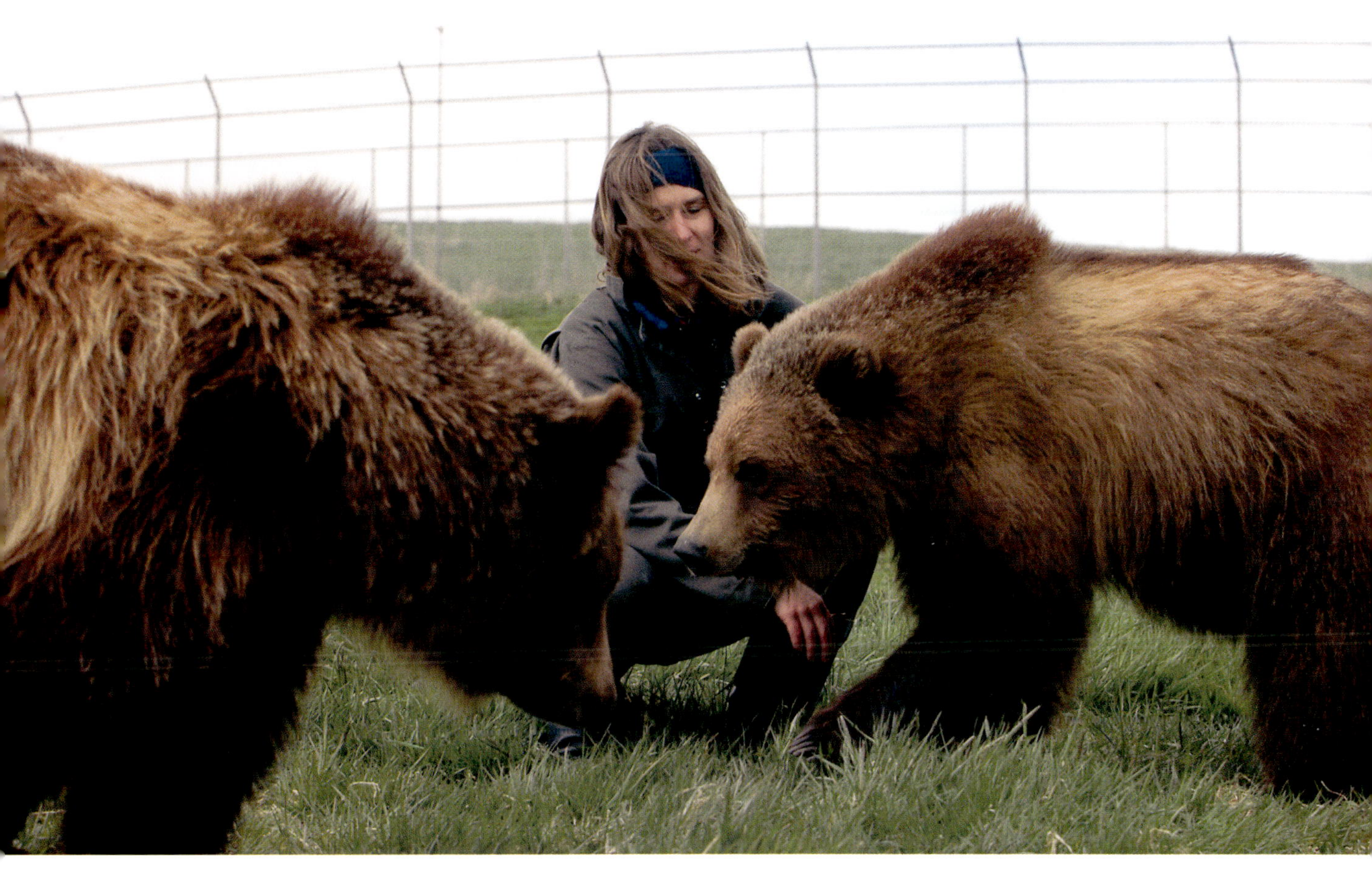

The WSU Bear Center, with six indoor pens and a fenced two-acre exercise yard, has taken in orphaned cubs from the Yellowstone Park area and other Northwest regions.

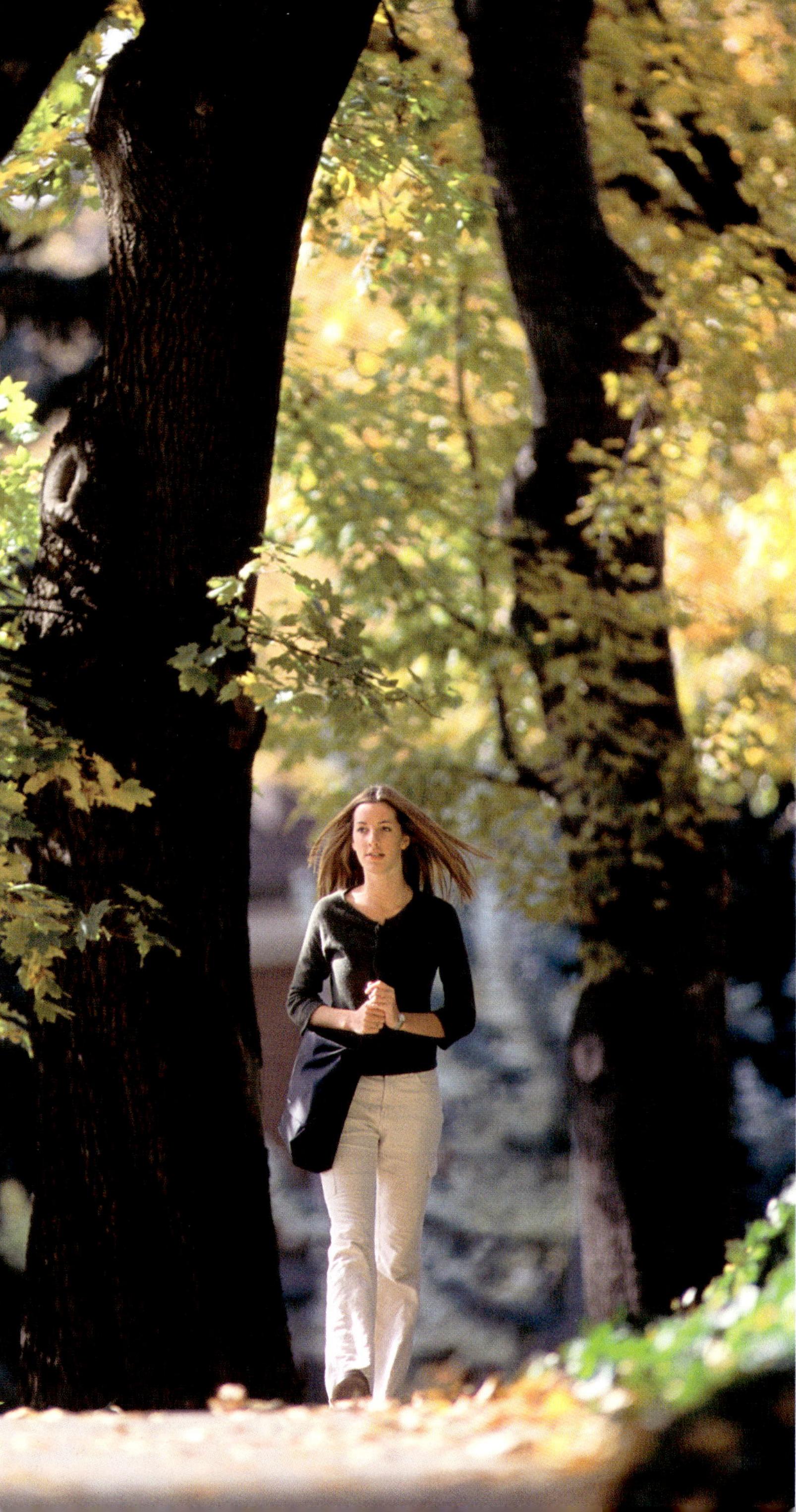

Long periods of warm
autumn weather are
typical in the Palouse.

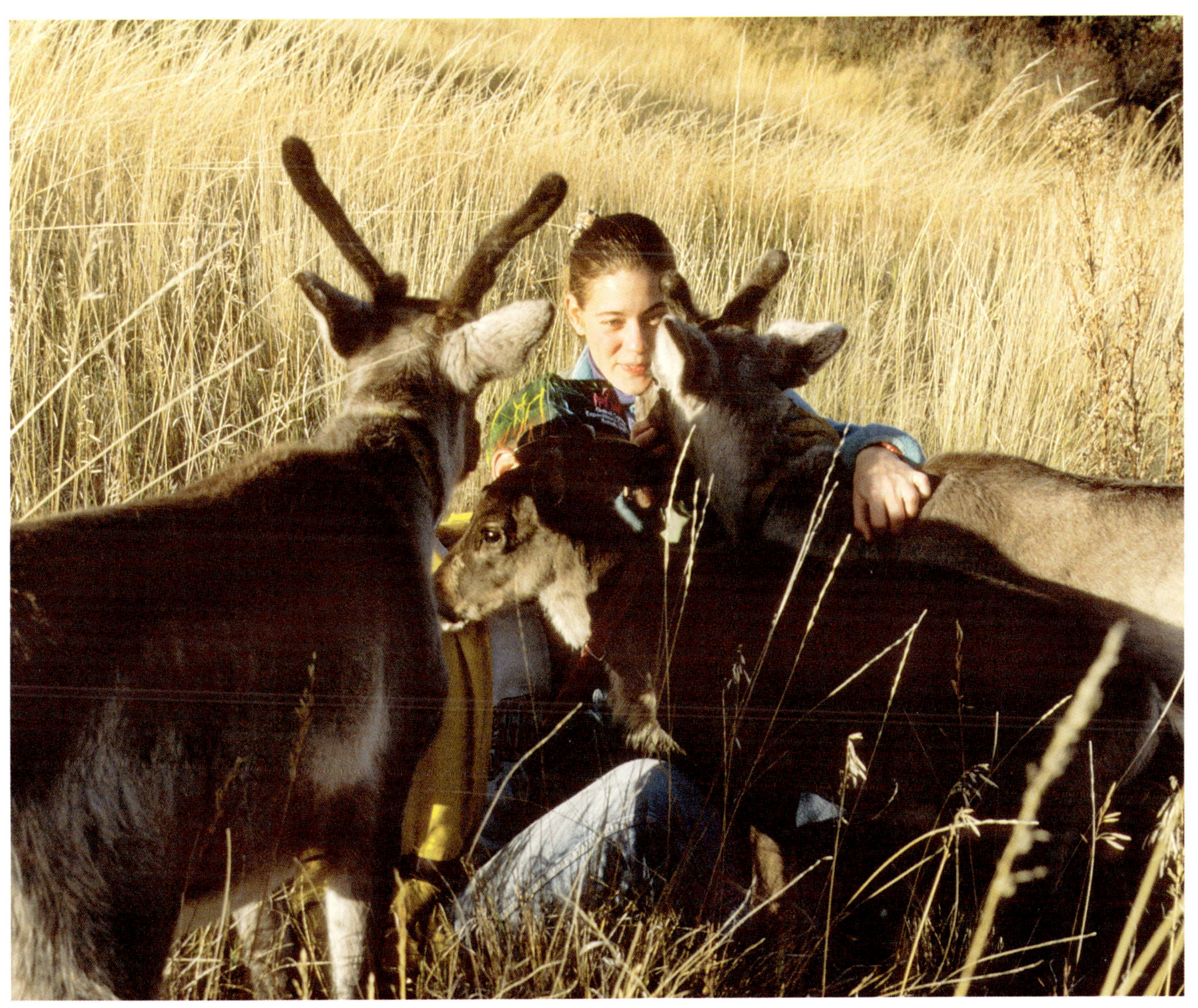

Caribou in a research plot
nuzzle two students.

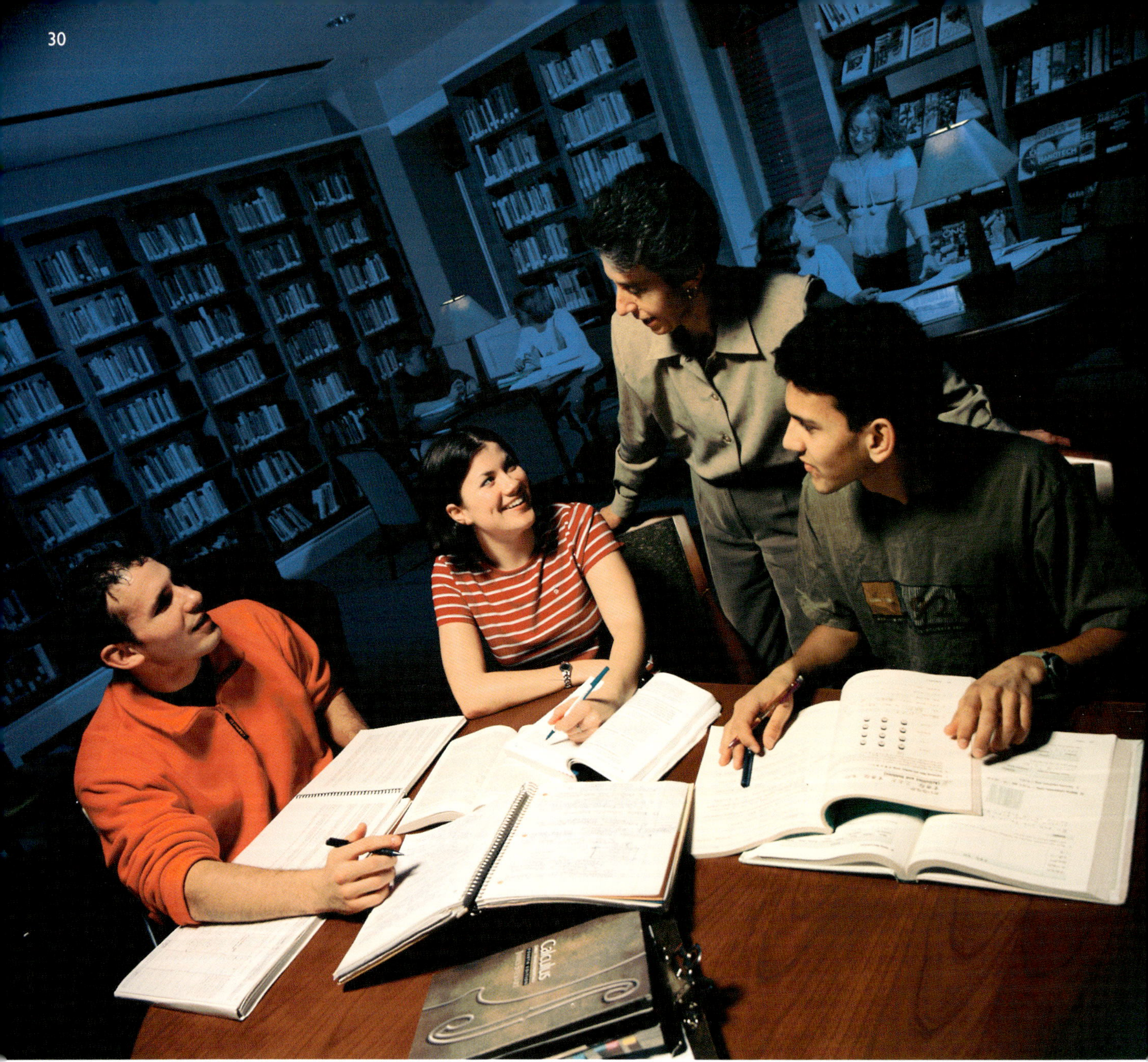

A University Honors College assistant dean converses with students in the library at the Honors Hall living and learning facility.

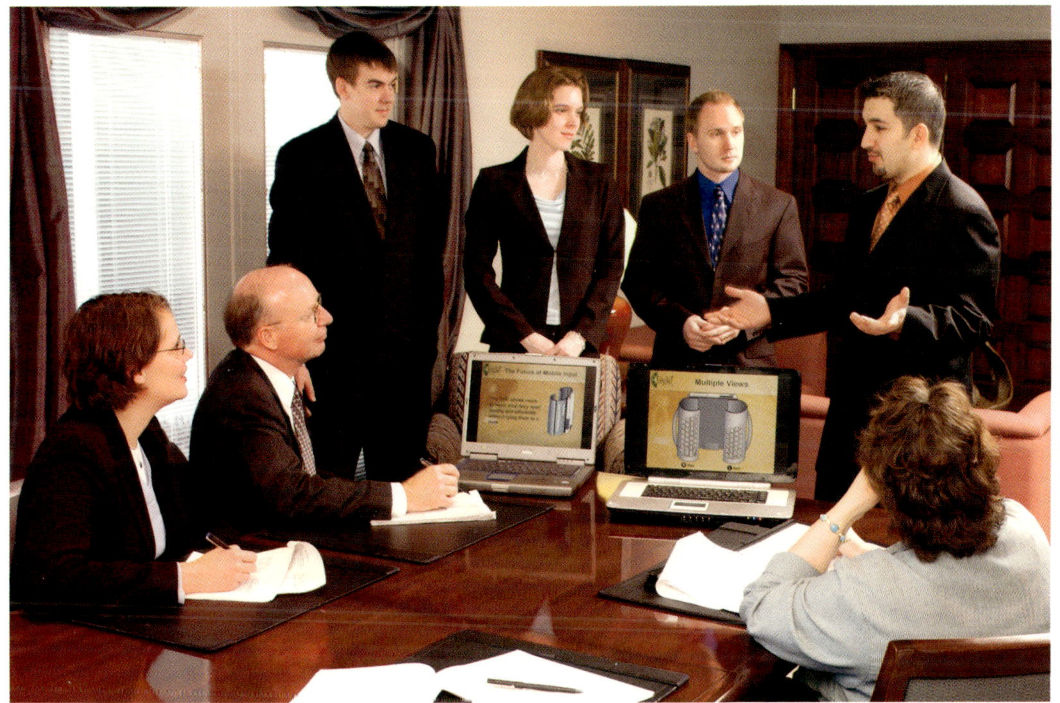

The luxurious Past Presidents Room at the Lewis Alumni Centre provides a fine boardroom setting for a business plan competition sponsored by the Center for Entrepreneurial Studies.

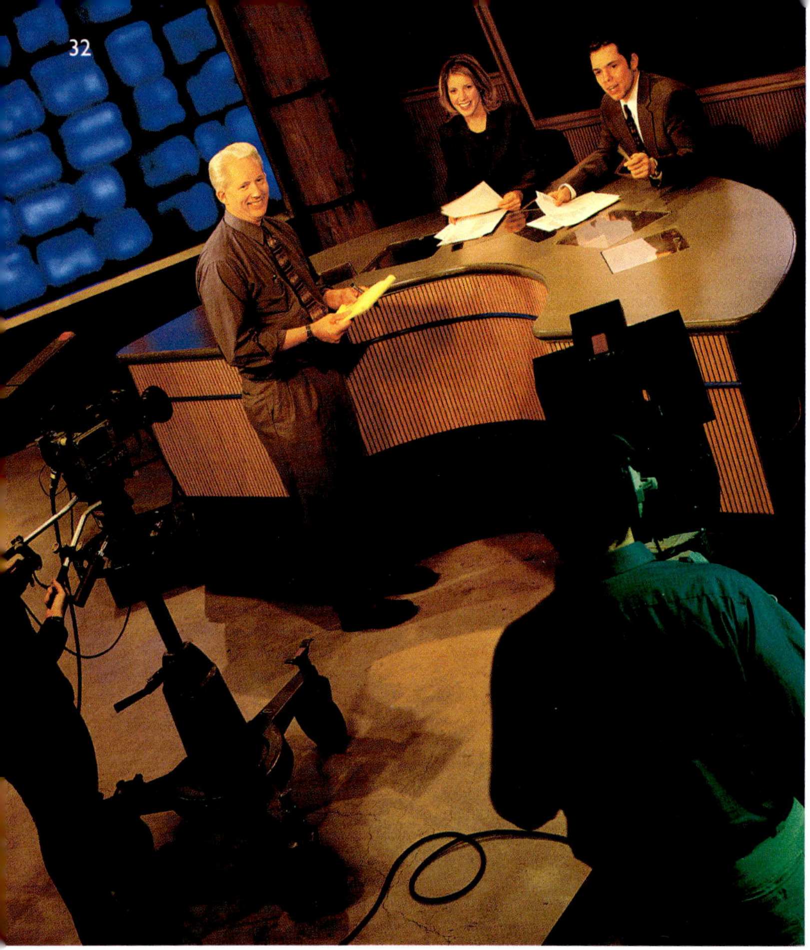

Edward R. Murrow School of Communication offers the only comprehensive broadcasting curriculum in the state of Washington. Here, a professor assists a student-run Cable 8 Productions newscast, where team members write, produce, and direct their own programming seven days a week.

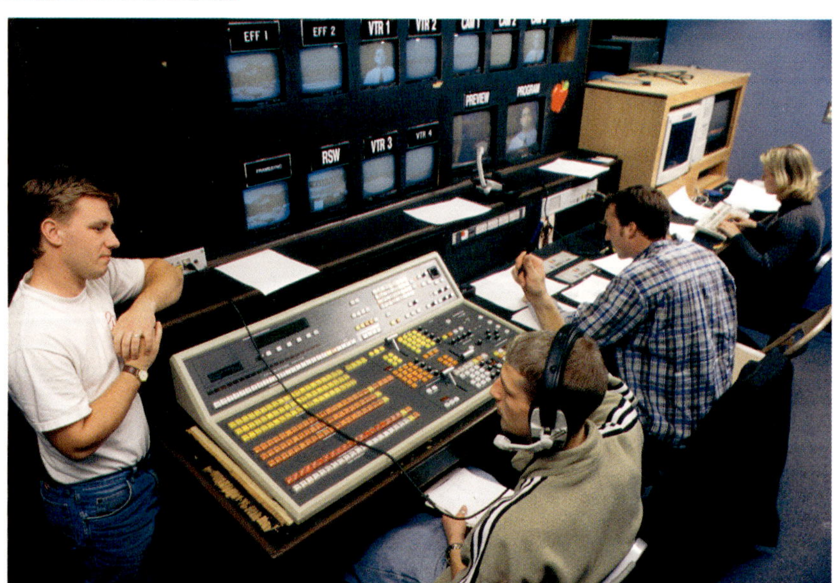

The KWSU TV production control studio.

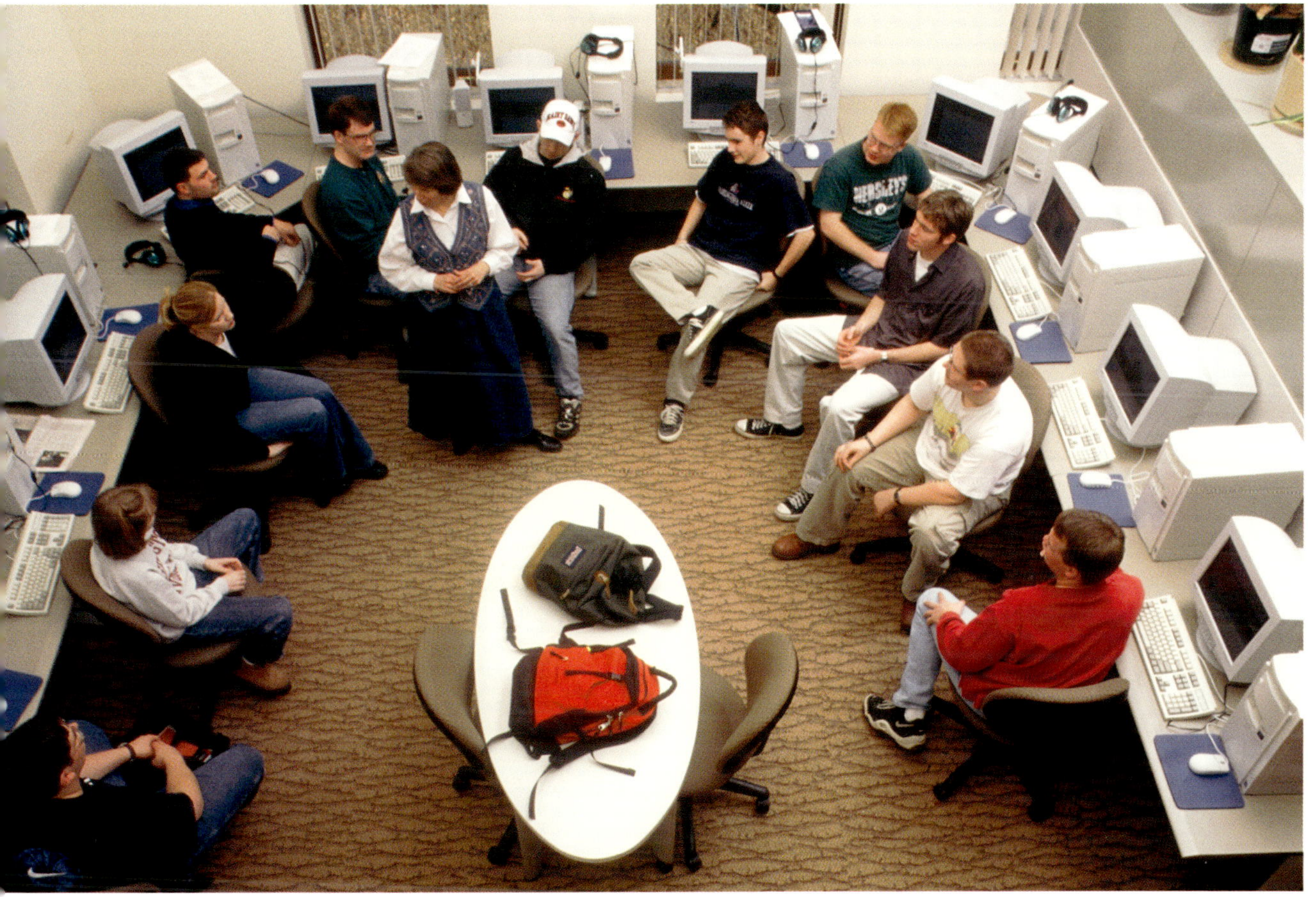

This foreign language
computer lab
is typical of the
University's emphasis
on technology.

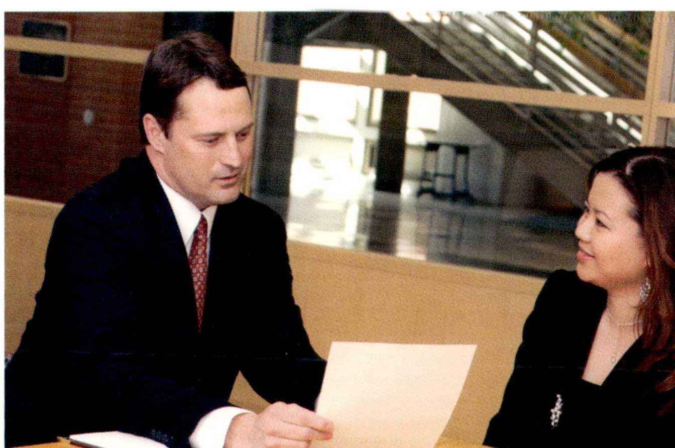

An undergraduate in a
mock job interview with
a WSU financial officer
at the Professional
Development Center.

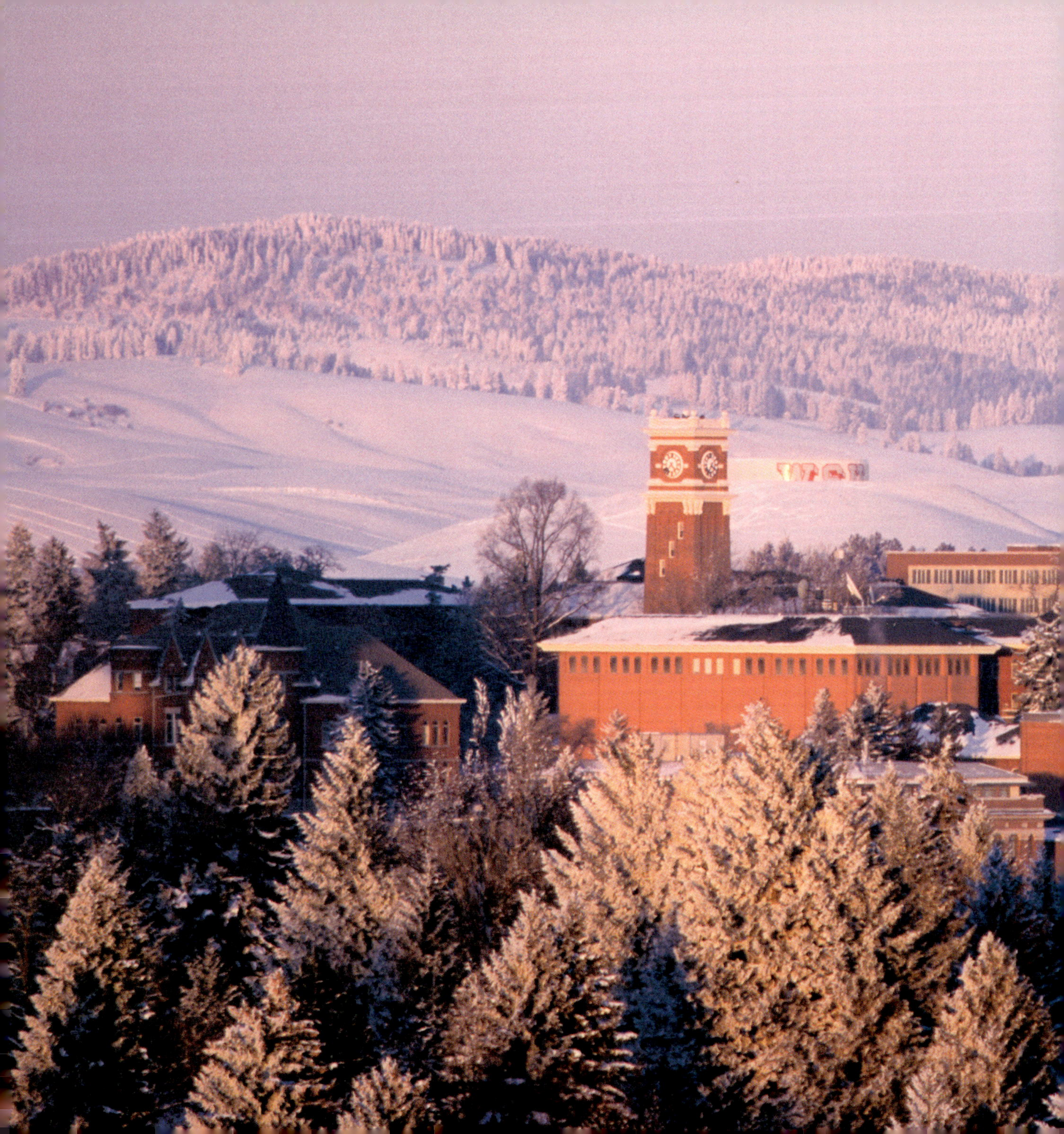

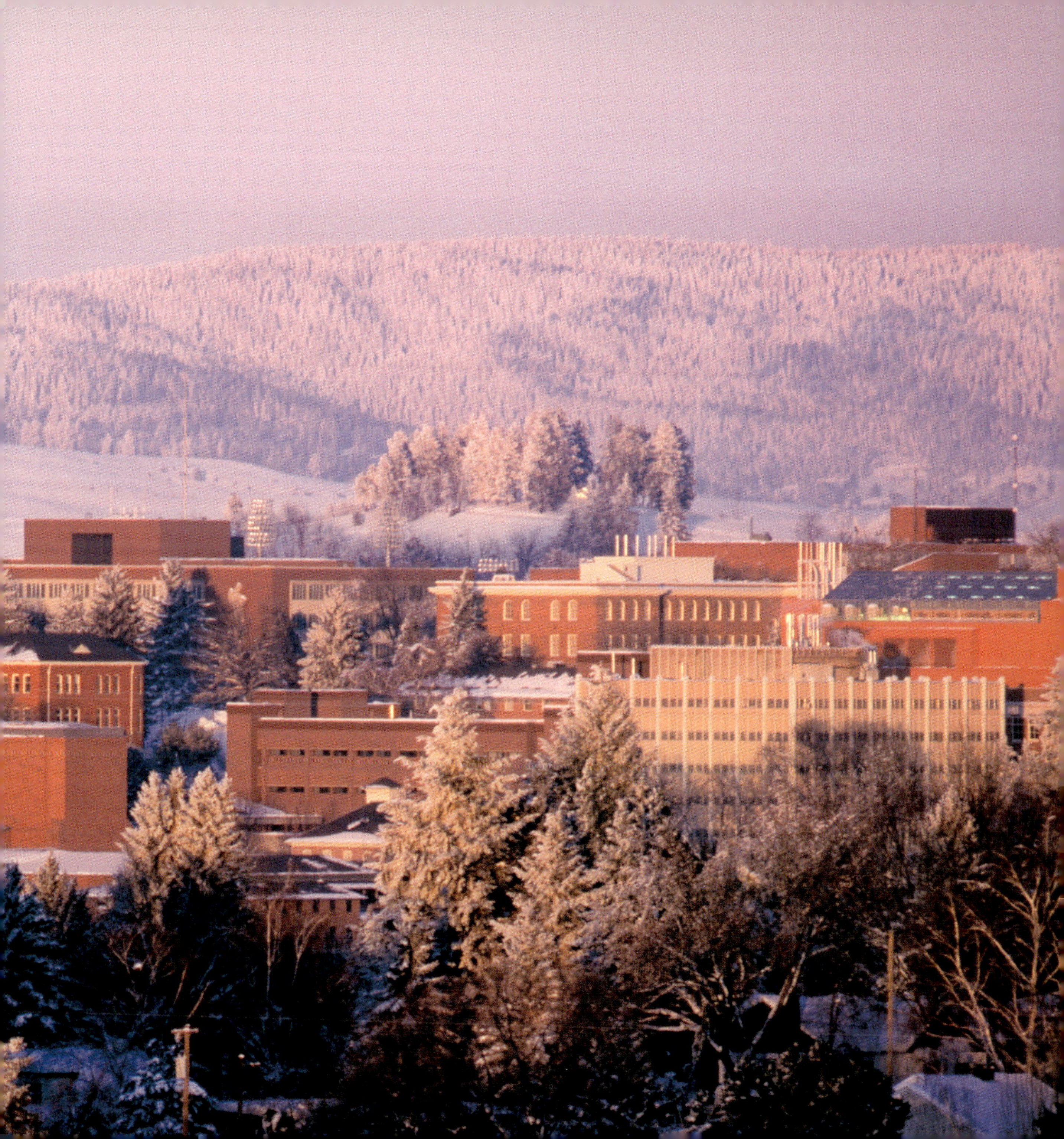

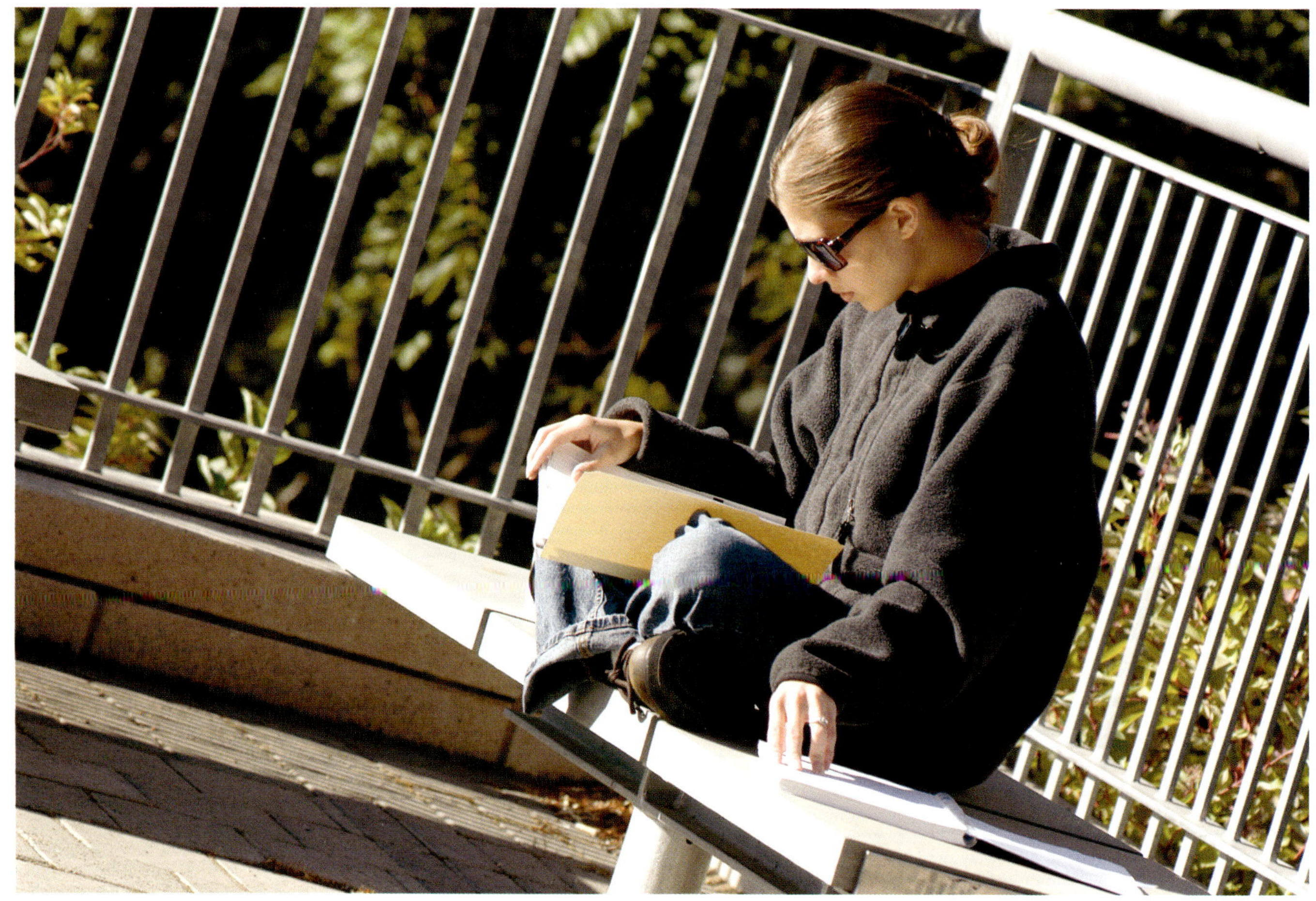

Warm sunshine and dark glasses are all
that is needed for studying outside.

Overleaf:
Alpenglow illuminates the
campus in late afternoon.

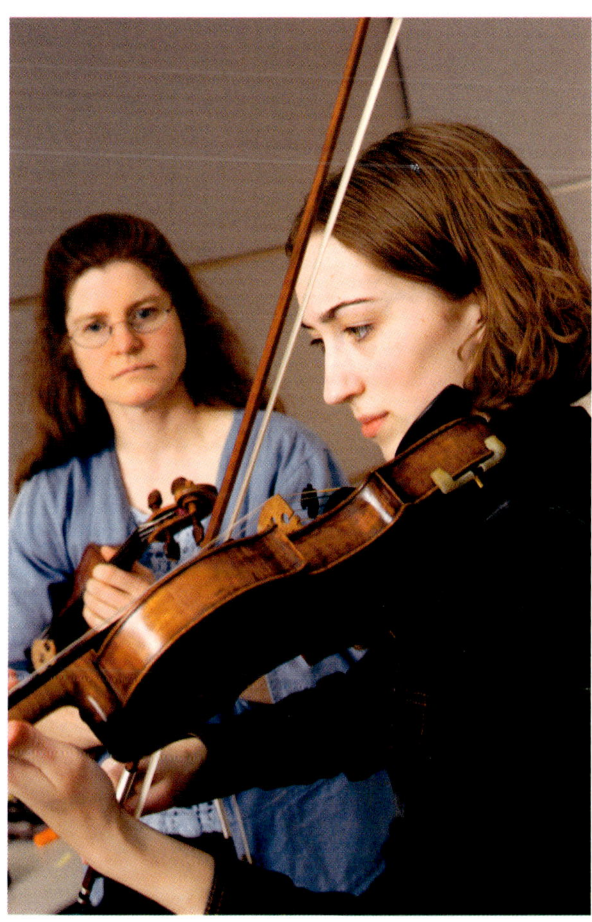

A music professor closely
observes a violinist.

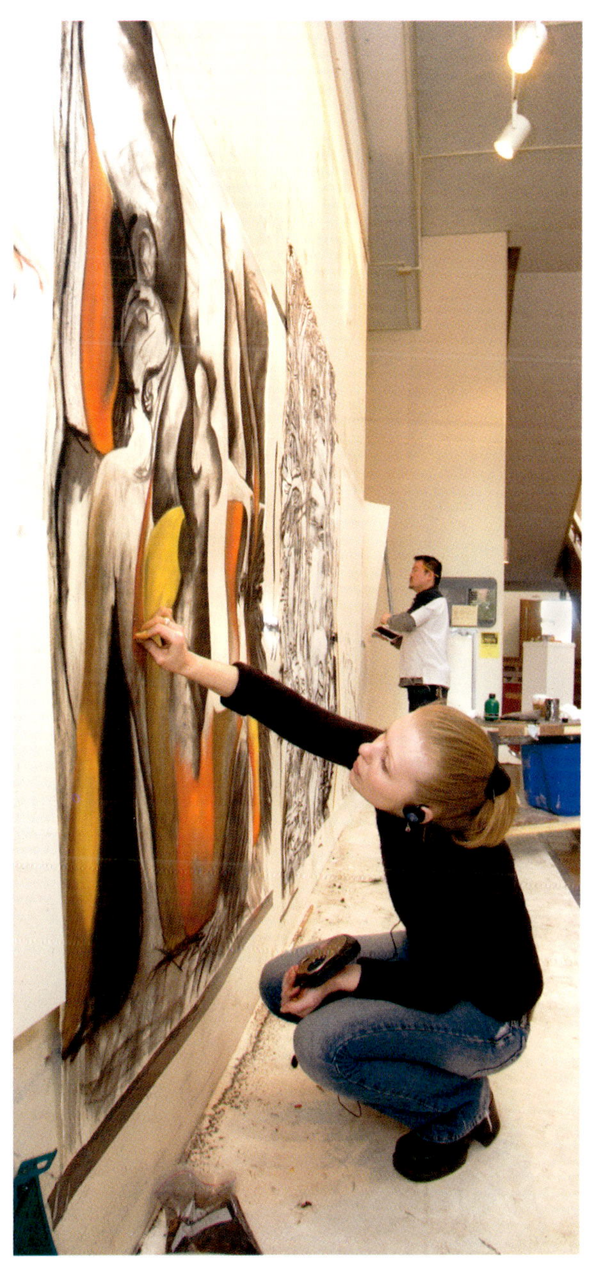

Fine Arts majors participate in
"Draw till You Drop."

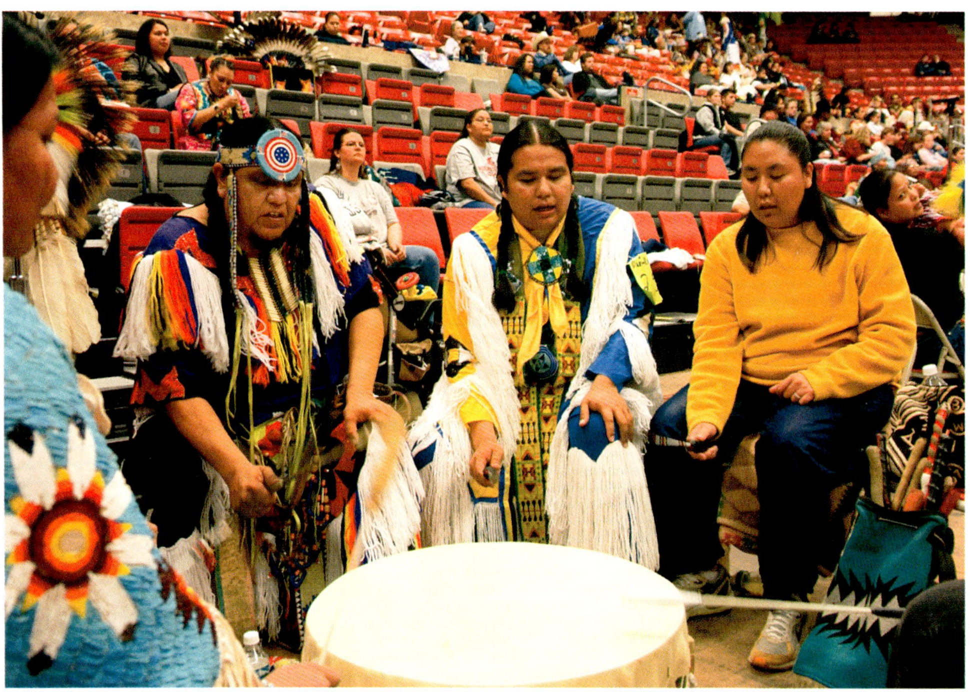

Southeast Washington was the traditional homeland of the Palouse and Nez Perce peoples, breeders of the famous Appaloosa horse. Descendants annually attend the Pah-Loots-Pu Celebration in the Beasley Performing Arts Coliseum for ceremonial and competitive dancing.

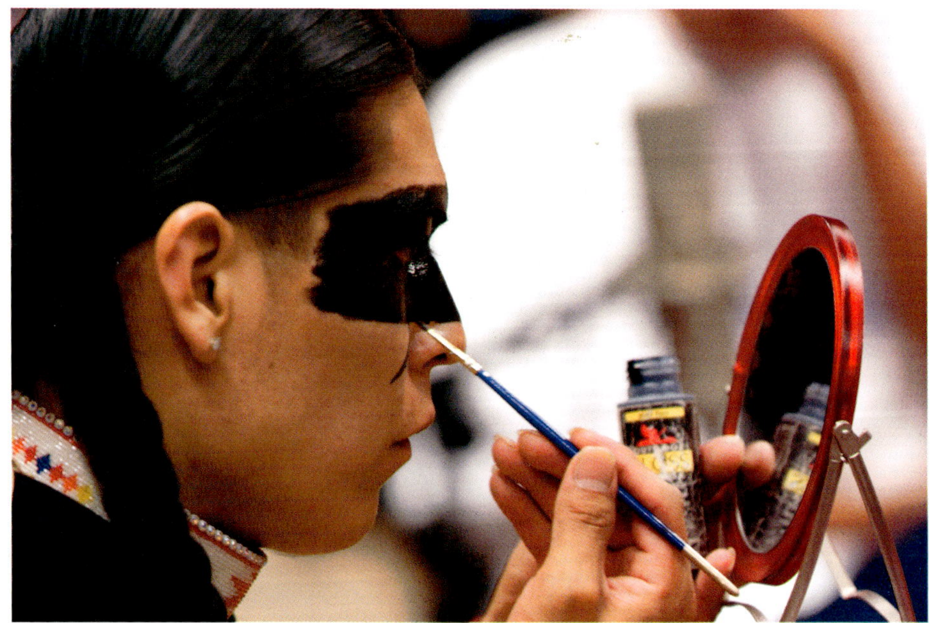

A steady hand applies final preparations for the opening events.

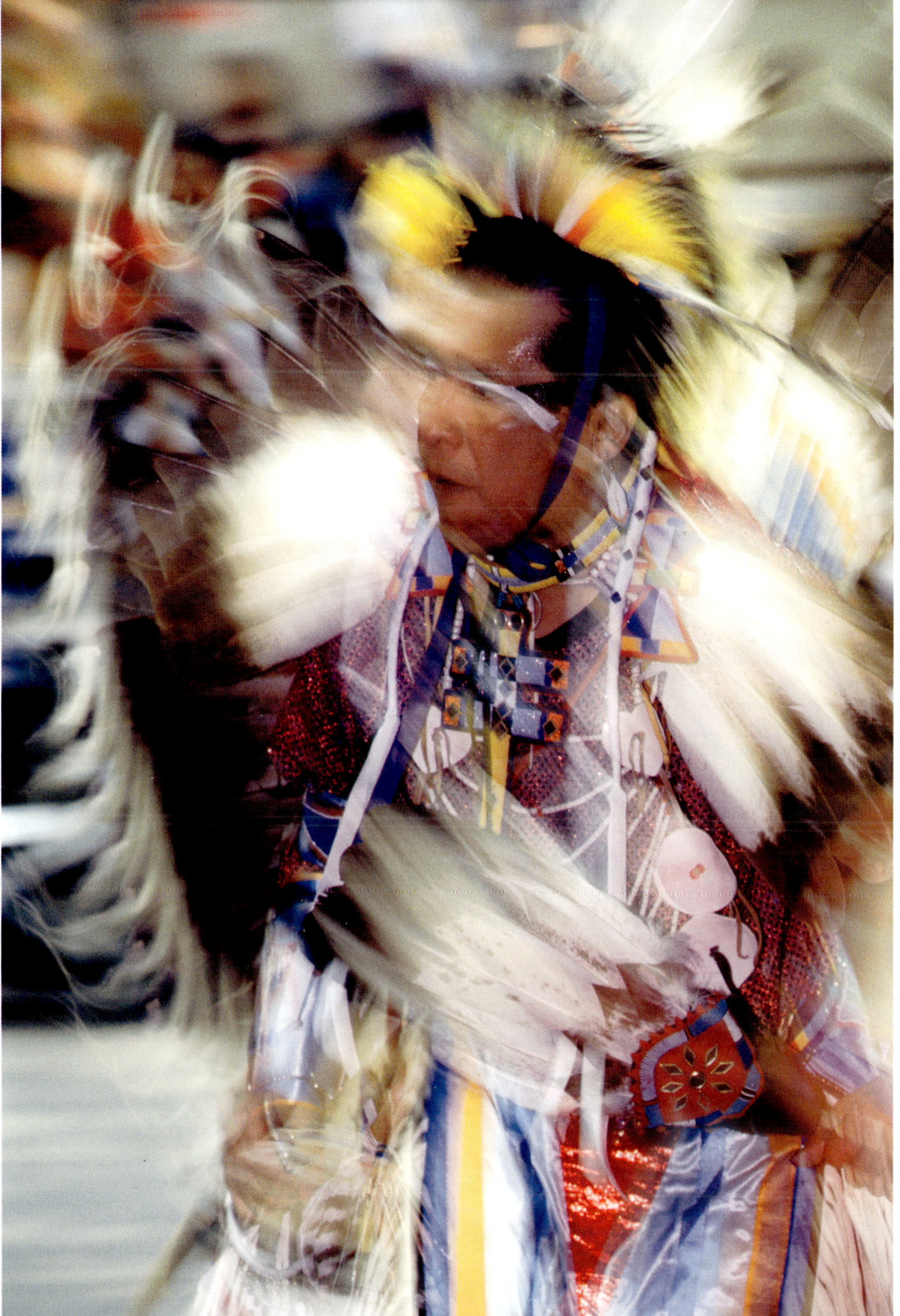

Native American dancers and singers from throughout the Inland Northwest attend the Pow Wow.

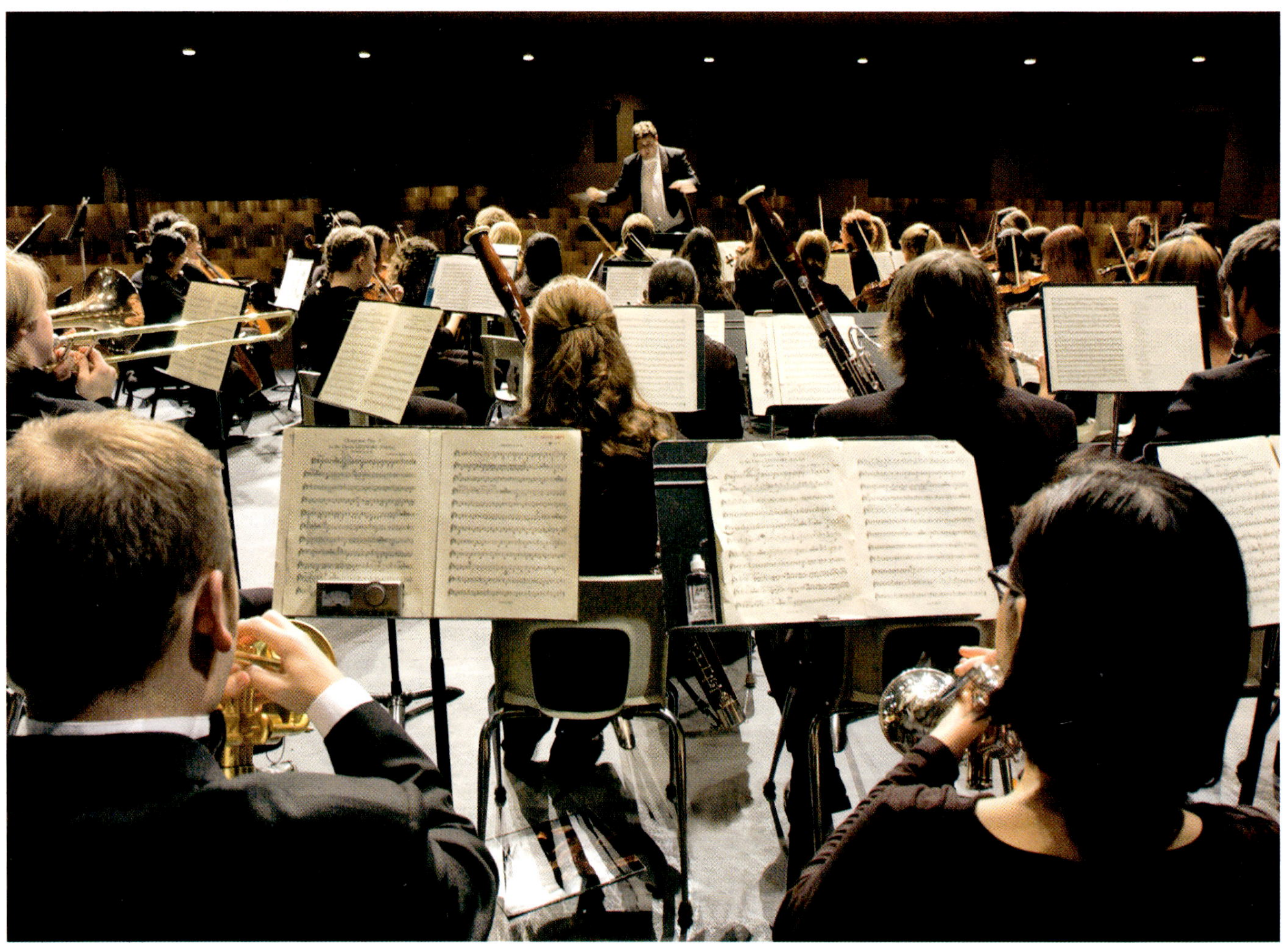

The WSU Orchestra
rehearses for a concert.

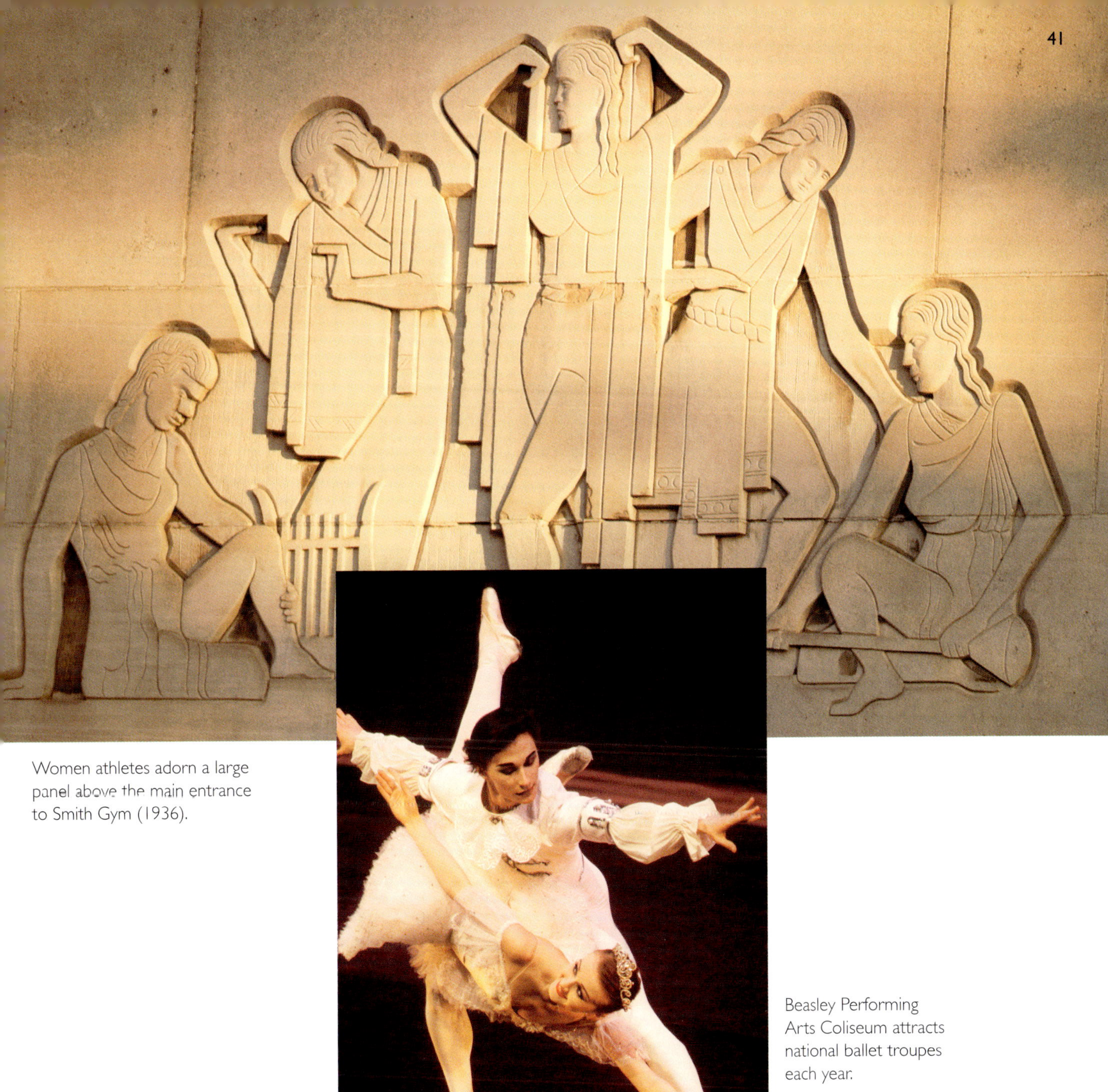

Women athletes adorn a large panel above the main entrance to Smith Gym (1936).

Beasley Performing Arts Coliseum attracts national ballet troupes each year.

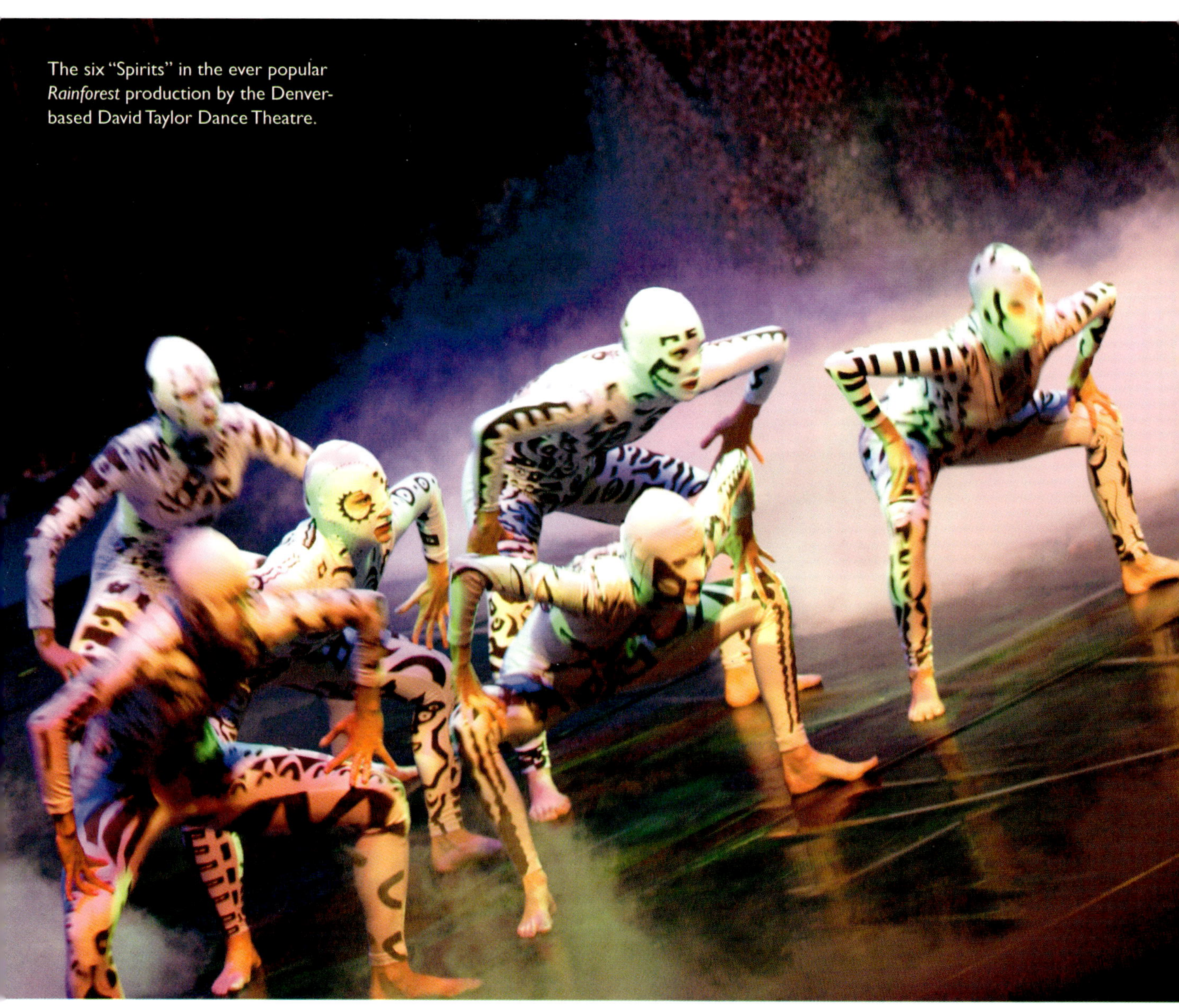

The six "Spirits" in the ever popular *Rainforest* production by the Denver-based David Taylor Dance Theatre.

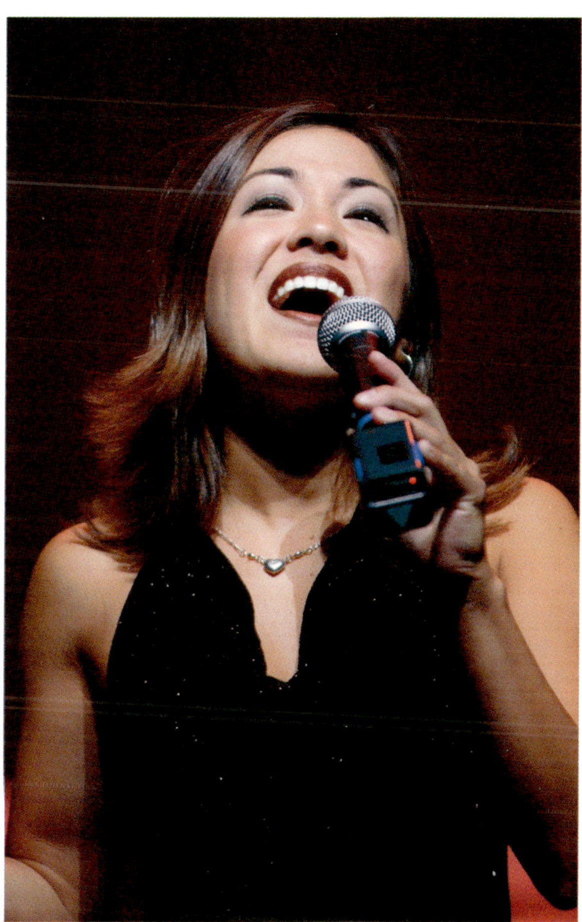

A member of the Crimson
Revue performs during the
Jazz Showcase.

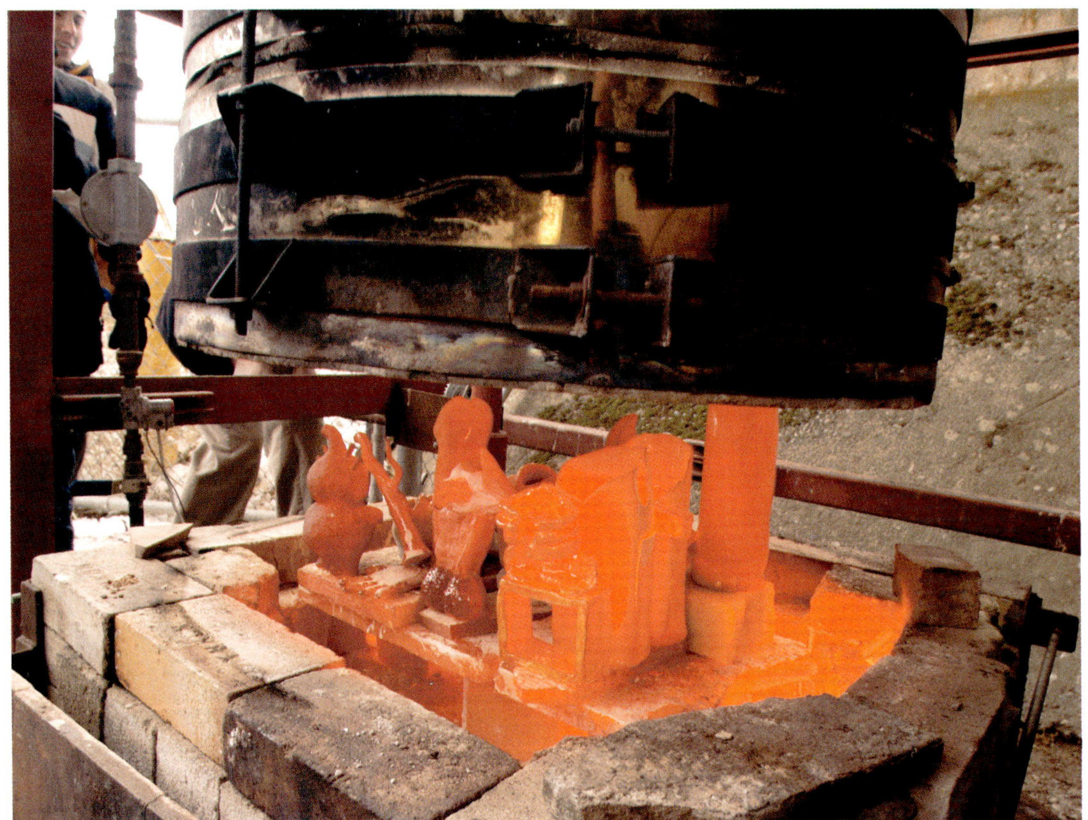

Fine Arts ceramic students
participate in a Raku firing.

"Around in Art" exhibit at the Museum of Art gallery.

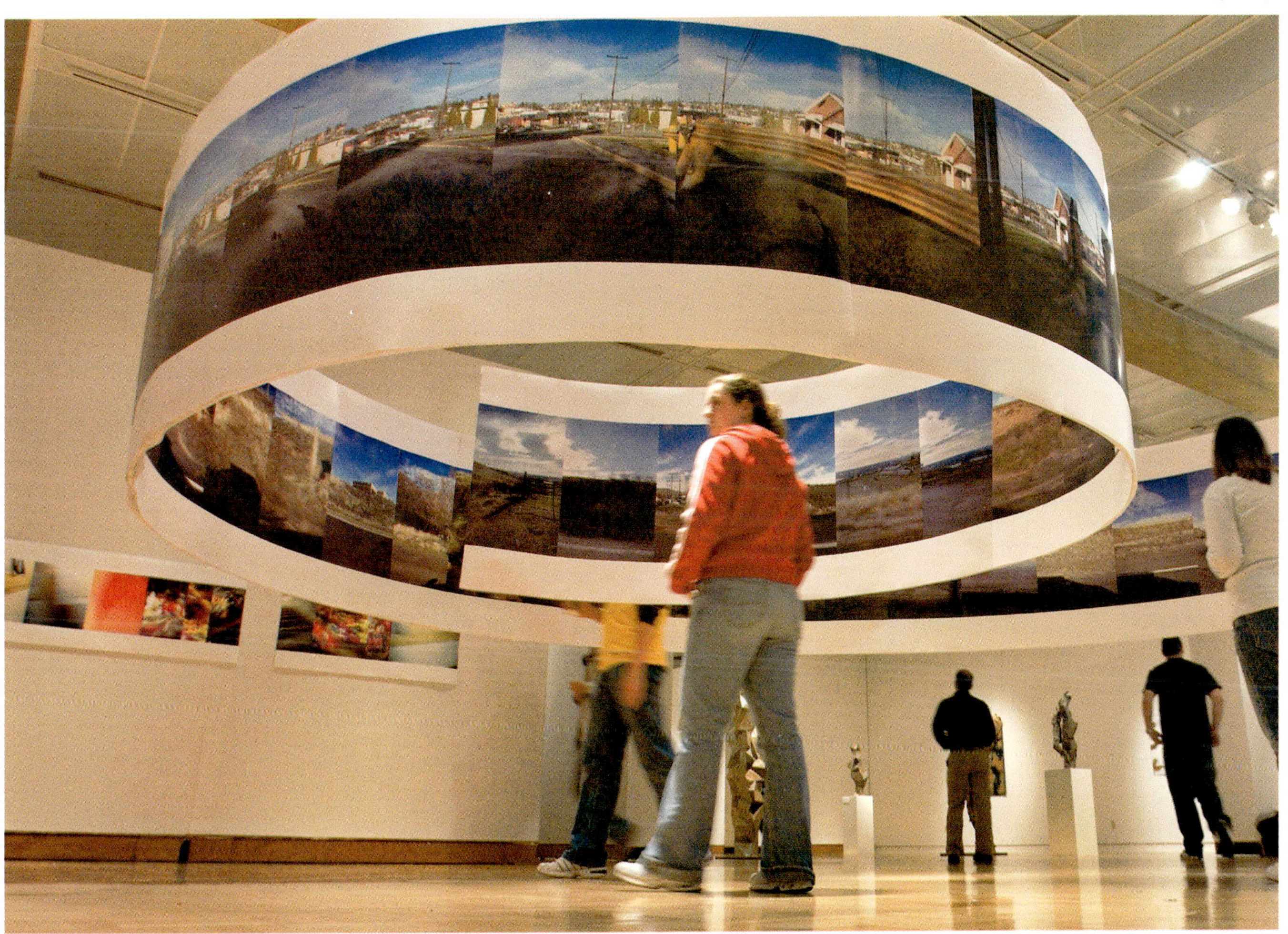

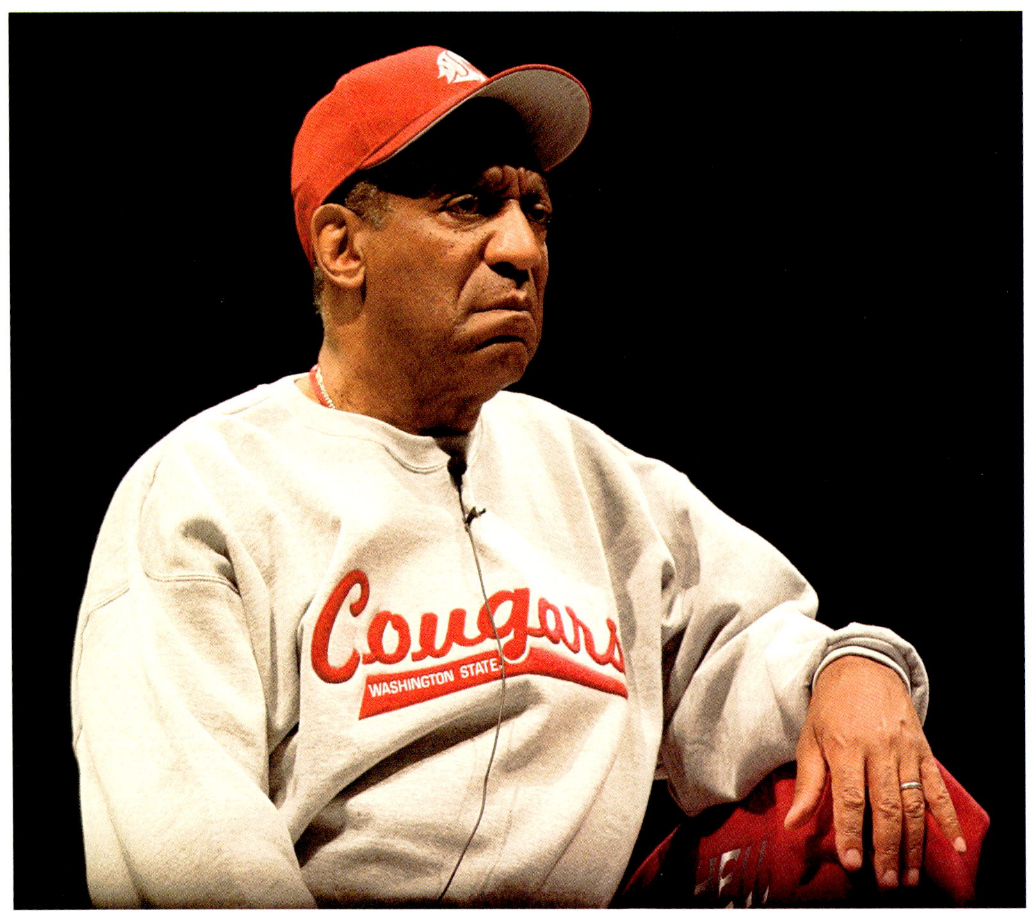

Bill Cosby entertains the
Mom's Weekend crowd.

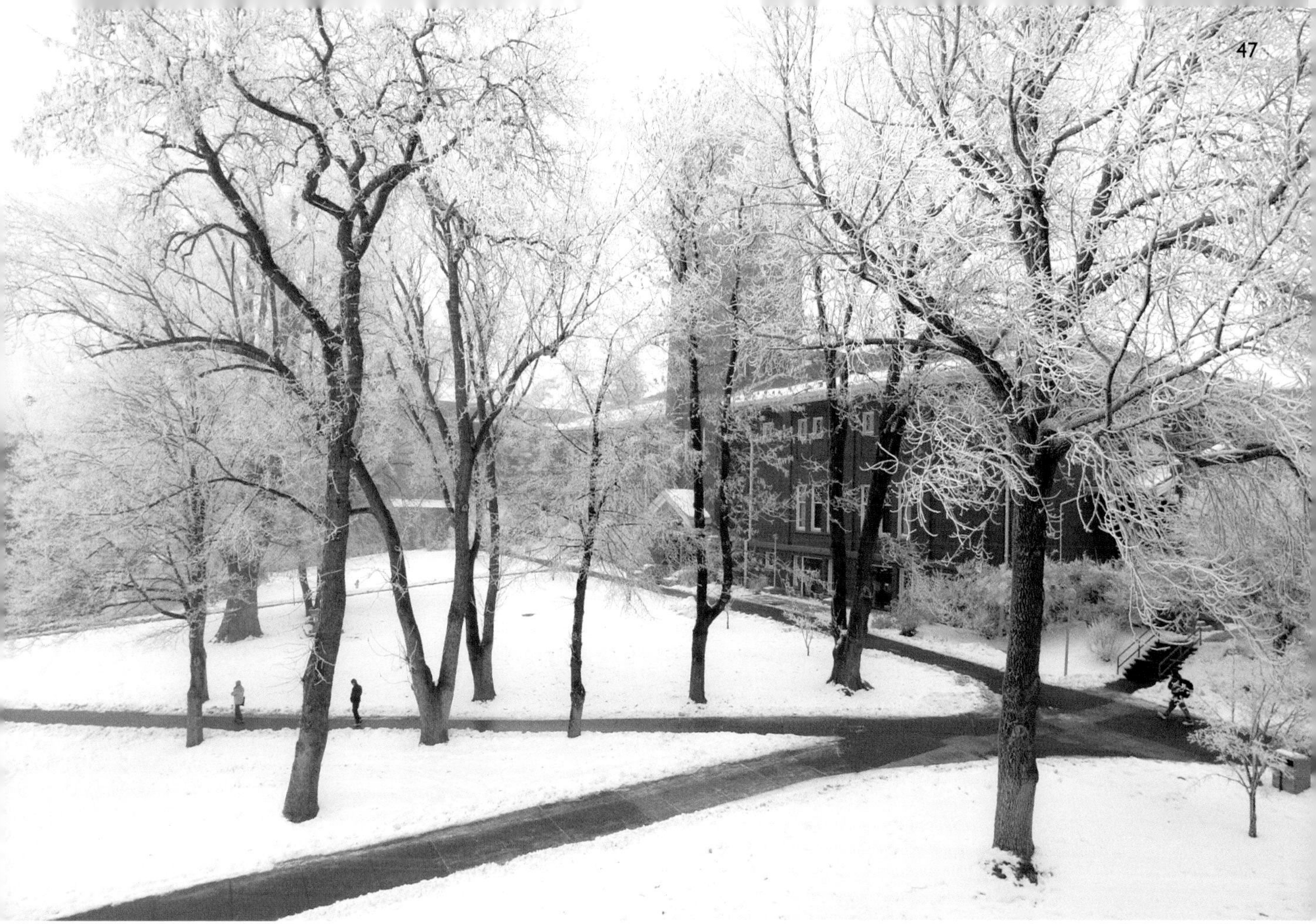

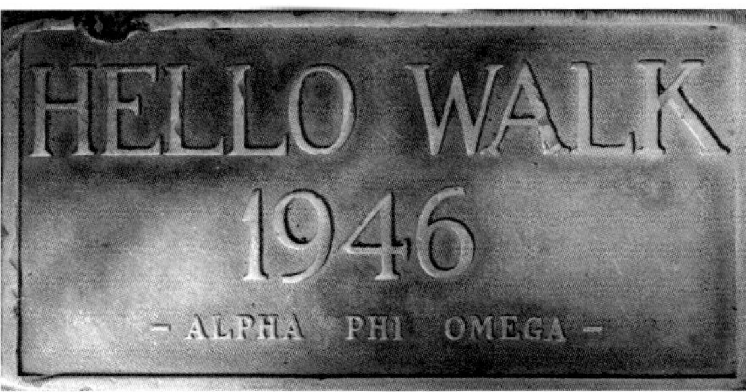

Bryan Hall auditorium provides an intimate venue for concerts, lectures, and other events. Hello Walk passes directly under the clock tower.

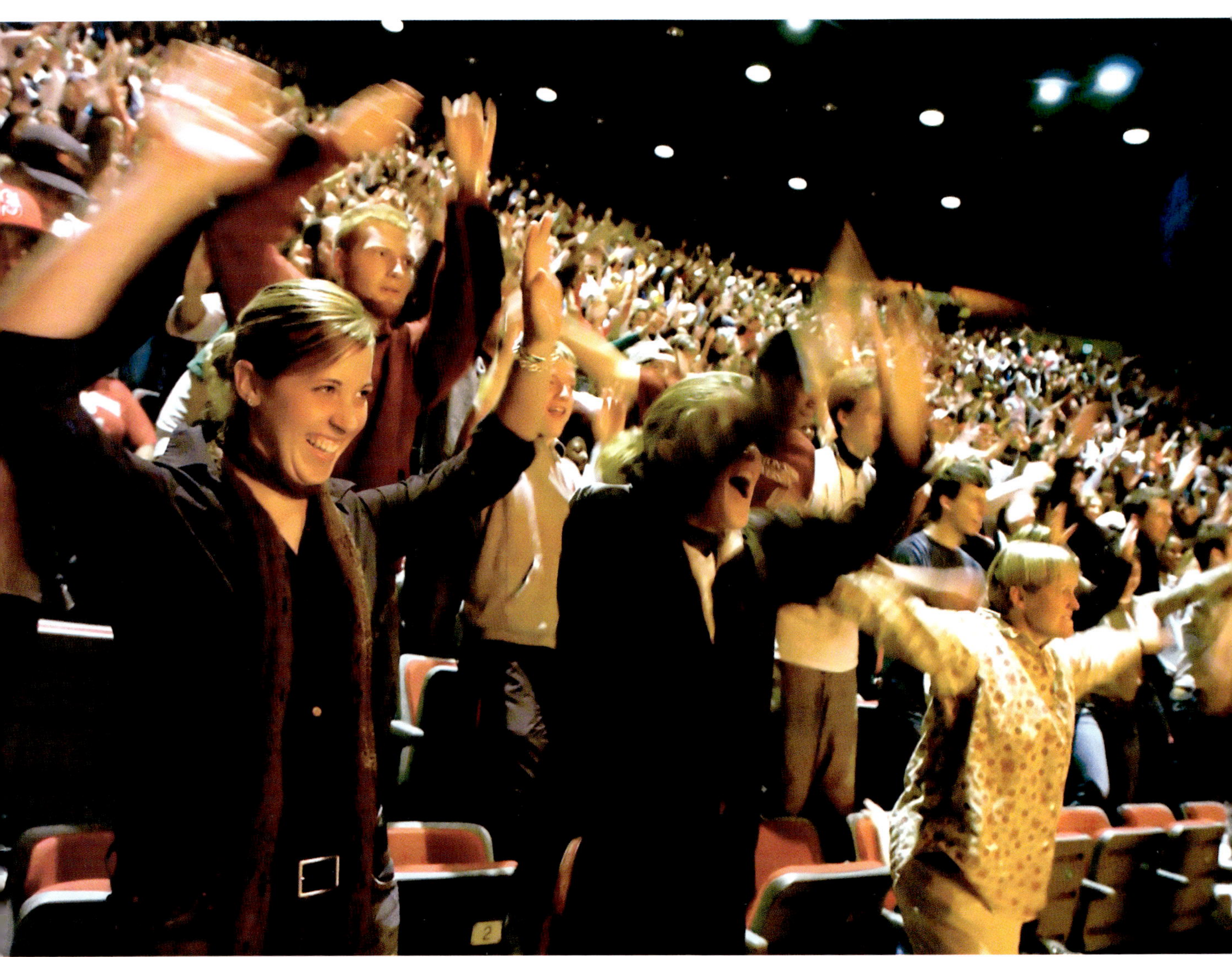

An enthusiastic audience responds at the
Step Afrika performance in Beasley Coliseum.

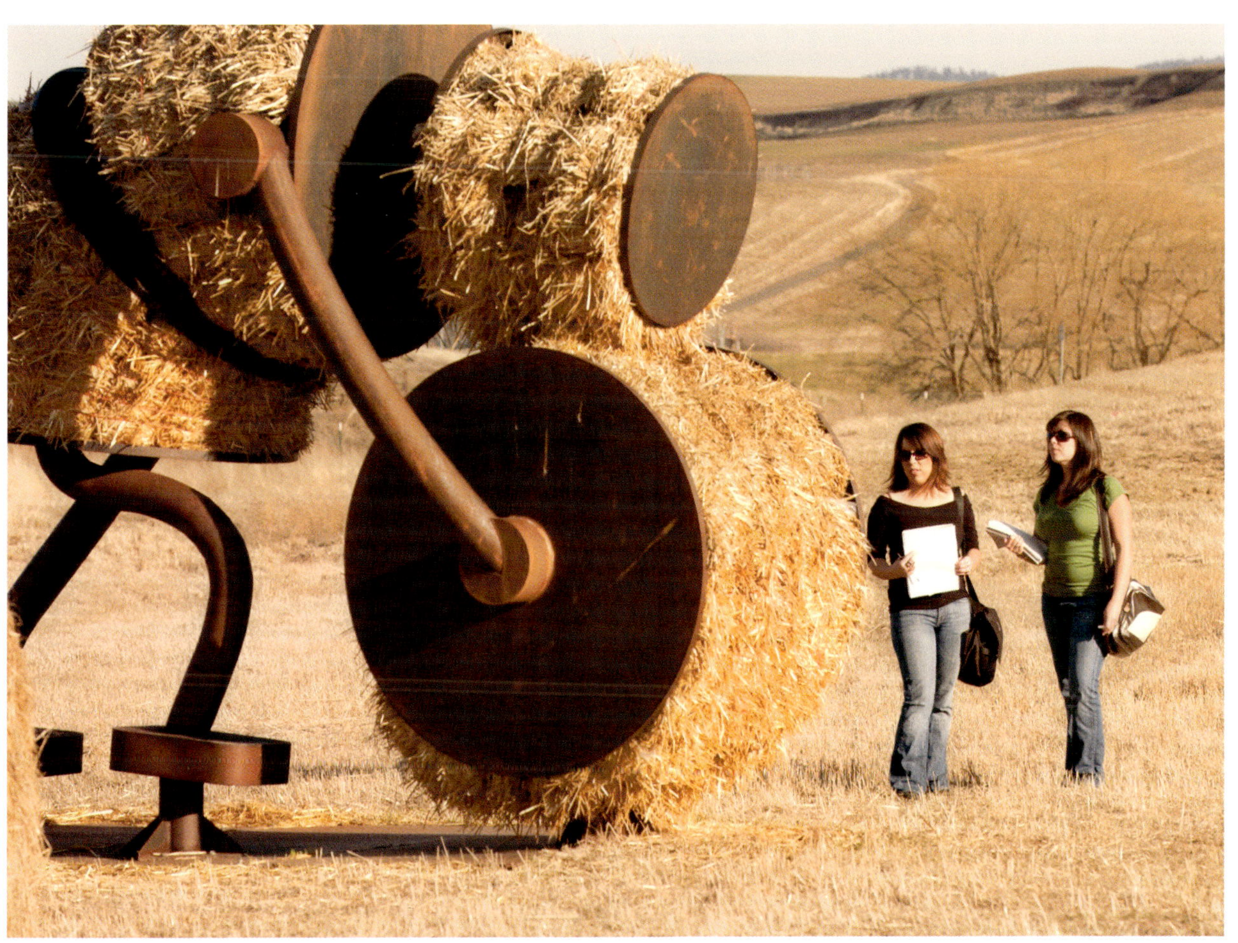

Students admire *Makin' Hay*, cast by artist Tom Otterness at the highly regarded Walla Walla Foundry. The steel sculpture was on temporary display in a field east of the Pullman campus.

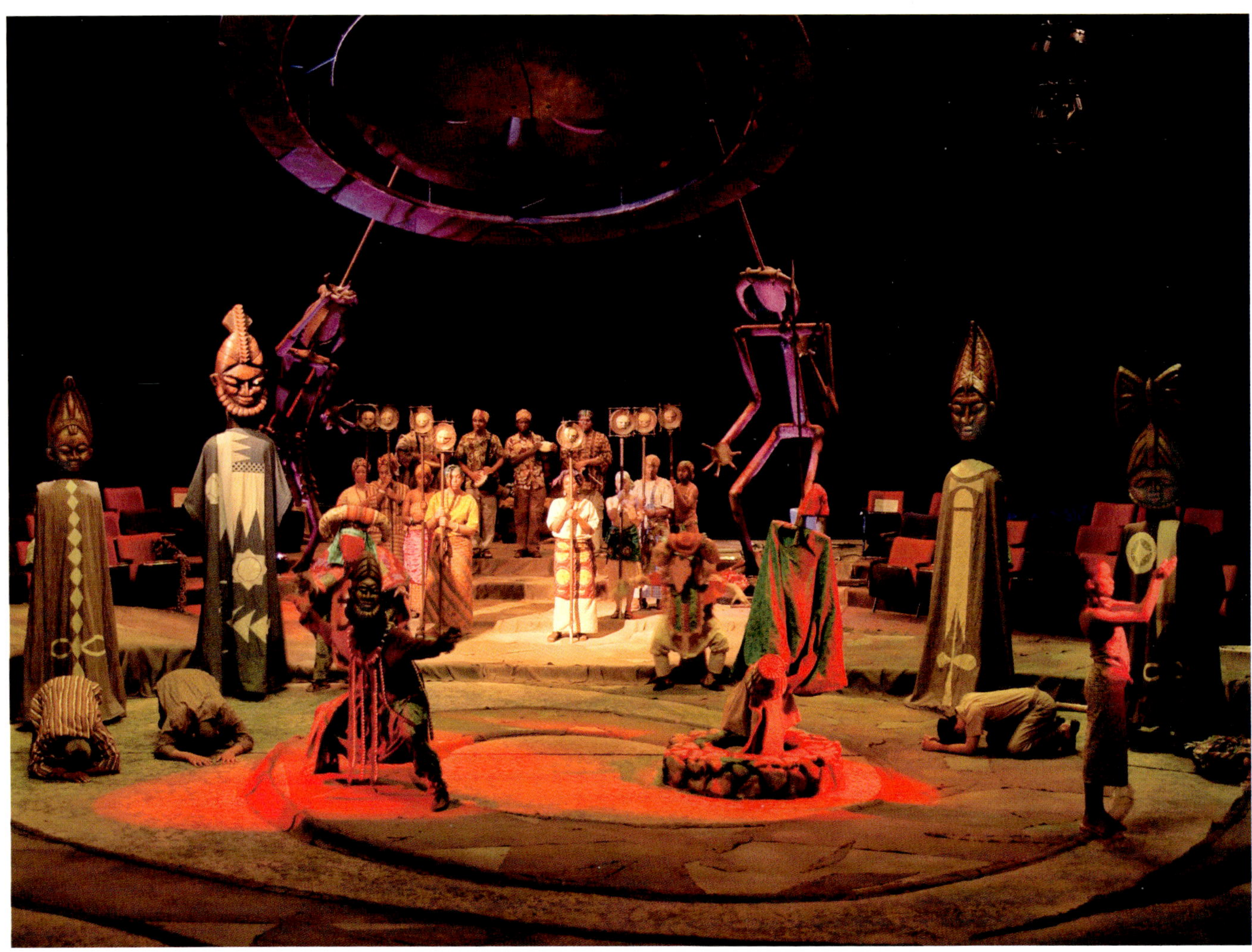

WSU Theatre's presentation of the celebrated *Death and the King's Horseman* by African writer Wole Soyinka. The Nobel Laureate attended the presentation of his play at the Pullman campus.

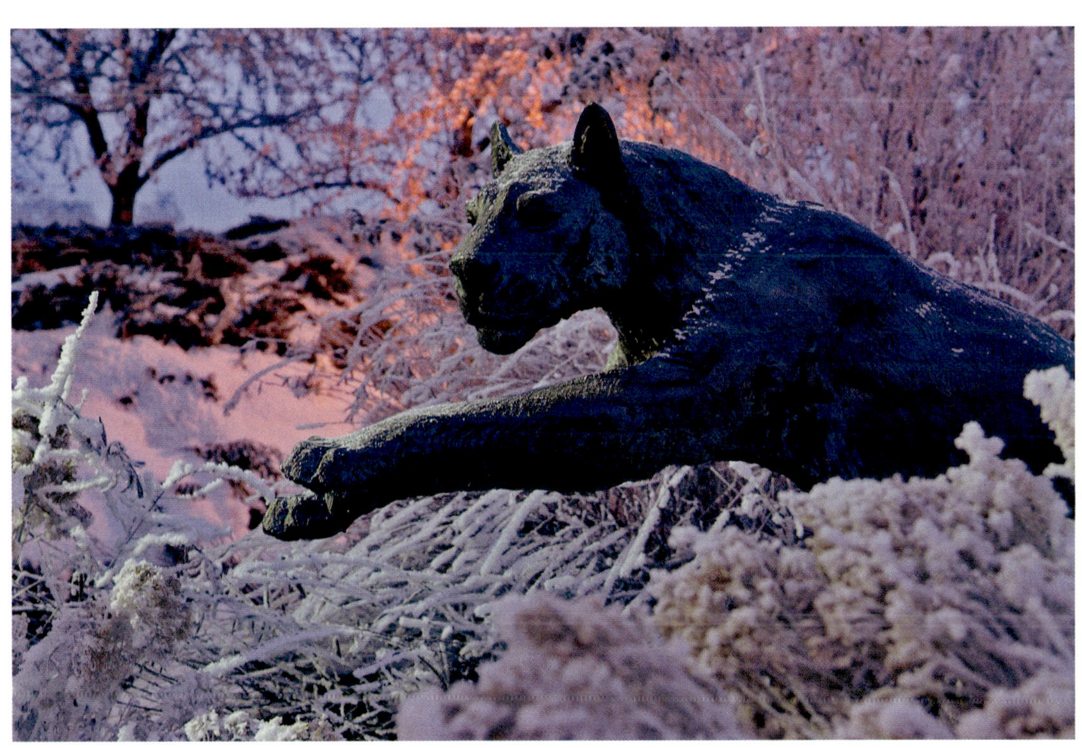

Lewis Alumni Centre
bronze cougar.

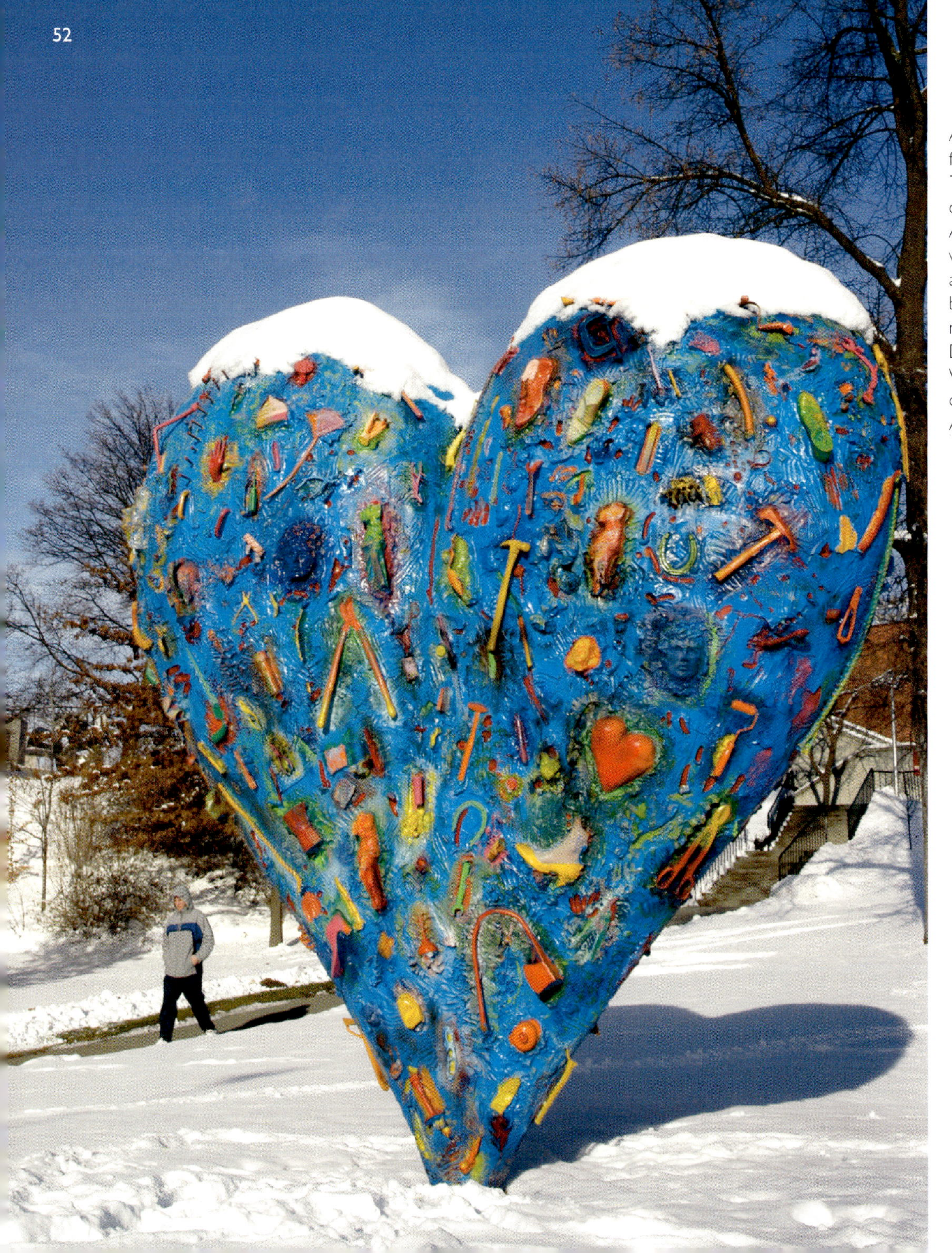

Art is meant to engender feeling, and the gigantic *Technicolor Heart* succeeds quite well in this regard. A splash of color in wintertime, people either admire it or loathe it. This bronze sculpture by the noted New York artist Jim Dine was cast at the Walla Walla Foundry and is part of the WSU Museum of Art outdoor collection.

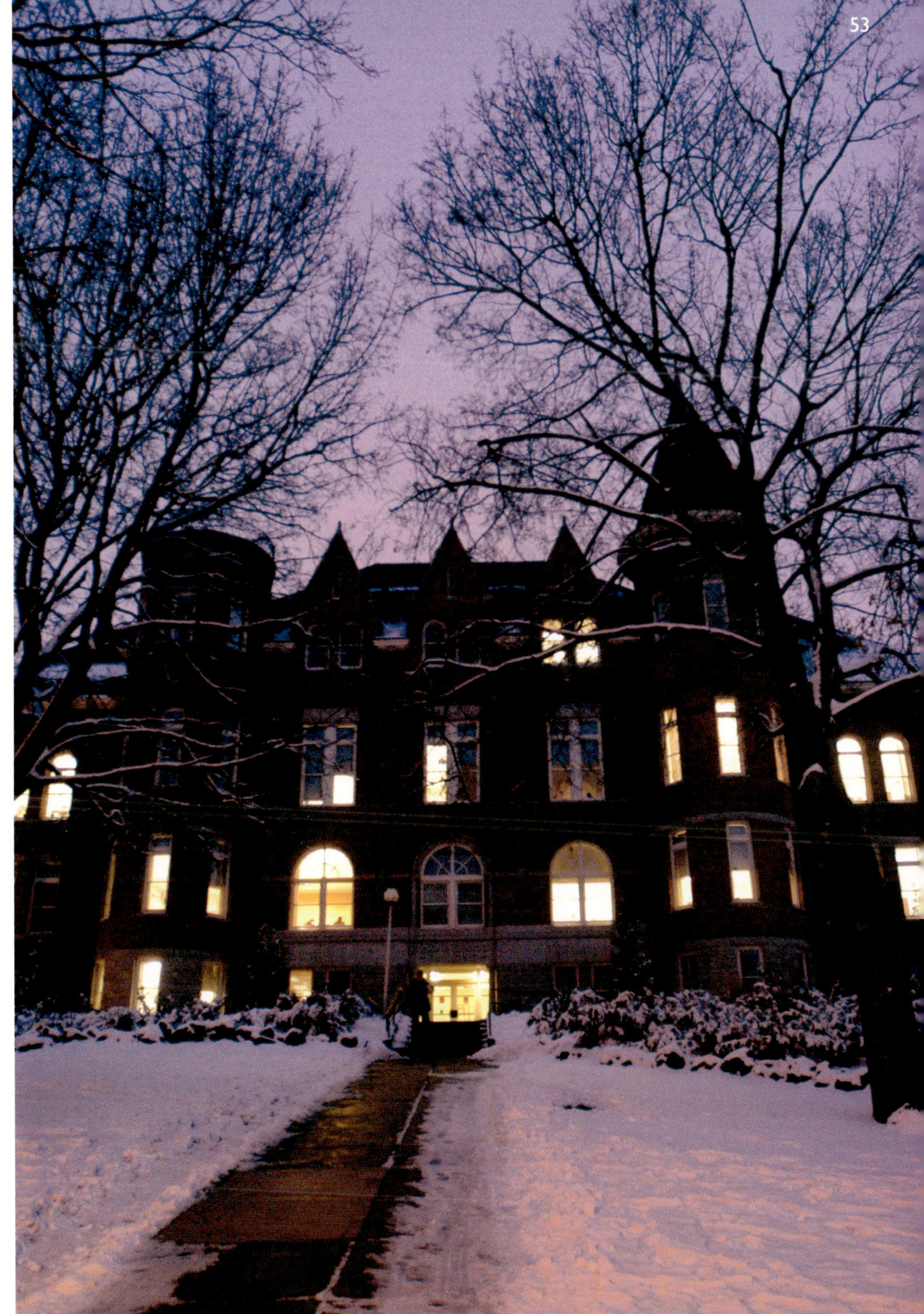

With its attractive Victorian Romanesque character, Thompson Hall signified a secure future for the new college in 1895, and served as the Administration Building until 1968. The structure's red brick was derived from clay deposits located just a few feet from the building site. The granite trim came from a Spokane area quarry.

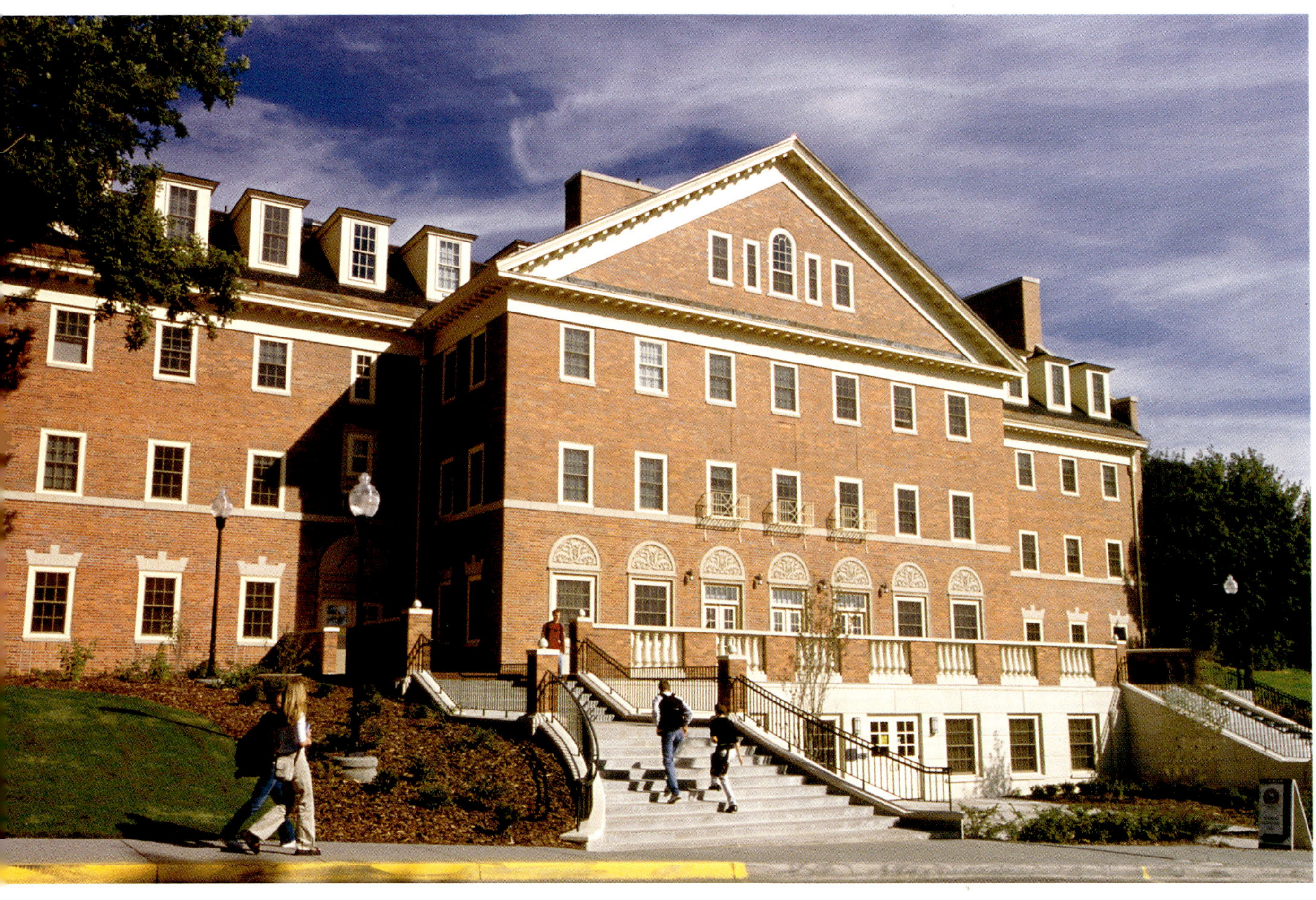

Dating from 1928, Honors Hall displays the fine brick masonry that has characterized the core campus area since WSU's founding. And, as with many structures erected between 1905 and 1943, it exhibits revivalist Classical and Georgian architectural elements. Most buildings of this era were the designs of architecture professors Rudolph Weaver and Stanley Smith.

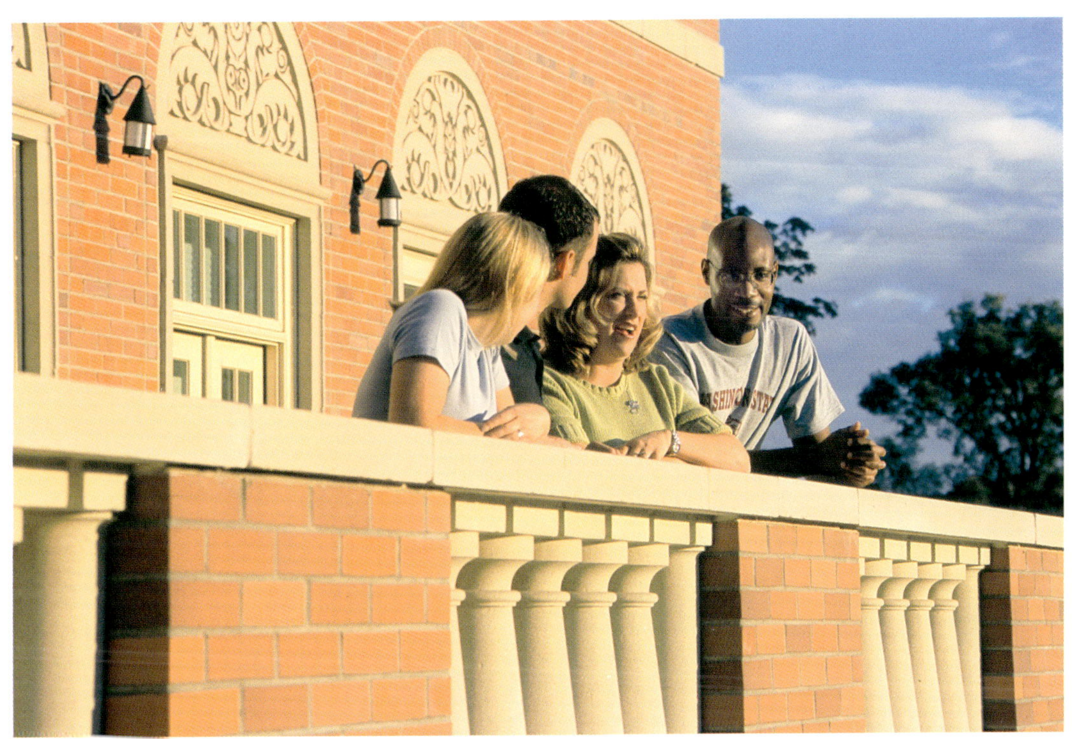

The hall houses a dynamic
mix of University Honors
College enrollees and non-
honors students, who share
living space, kitchenettes,
and lounge areas.

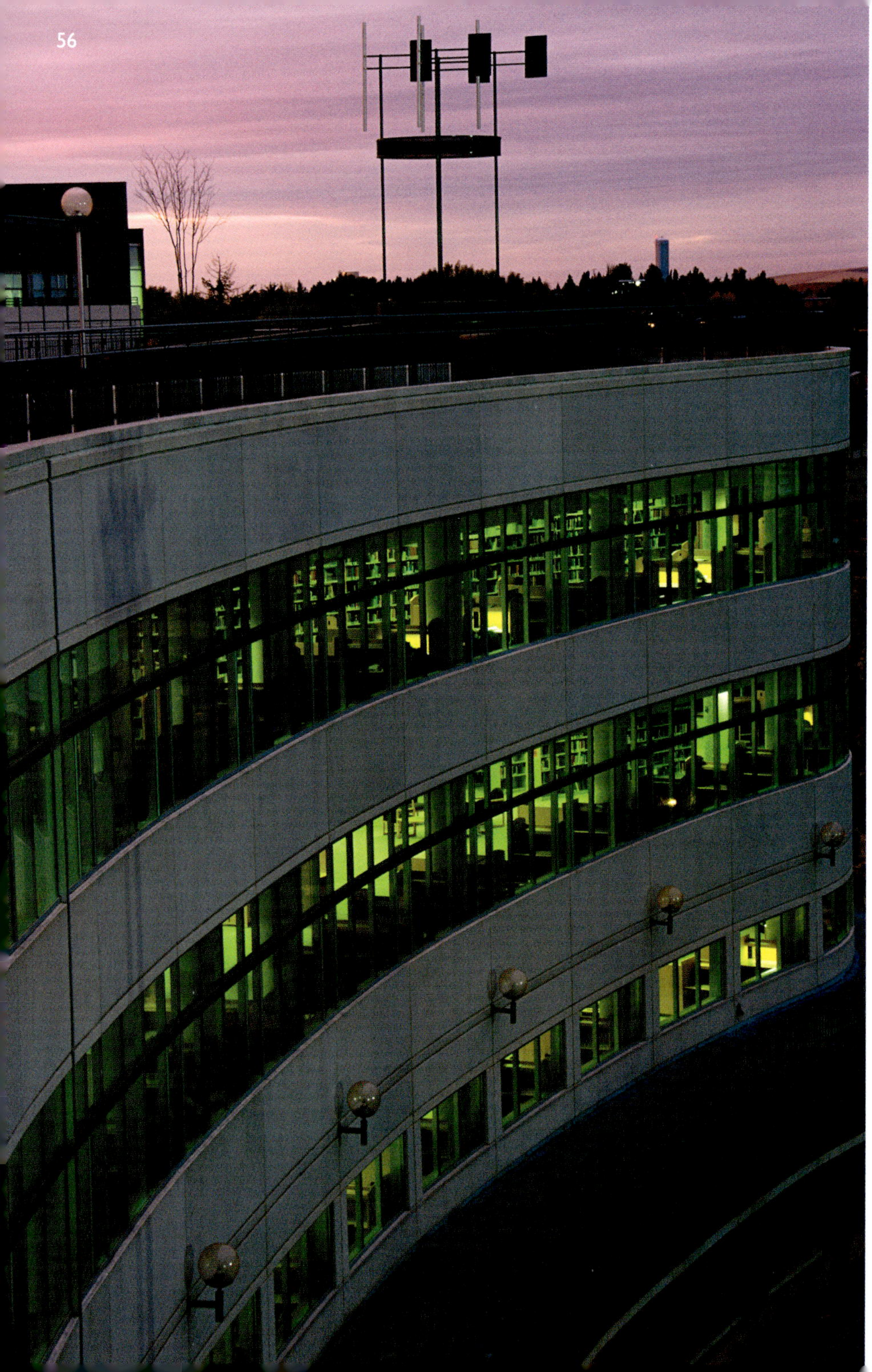

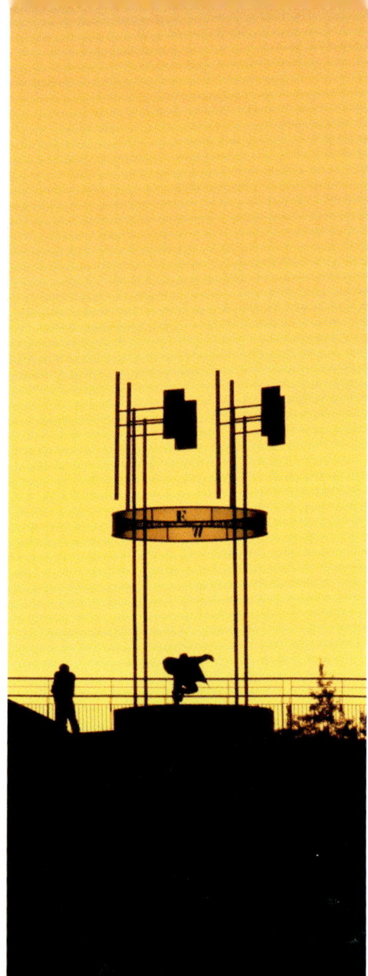

The Holland-Terrell Library's arched facade grandly overlooks Rogers Field and Martin Stadium. A harmonic wind-chime structure stands on top amongst rooftop walkways and lawns.

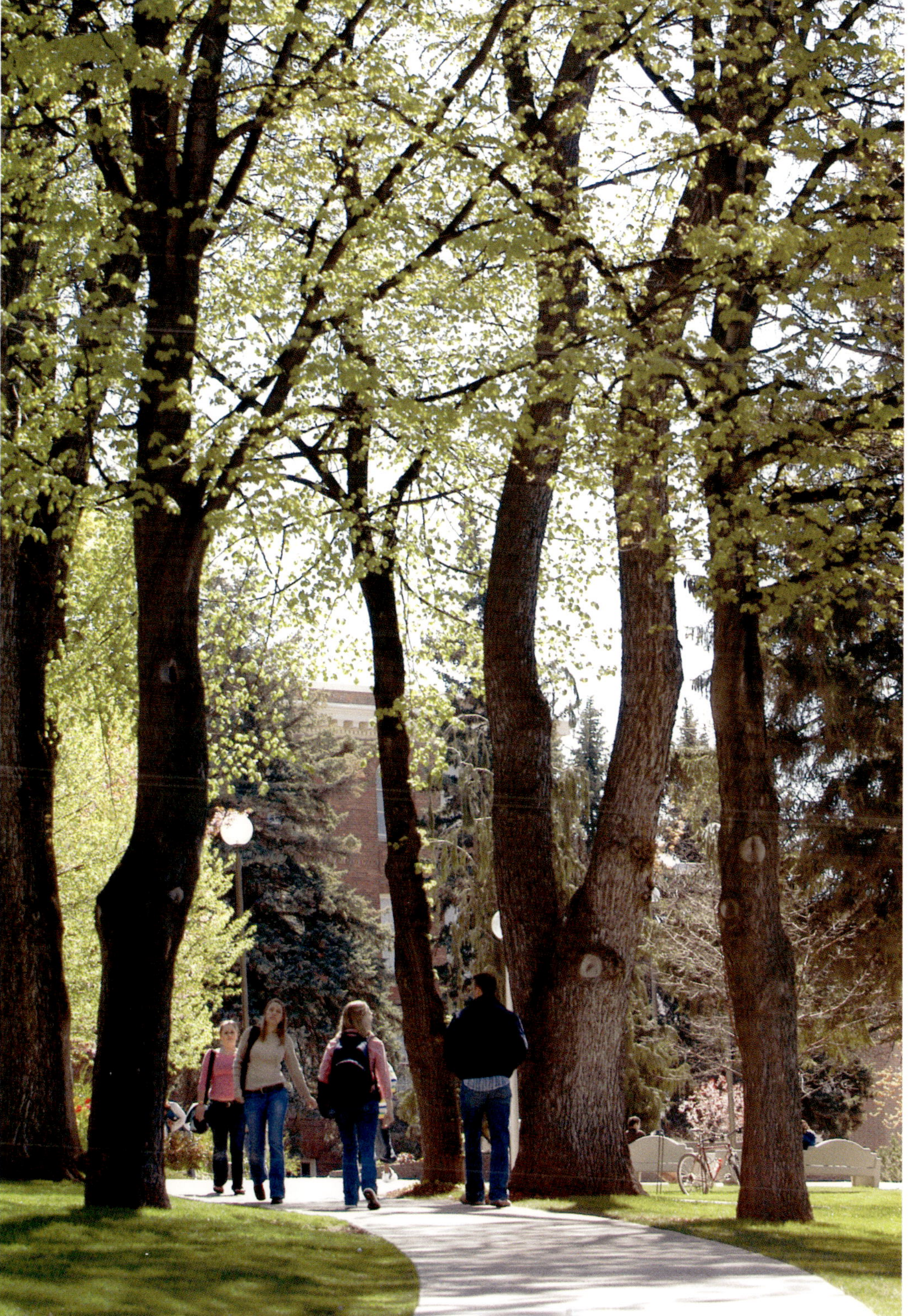

A campus walkway in springtime.

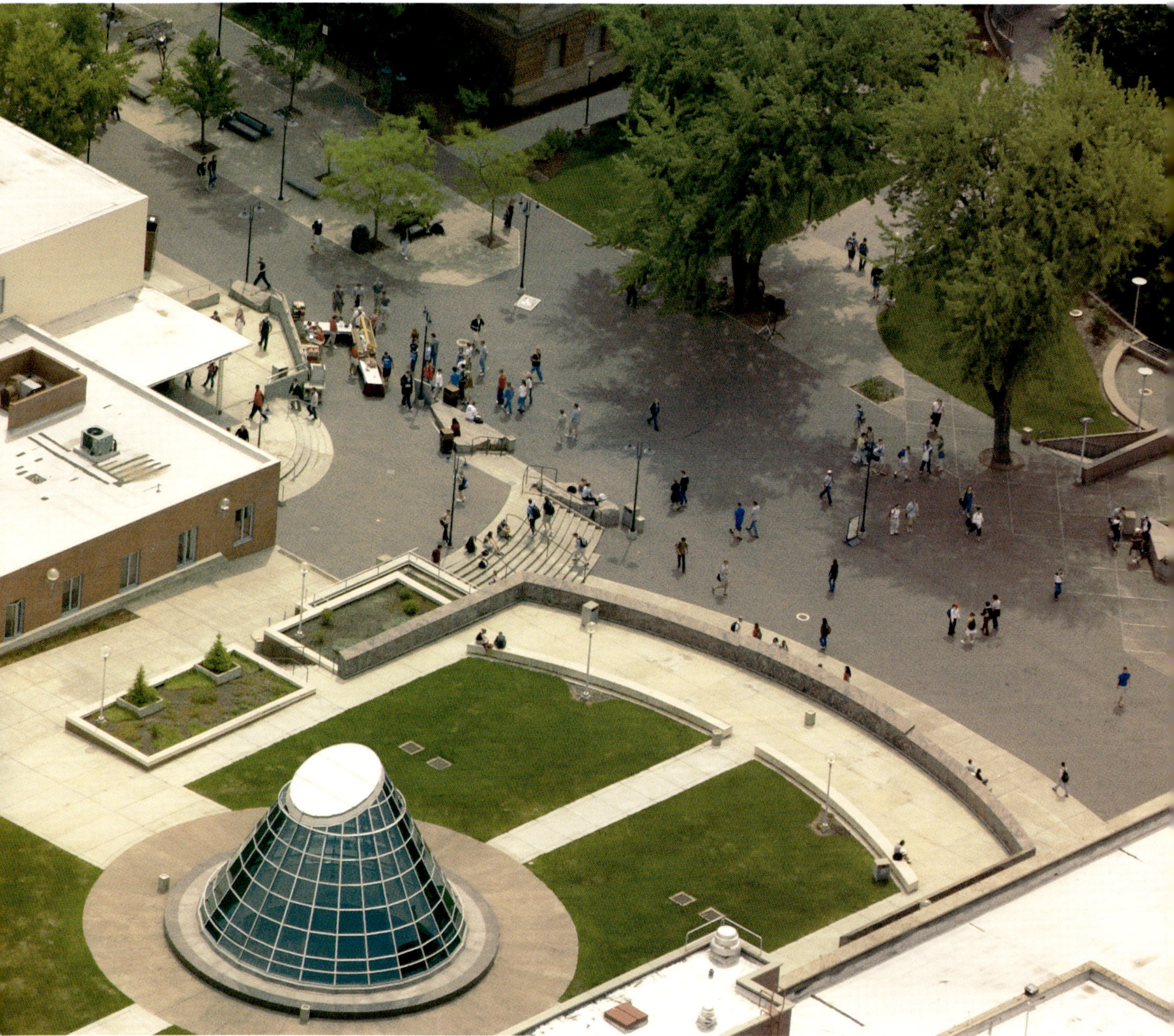

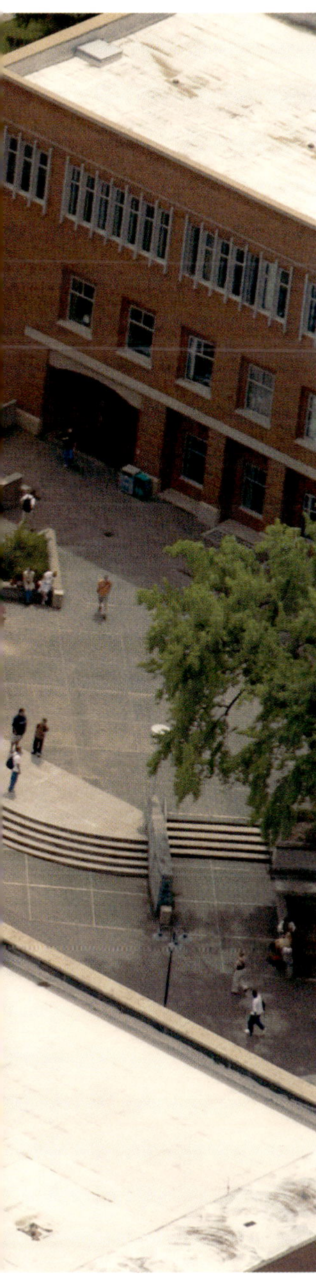

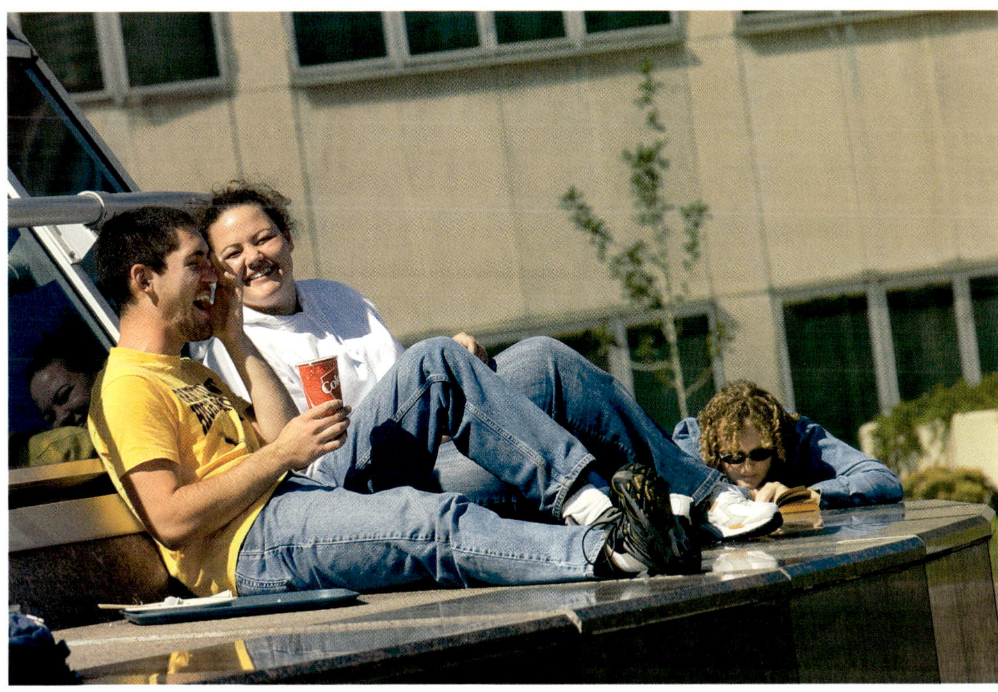

Terrell Mall and the library's landscaped roof—between classes the pedestrian friendly platform surrounding the library dome attracts students for conversation and study.

Jazz combo performing in the atrium, venue for a weekly noon music series beneath the library dome.

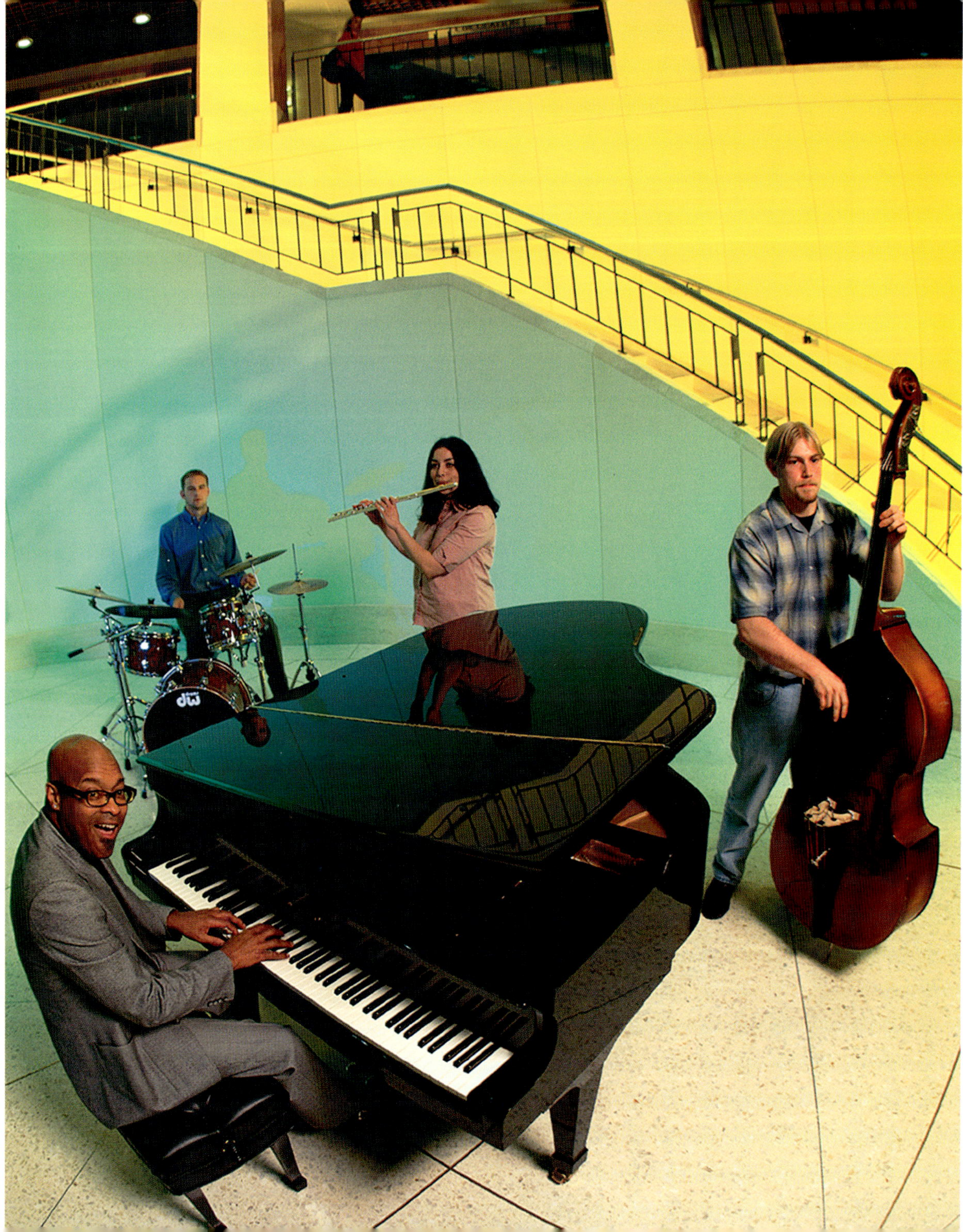

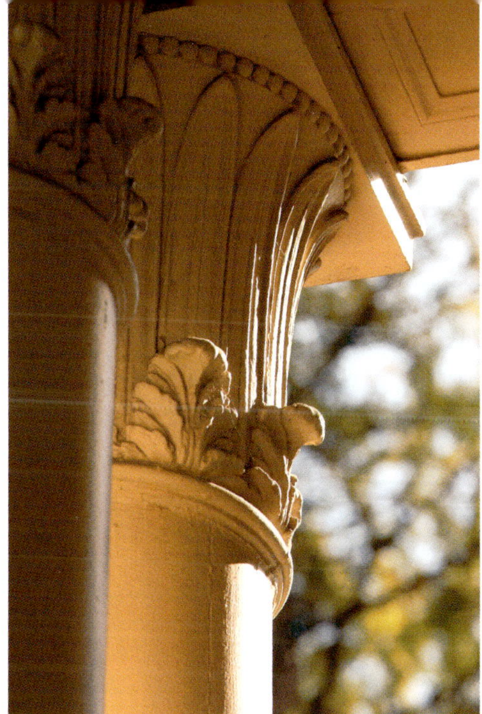

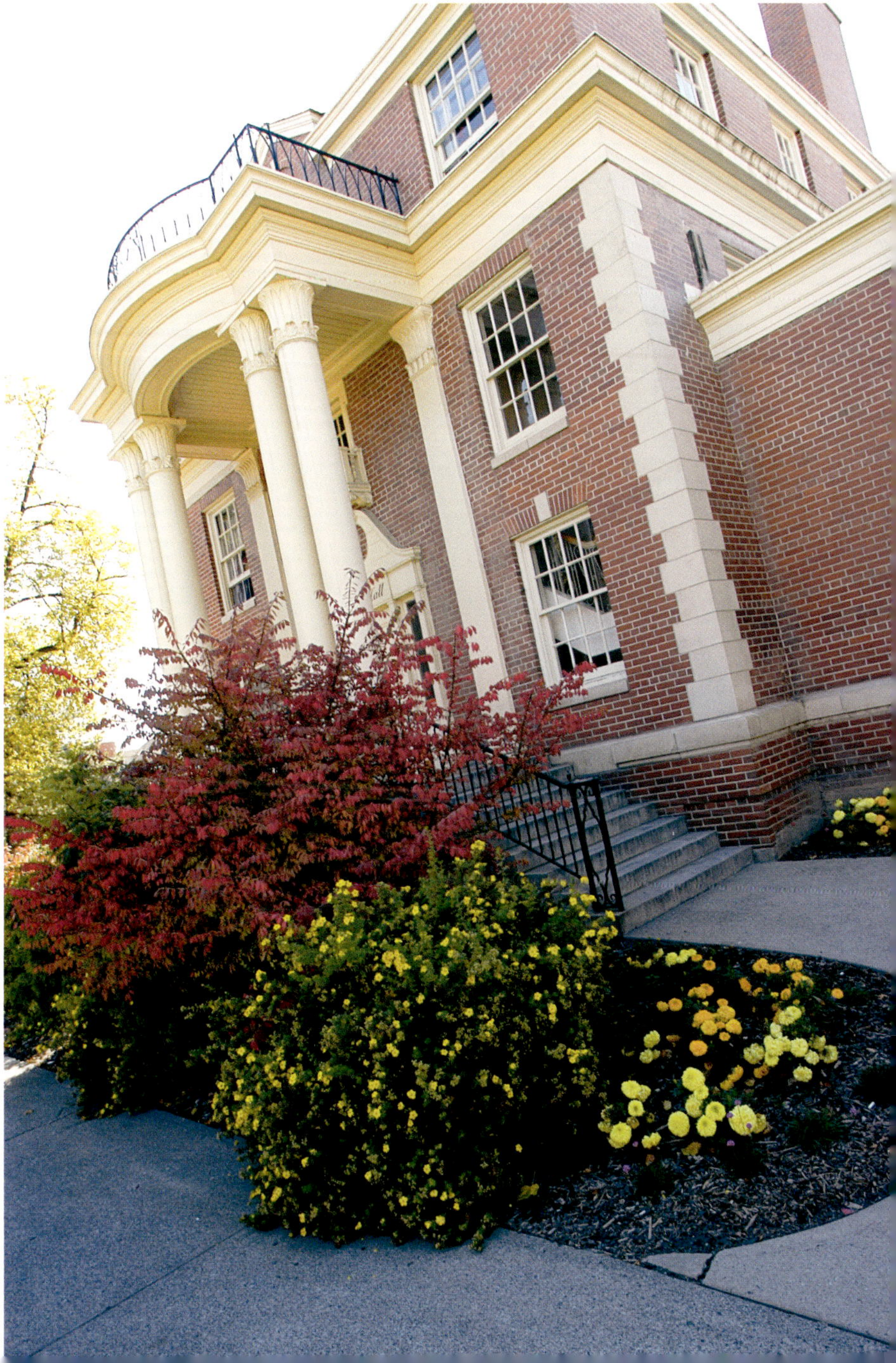

Springtime at the ornate
Wilmer-Davis Residence
Hall complex.

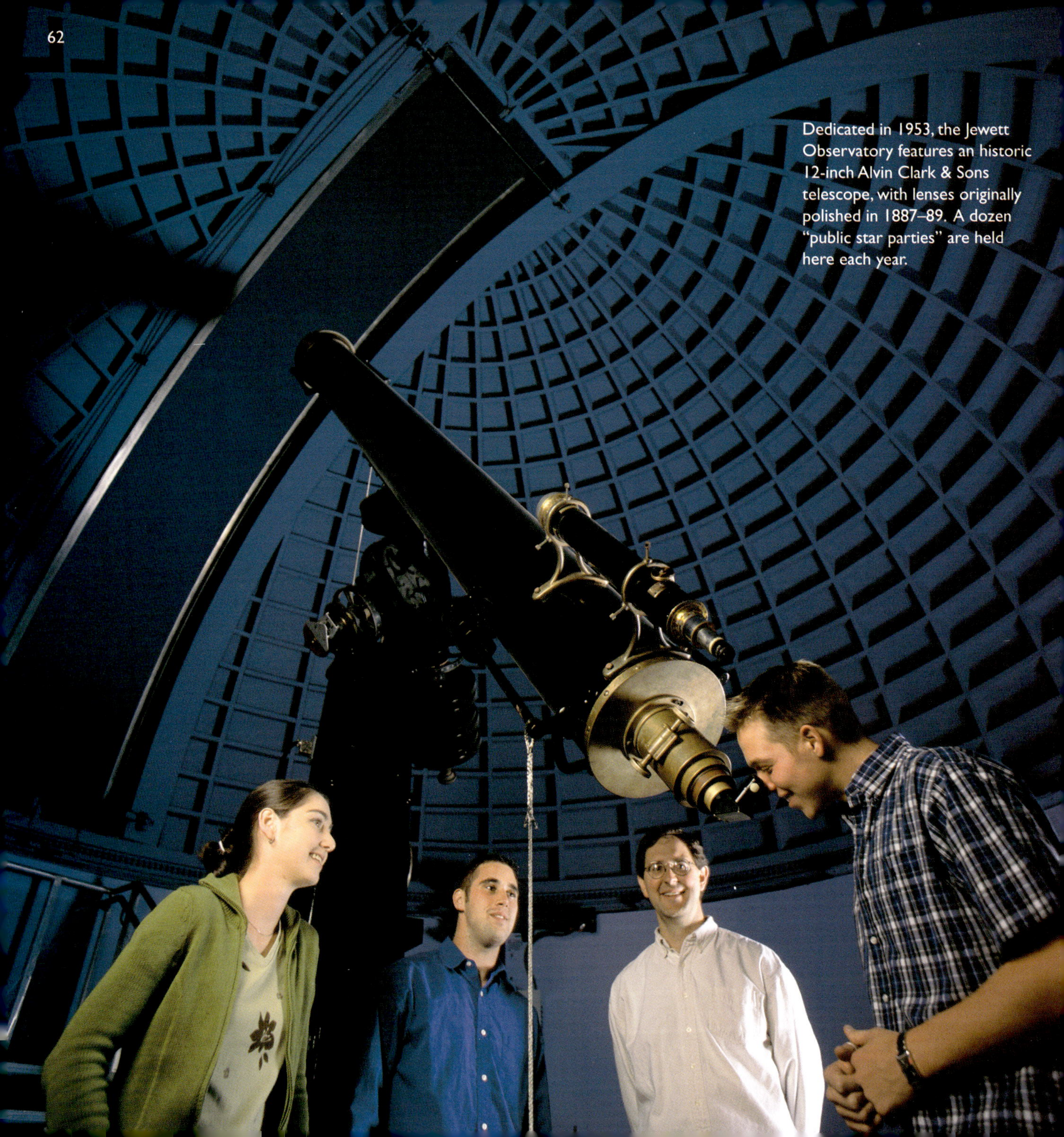

Dedicated in 1953, the Jewett Observatory features an historic 12-inch Alvin Clark & Sons telescope, with lenses originally polished in 1887–89. A dozen "public star parties" are held here each year.

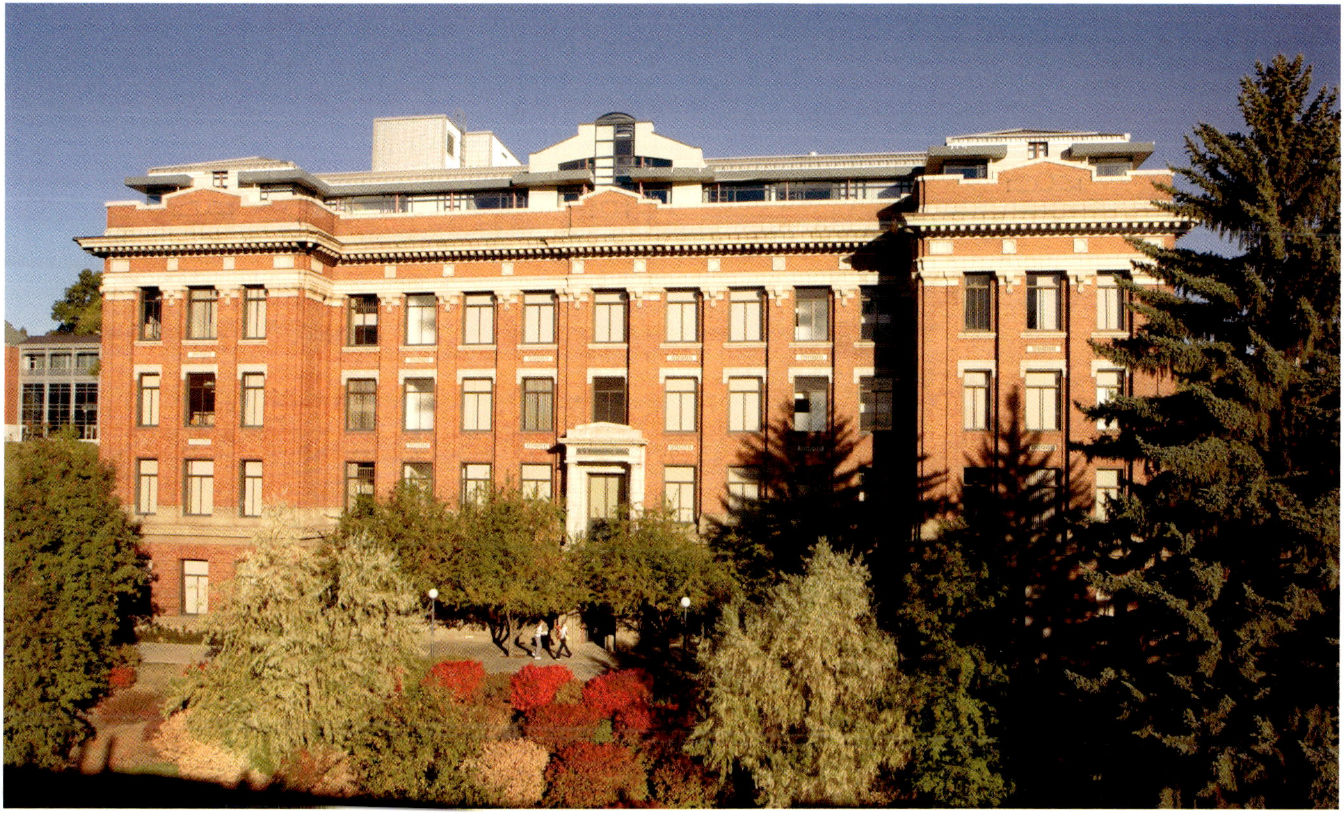

One of the nation's best-equipped architectural schools resides in Carpenter Hall (1926), where upper level majors have their own workstations with specialized computer software. Conveniently at hand are other vital resources, including a complete architecture library.

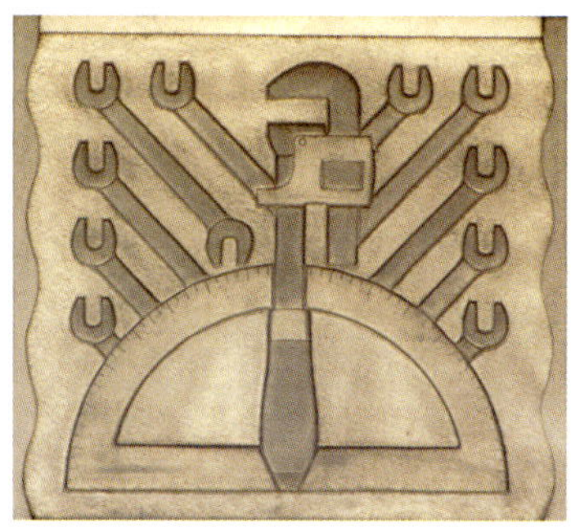

Metal wrench art over a door in Dana Hall (1947), a fitting tribute to the architectural and engineering shops, offices, and instruction housed in the building.

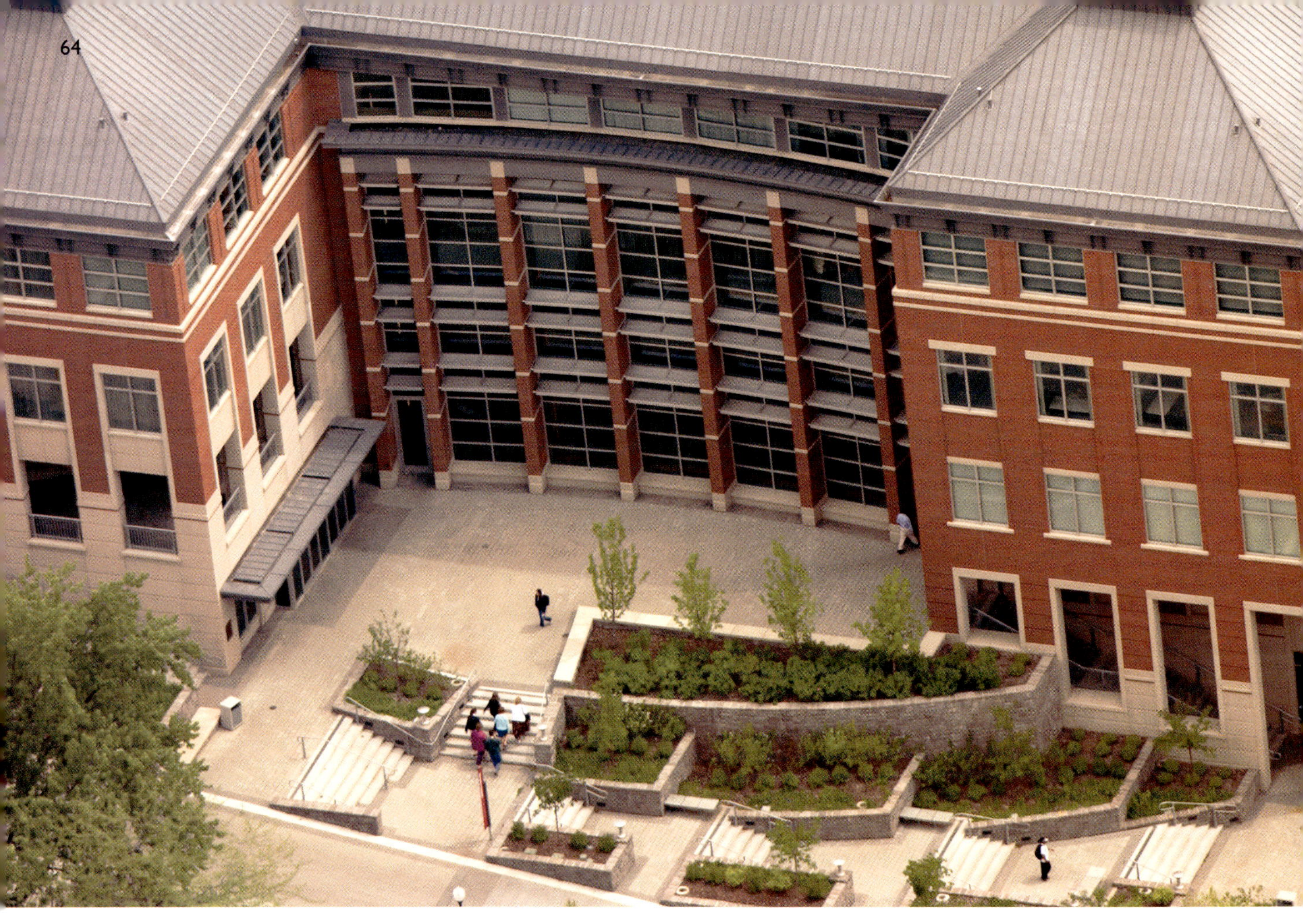

The 94,000 square-feet Smith Center for Undergraduate Education embodies WSU's commitment to academic success. Among its many state-of-the-art resources are walk-in tutorial services, online labs, a writing program, two auditoriums, 17 innovative and flexible classrooms, as well as additional specialty units.

Stairwell in the Smith Center—the name of the advanced educational facility commemorates Samuel H. Smith, WSU's eighth president (1985–2000).

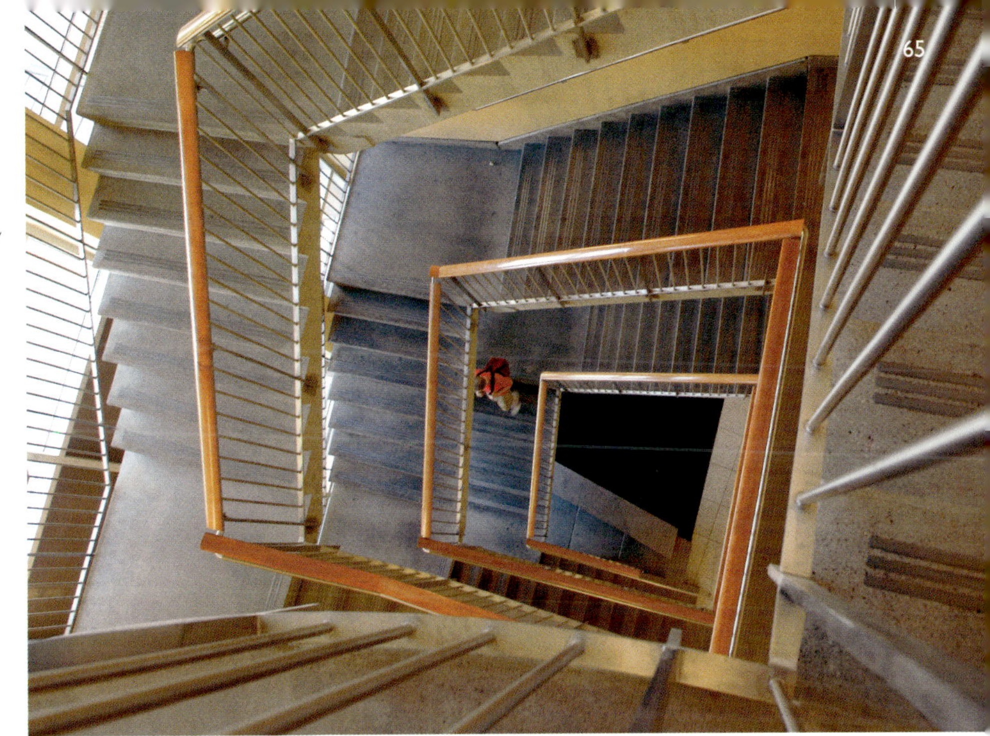

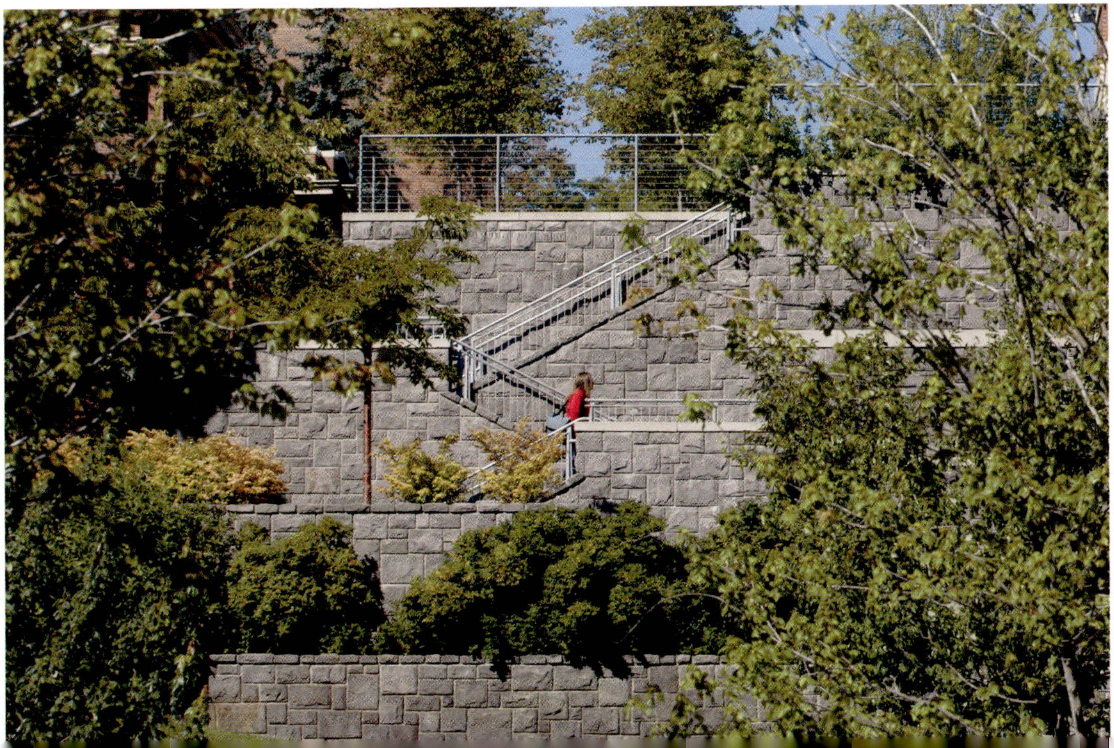

Student ascending steps outside of the Smith Center.

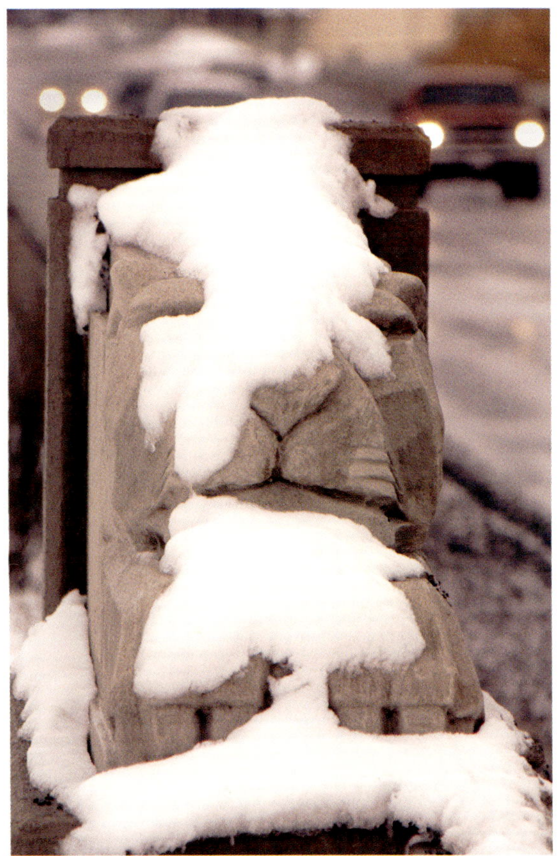

A cougar sculpture on Pullman's
Main Street overpass appears
disgruntled by the snow.

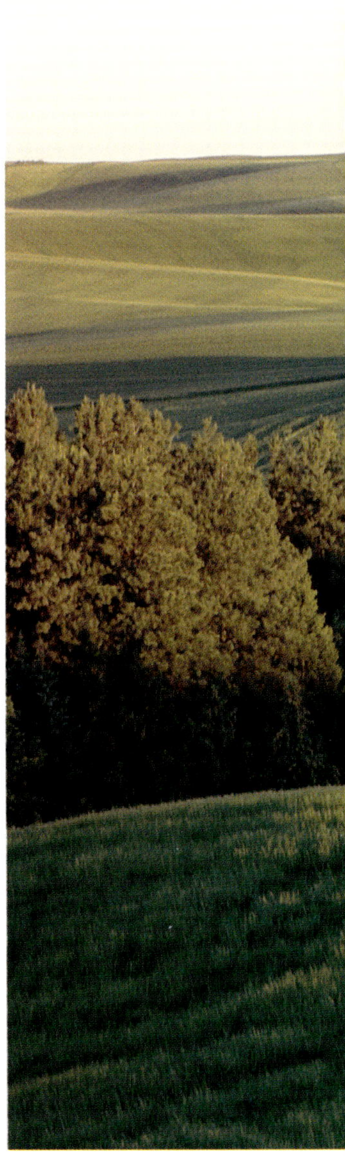

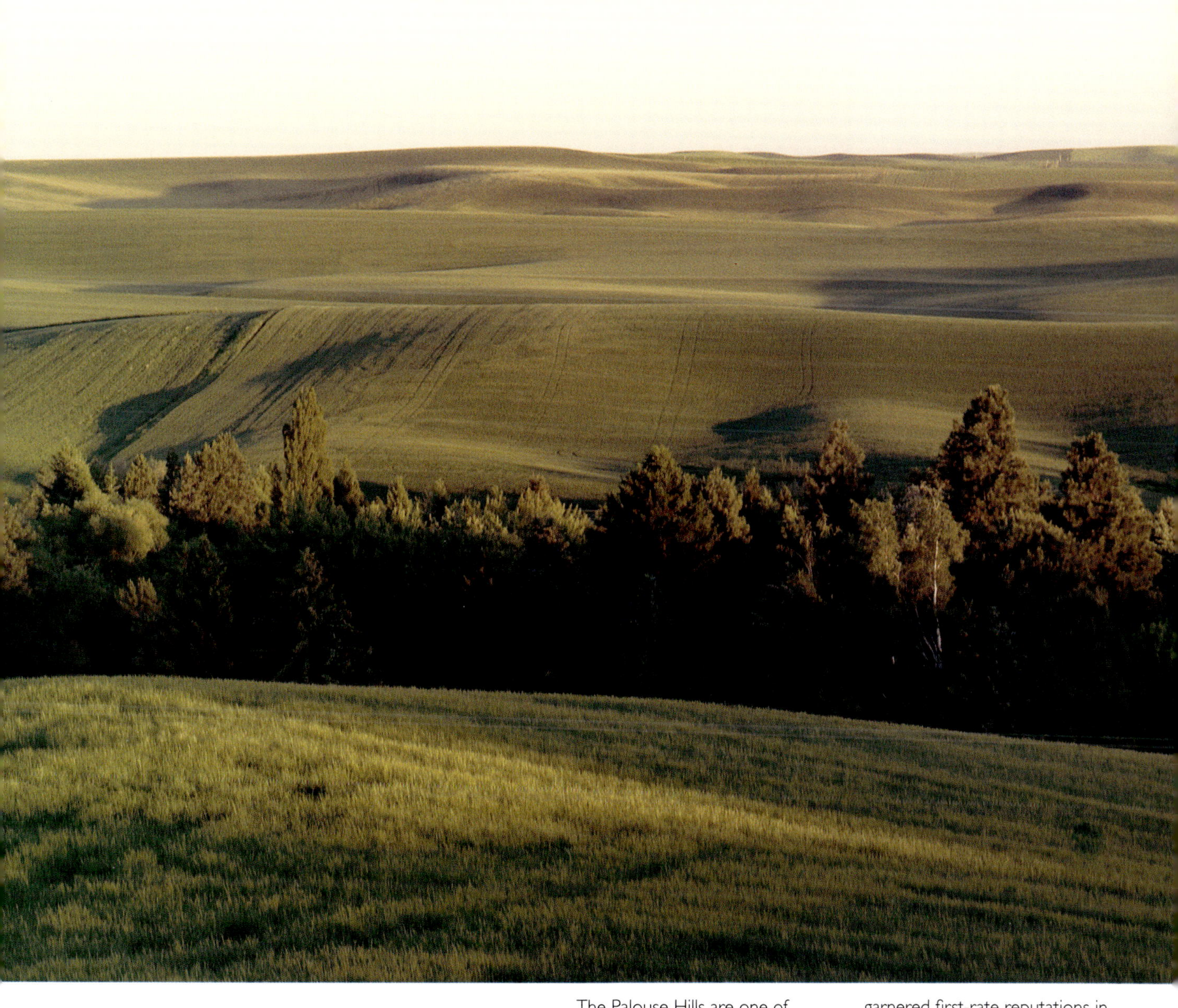

The Palouse Hills are one of America's major producers of wheat, dry peas, and lentils. WSU's agricultural programs have long garnered first-rate reputations in regional, national, and international research and instruction, and in statewide Extension Service.

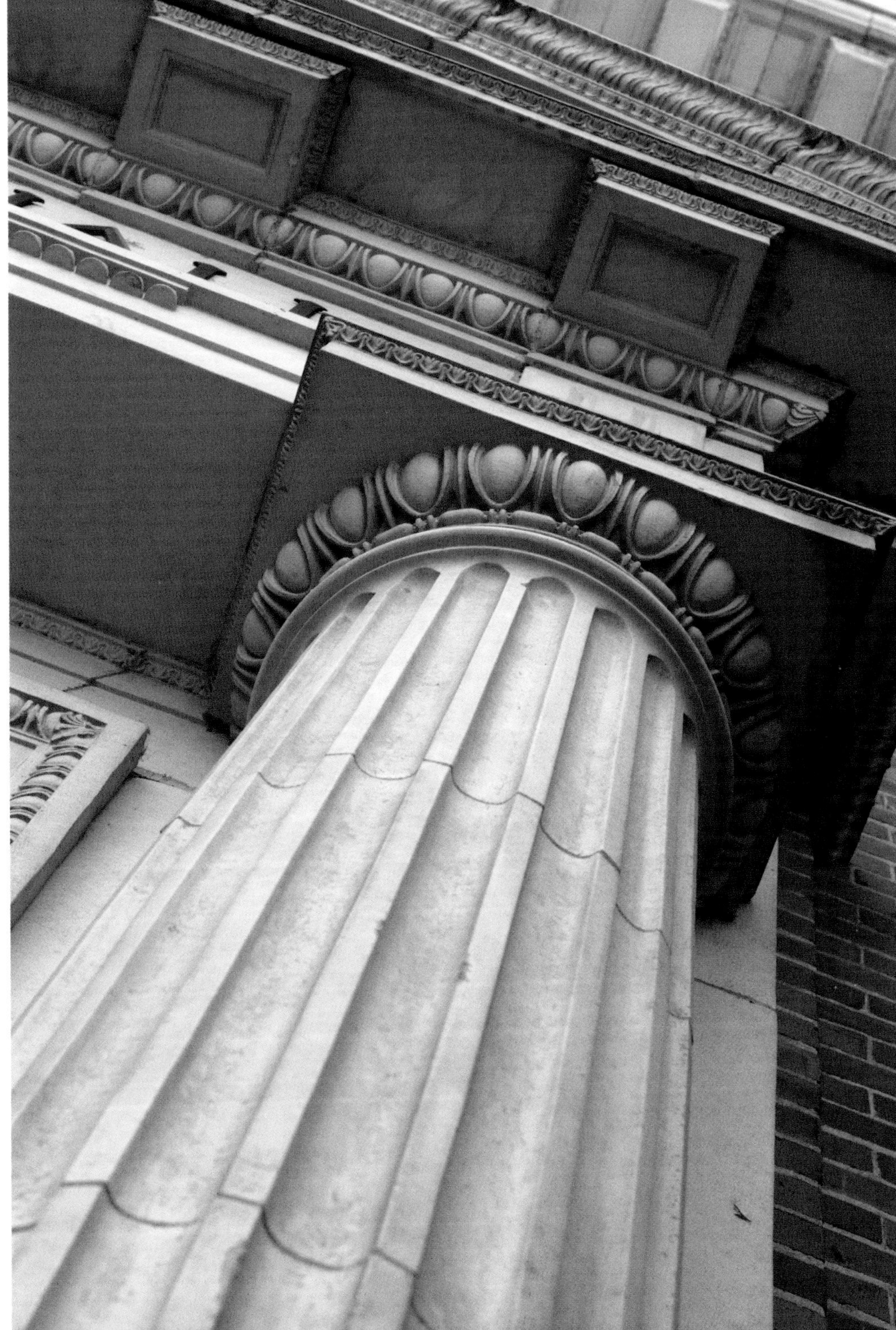

Detail of pillar gracing
Wilson Hall.

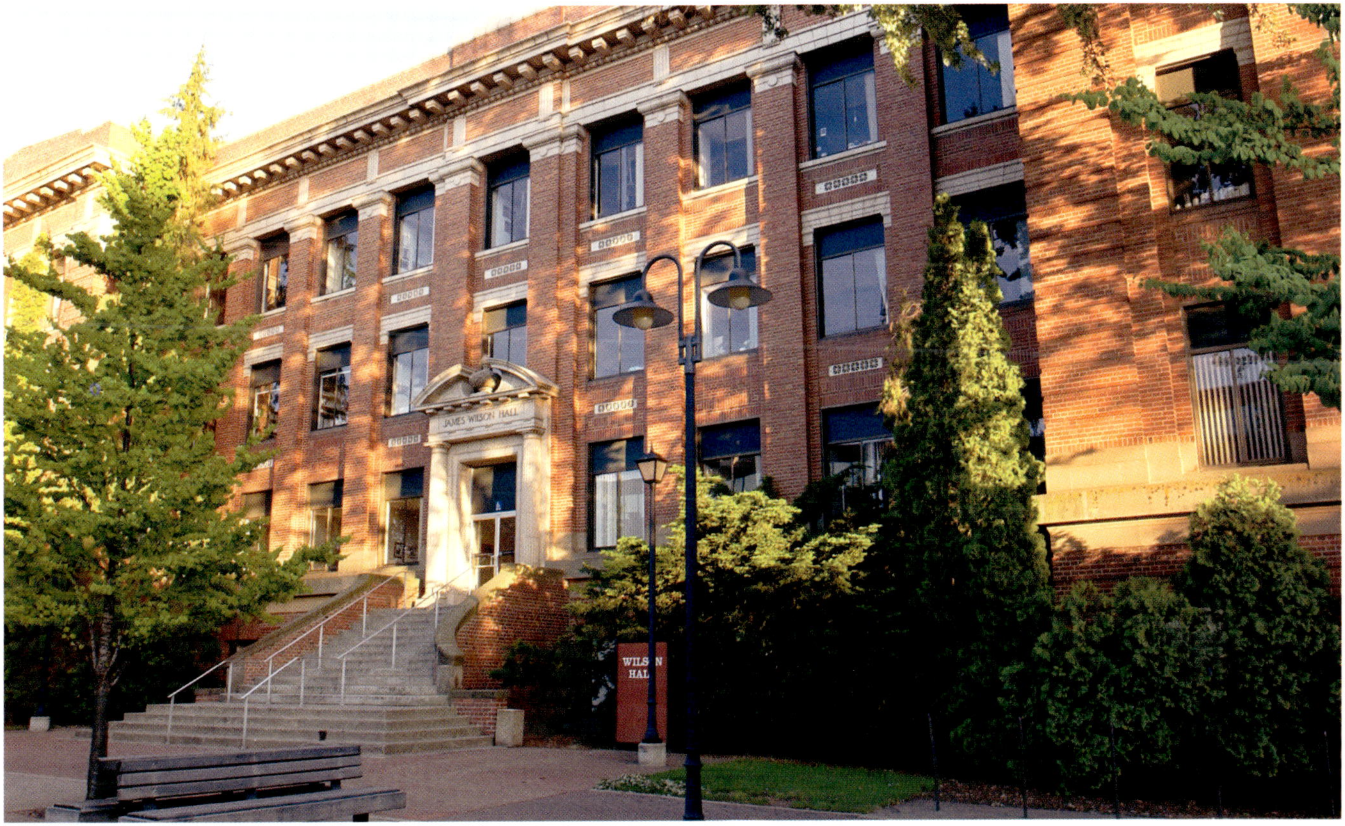

Wilson Hall stands in the warm glow of the setting sun. Named for James Wilson, a U.S. Secretary of Agriculture (1897–1913), the building originally served horticulture and agriculture programs. Today, Comparative Ethnic Studies, Women's Studies, History, and Sociology reside here.

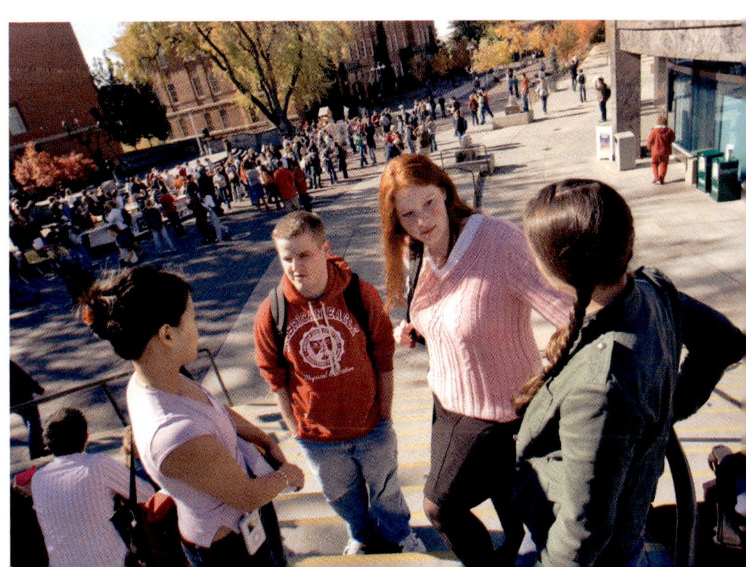

Friends gather on Terrell Mall, a popular campus crossroads. The buildings in this view include (left to right) Todd Hall, College Hall, and the Holland-Terrell Library.

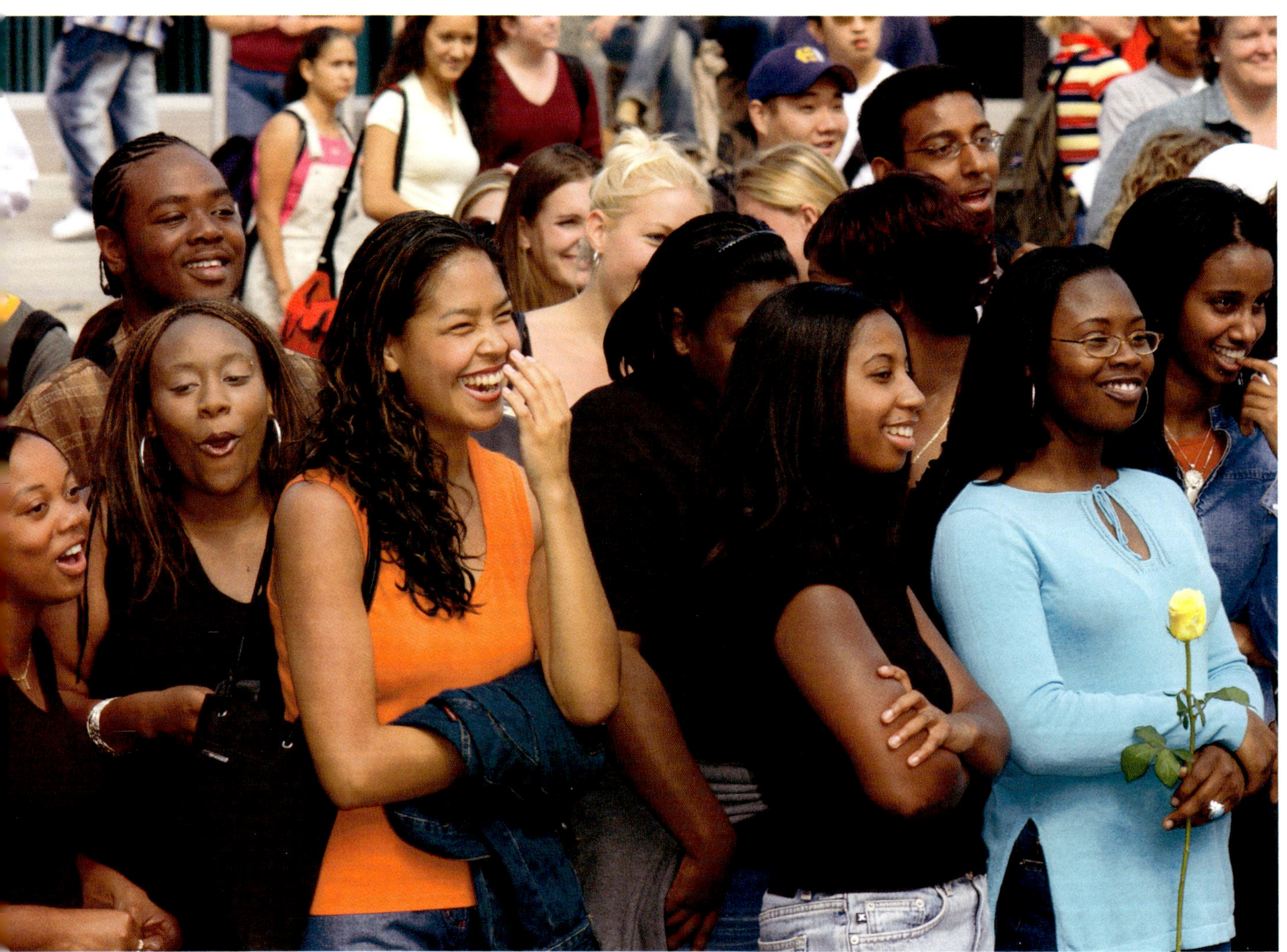

Terrell Mall crowd enjoying the antics of Greek Row
participants in the annual Fall Yard Show.

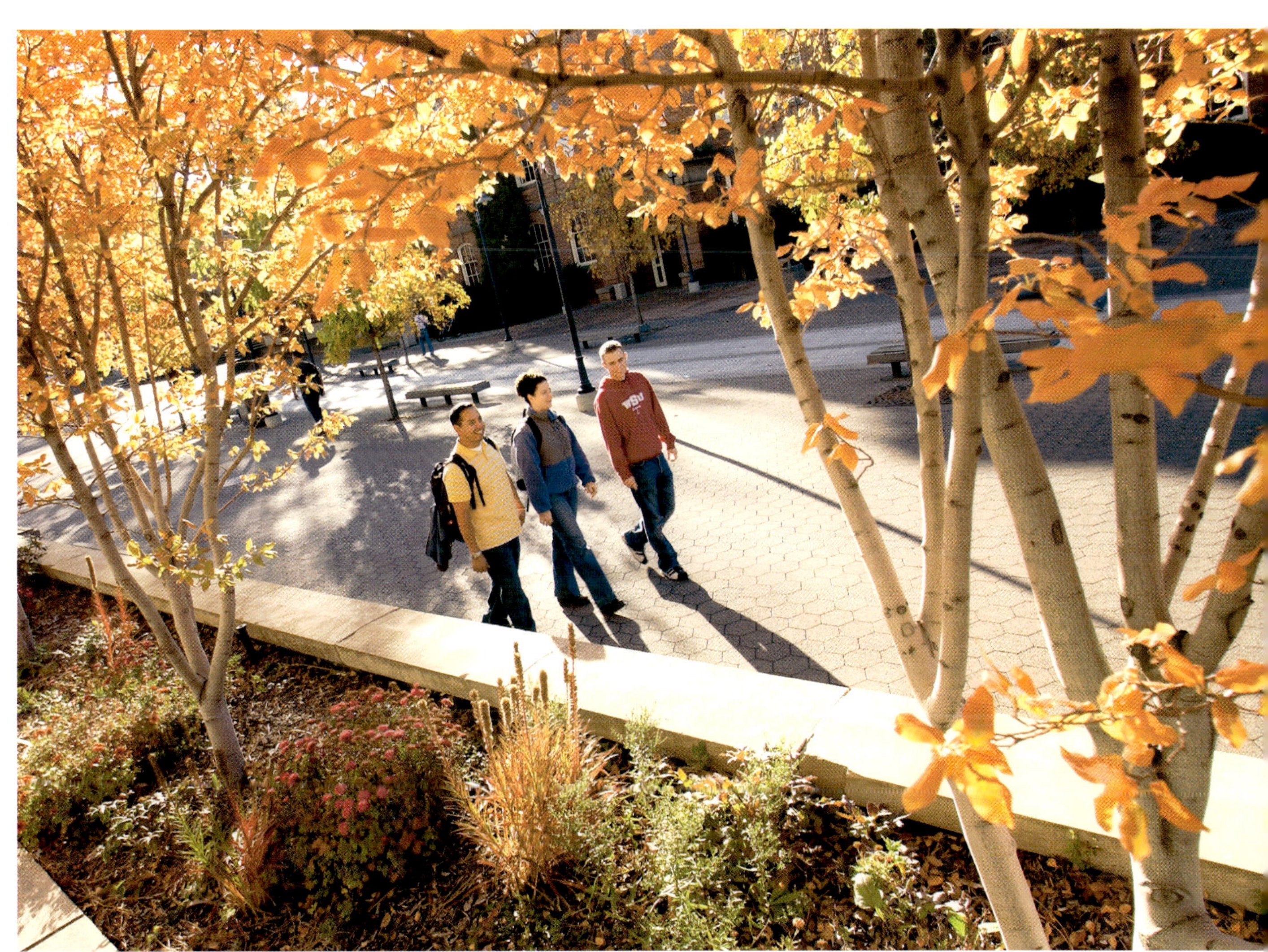

Blue-sky days and crisp clear nights characterize the long Palouse autumn.

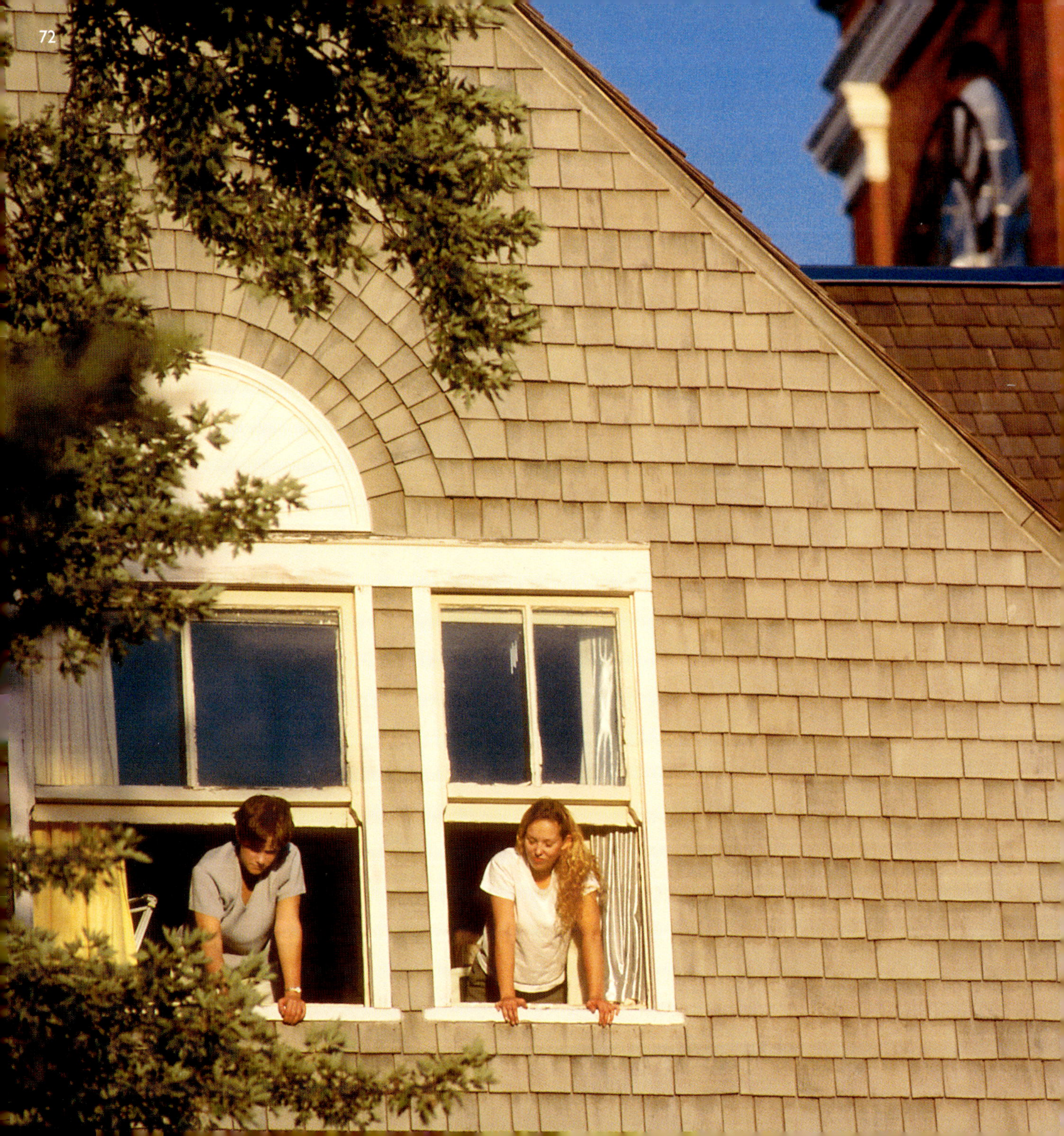

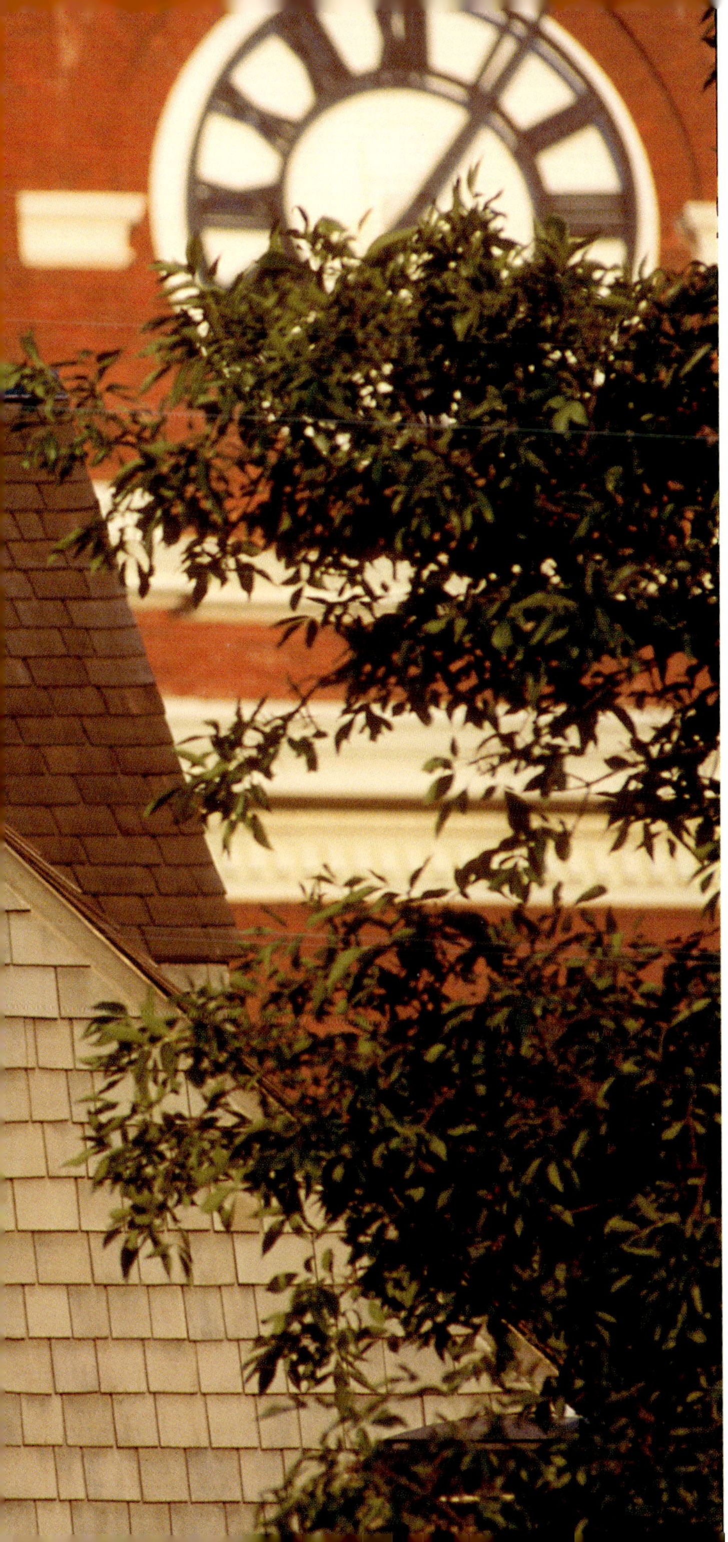

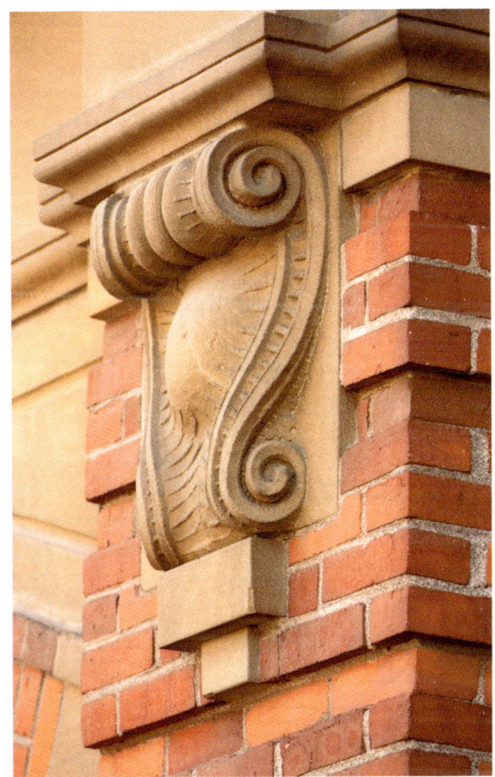

Concrete scroll detail at the entrance to College Hall (1909), home to the Department of Anthropology and the Museum of Anthropology.

Undergraduates at Stevens Residence Hall (1895), with Bryan Tower looming in the background.

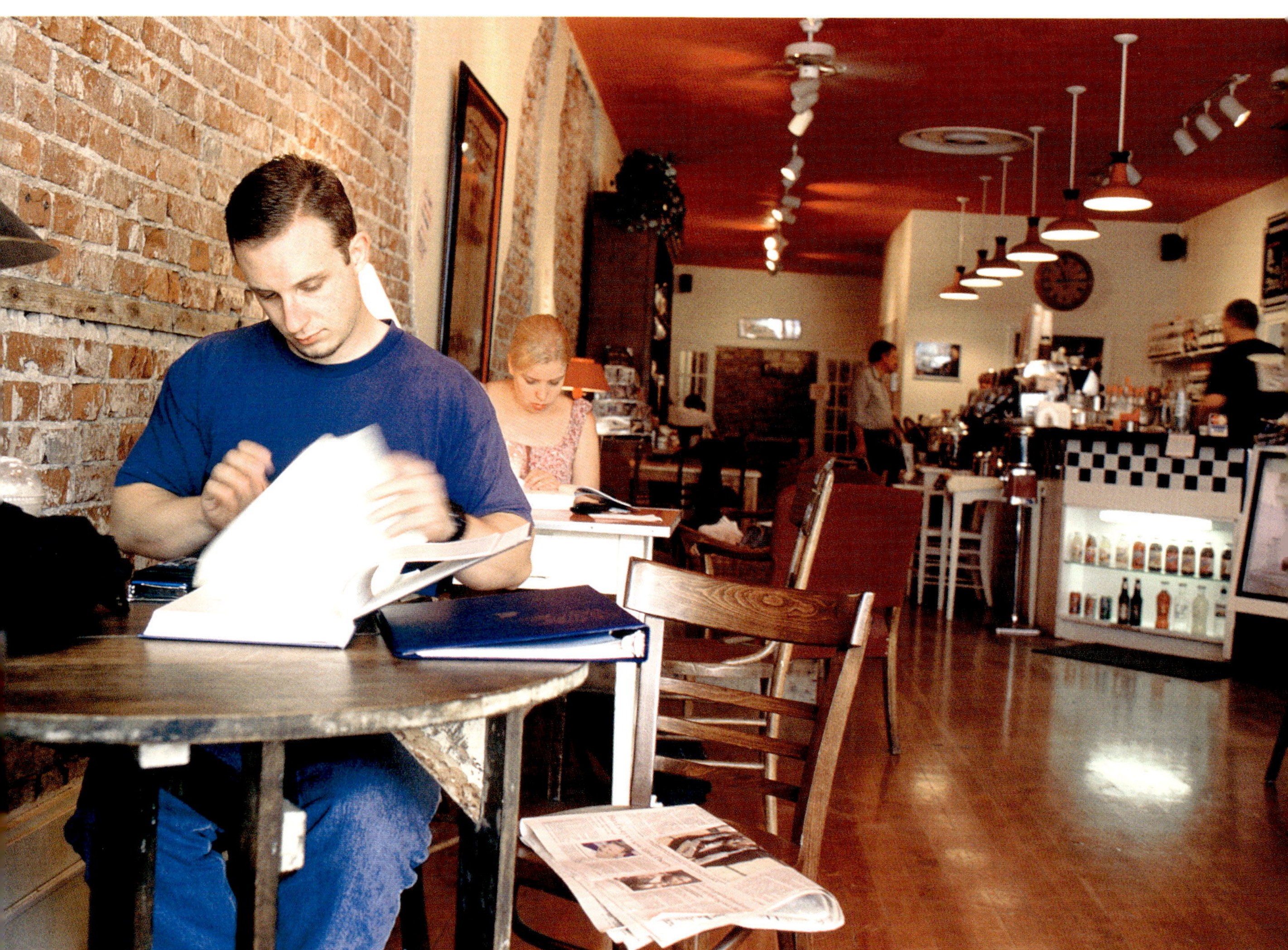

Students can be found studying in favored
nooks and crannies throughout the Pullman
community, as in this downtown coffee shop.

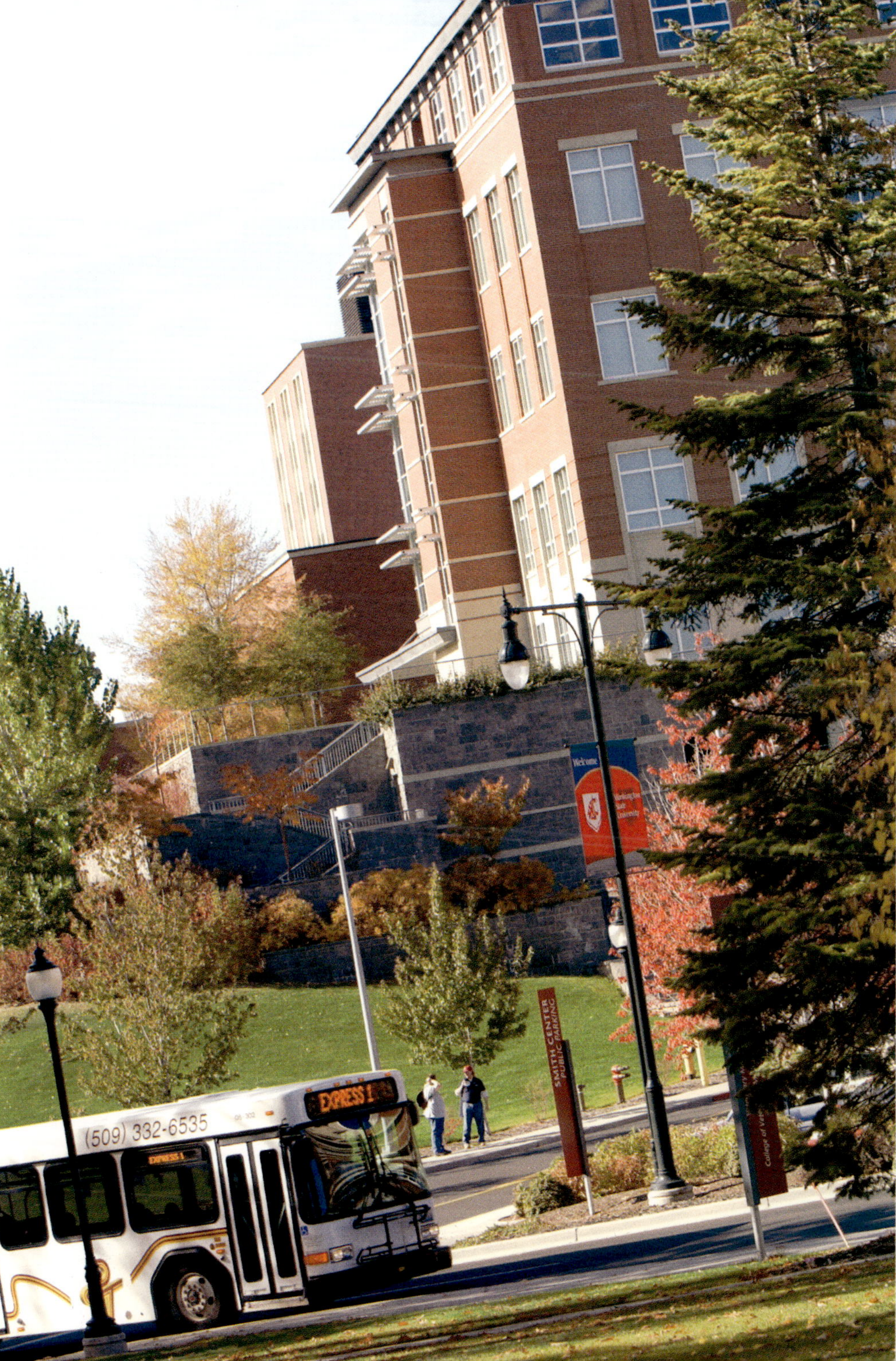

One of the busses from Pullman's city wide transit system—extensively ridden by students—passes by the Smith Center on Stadium Way.

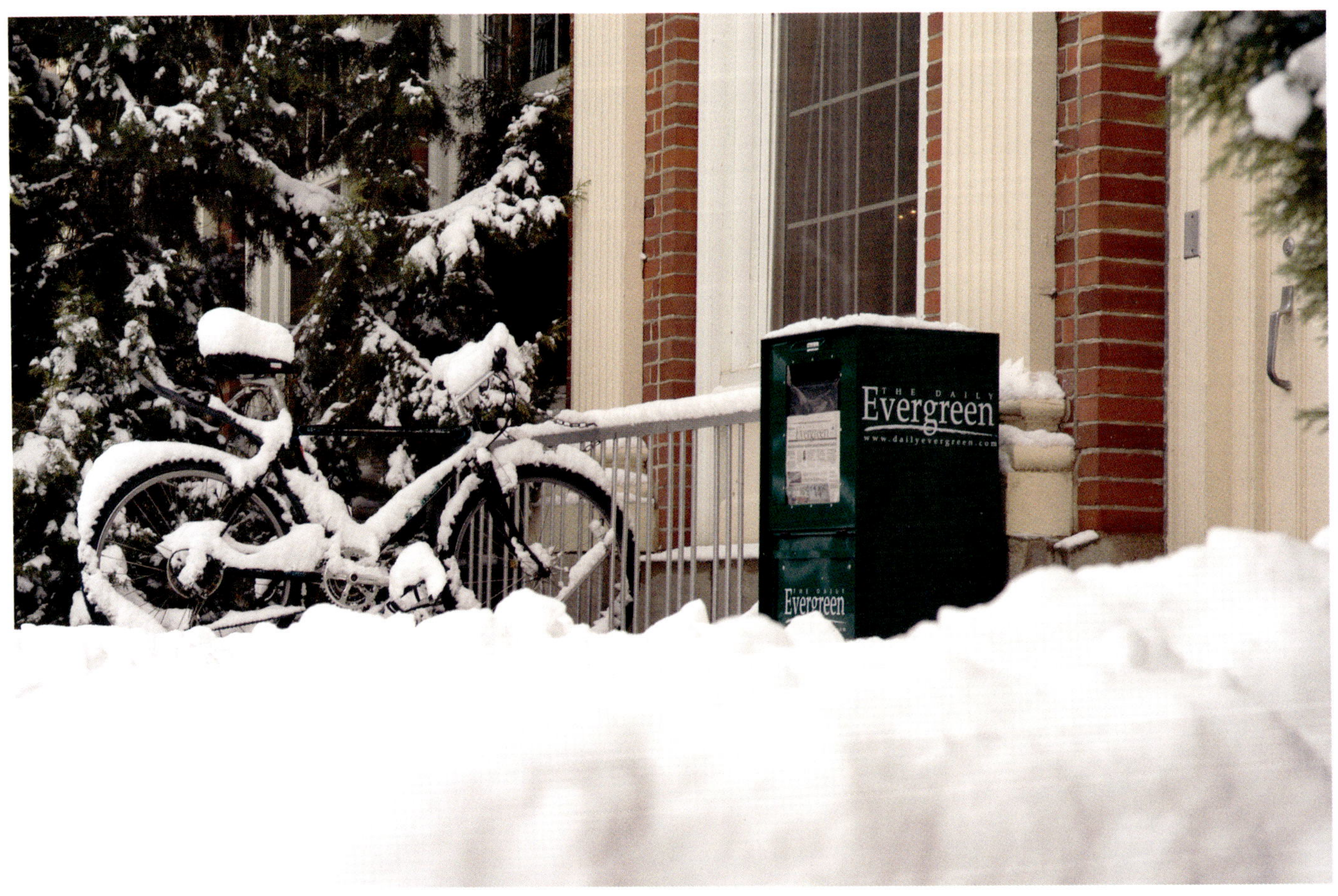

Entrance to Stimson Residence Hall with a dispenser for *The Daily Evergreen*, WSU's student newspaper.

The Bryan clock tower lights up as the sun drops over the Columbia Basin horizon.

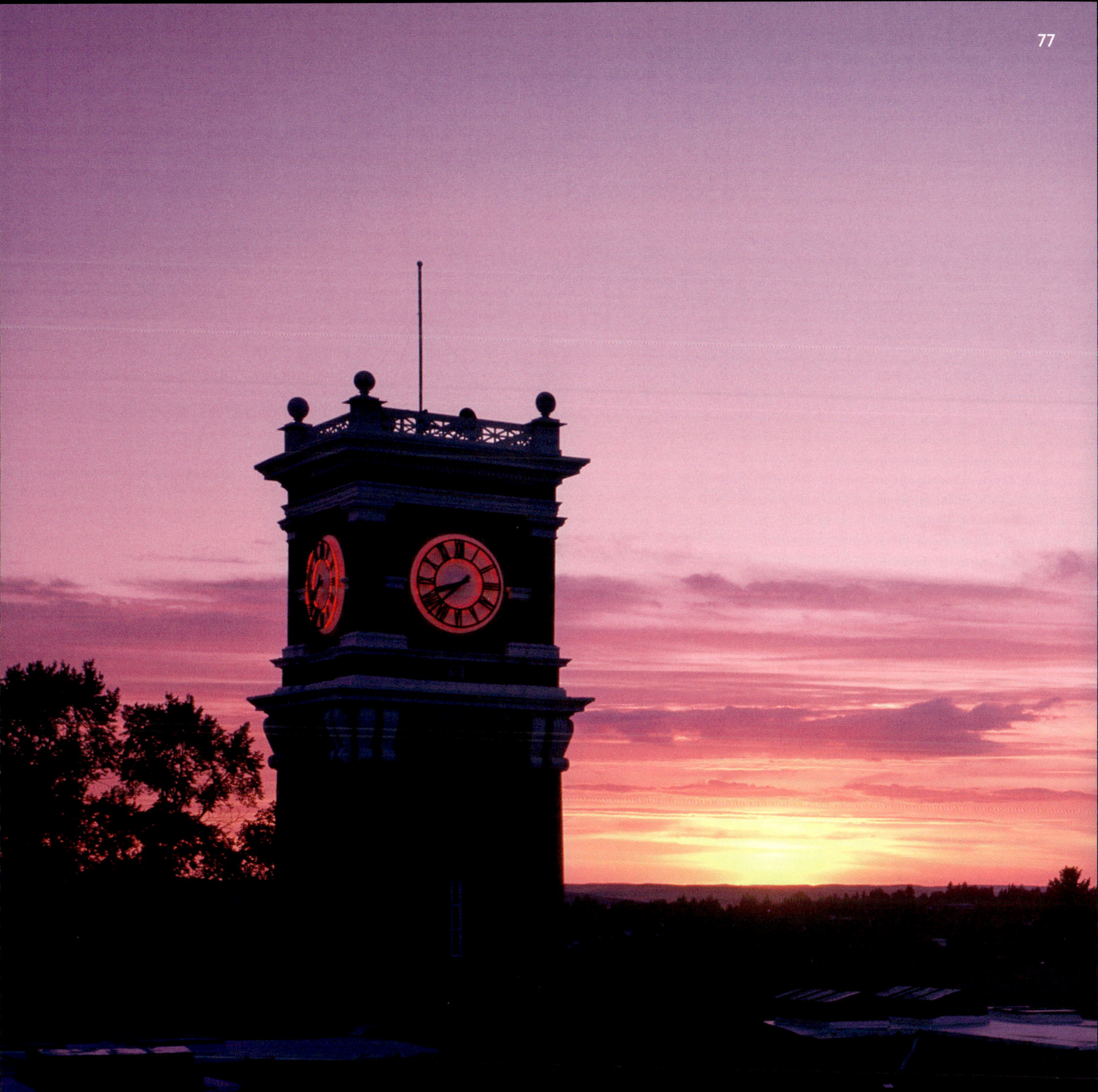

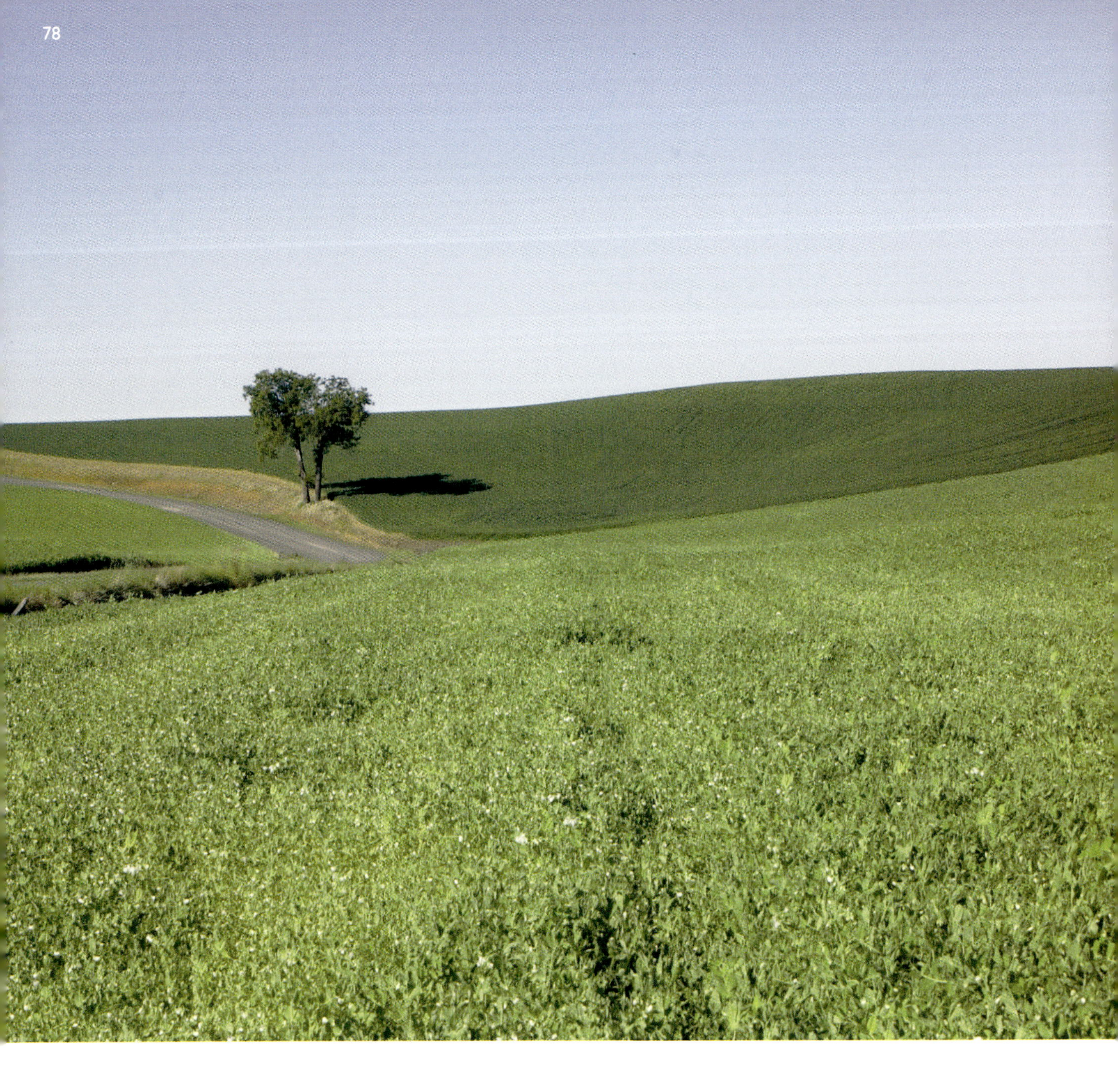

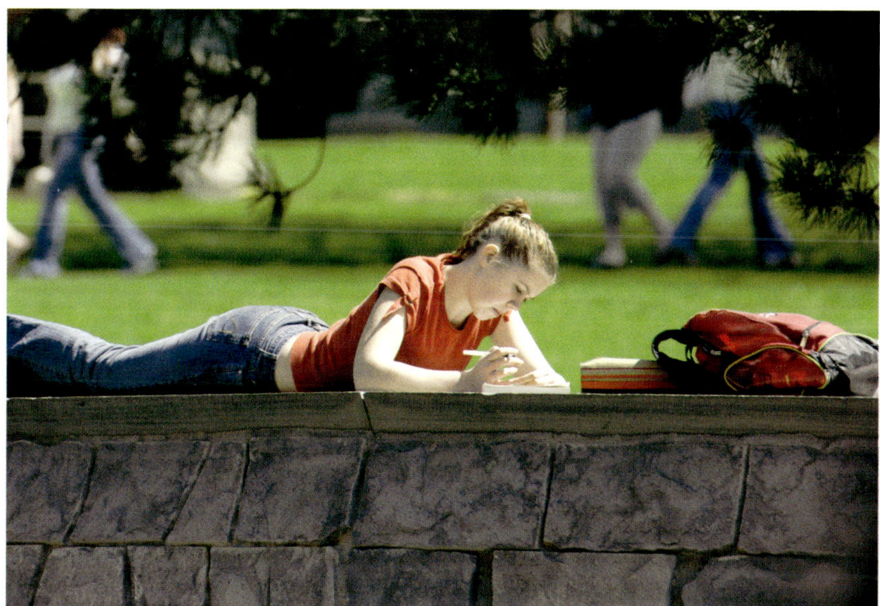

Reading in the reflective environs of the WSU Veterans Memorial.

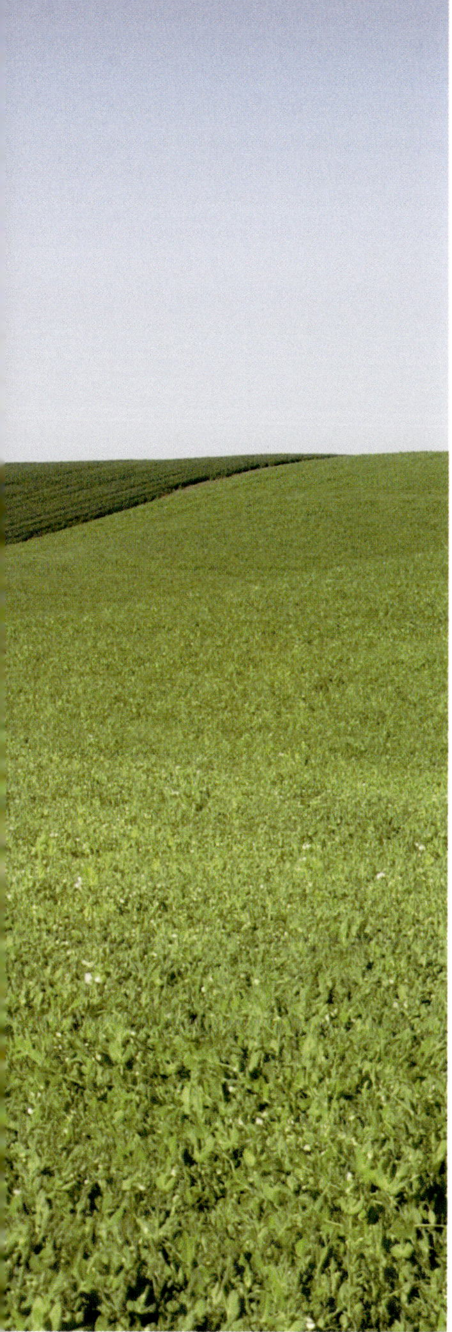

A verdant springtime pea field, with a grain crop in the distance. Large-scale farming in the Palouse prairieland dates back to the 1870s and 1880s.

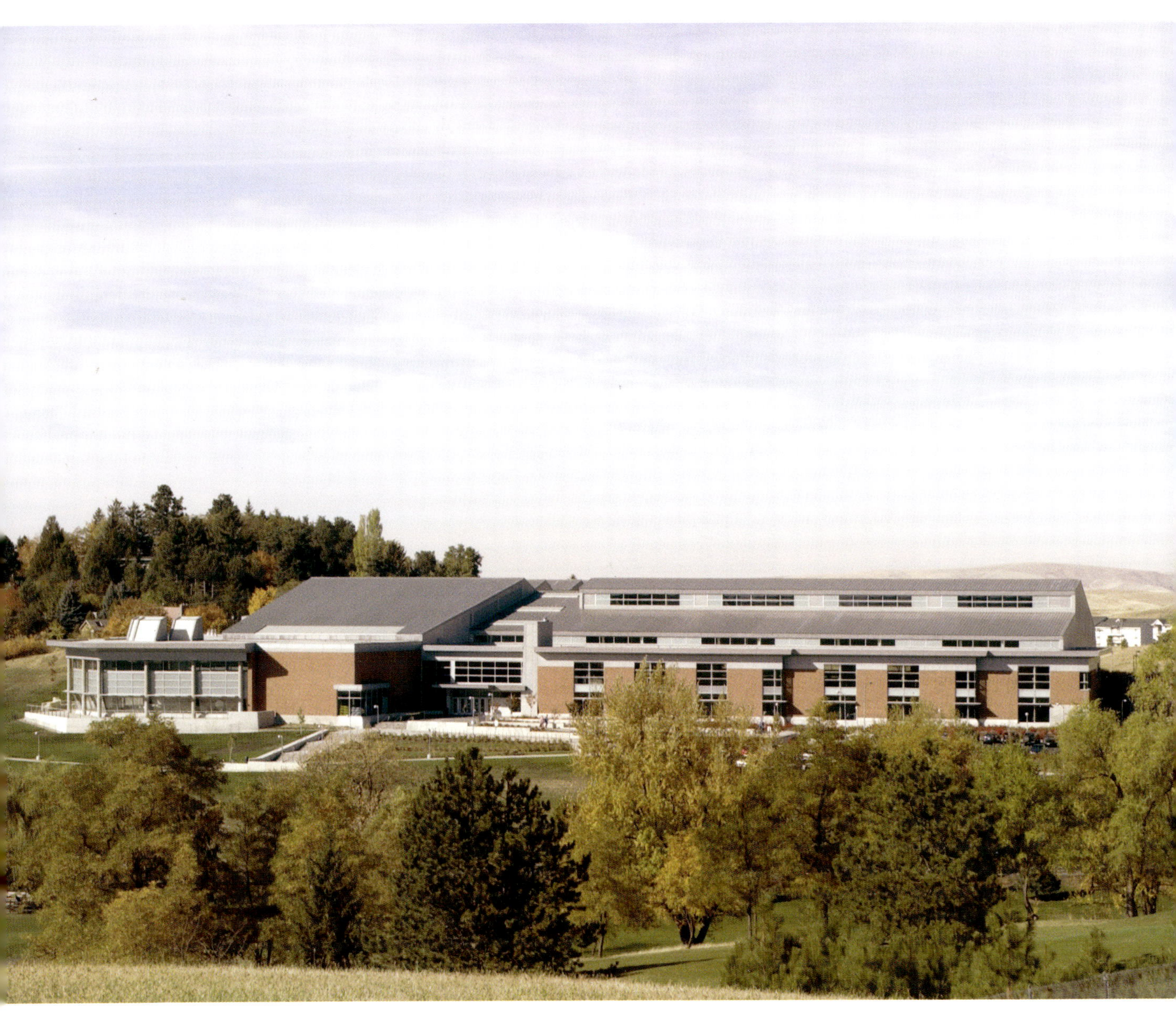

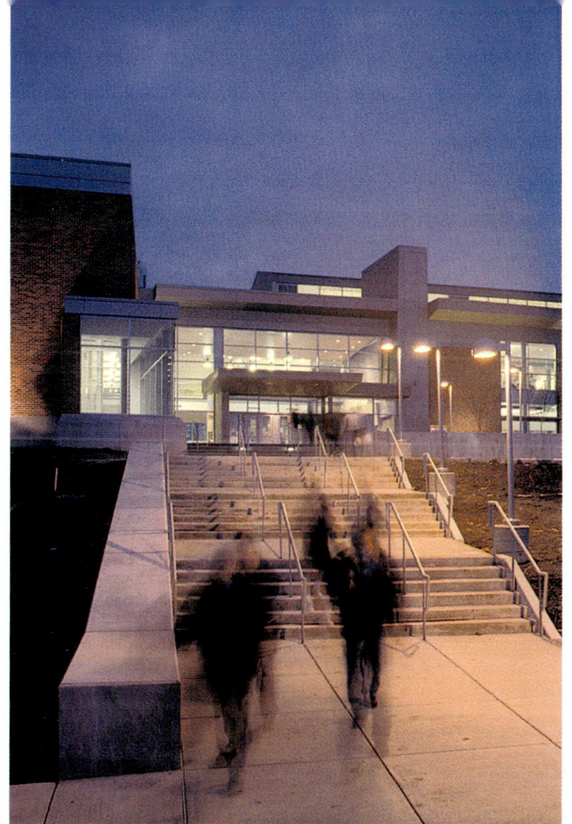

A favored destination for students, faculty, and staff alike, the doors at the Student Recreation Center (SRC) constantly revolve. The facility has won recognition from such organizations as the Engineering Society of North America, the Washington Parks and Recreation Association, *Athletic Business*, and the National Intramural Recreation Sports Association.

The SRC includes seven gymnasiums, four racquetball courts, three martial arts and aerobic workout rooms, a 17,000-square-feet fitness training area, a five-lane lap pool, a four-lane track, hot tub, and fireside lounge.

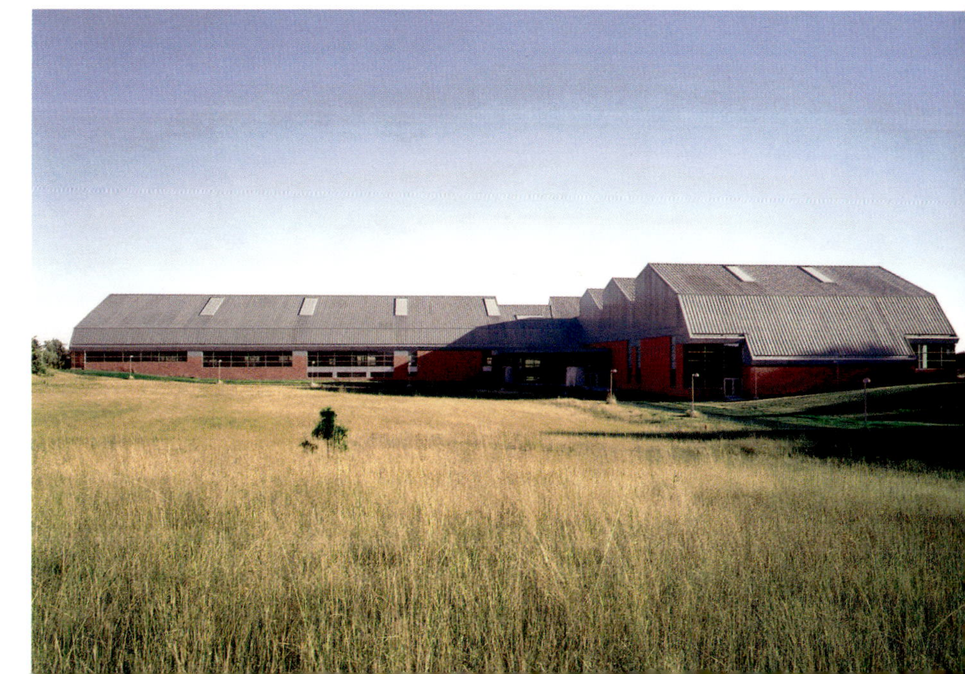

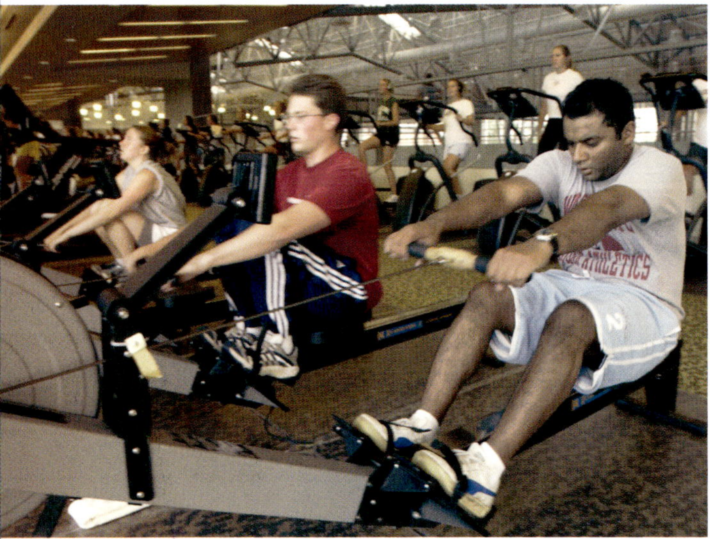

Hard workouts are common on scores of exercise and lifting equipment.

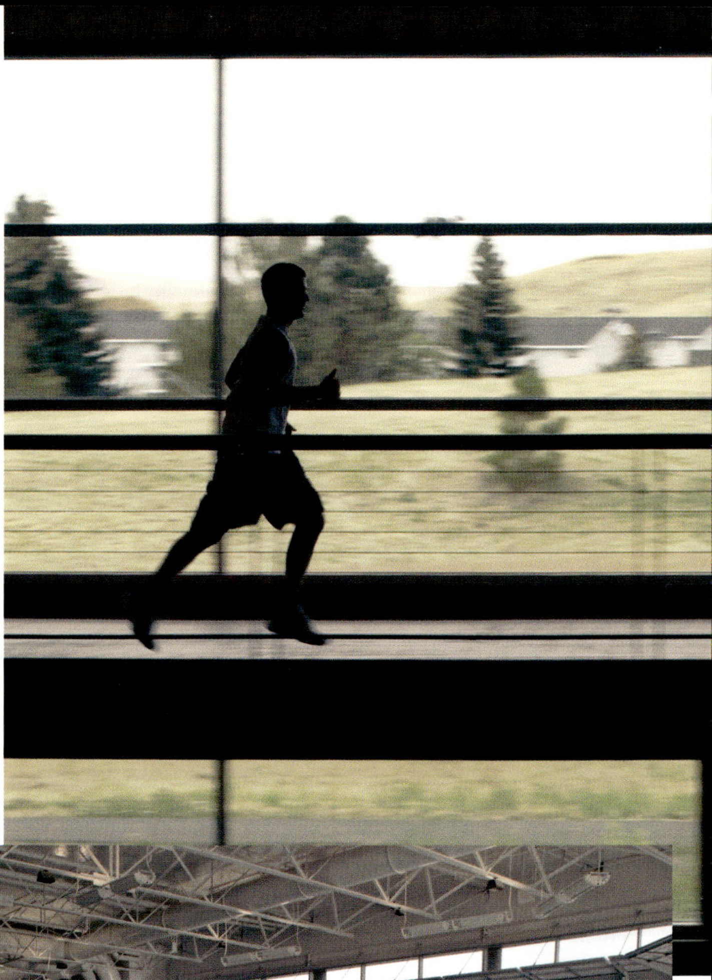

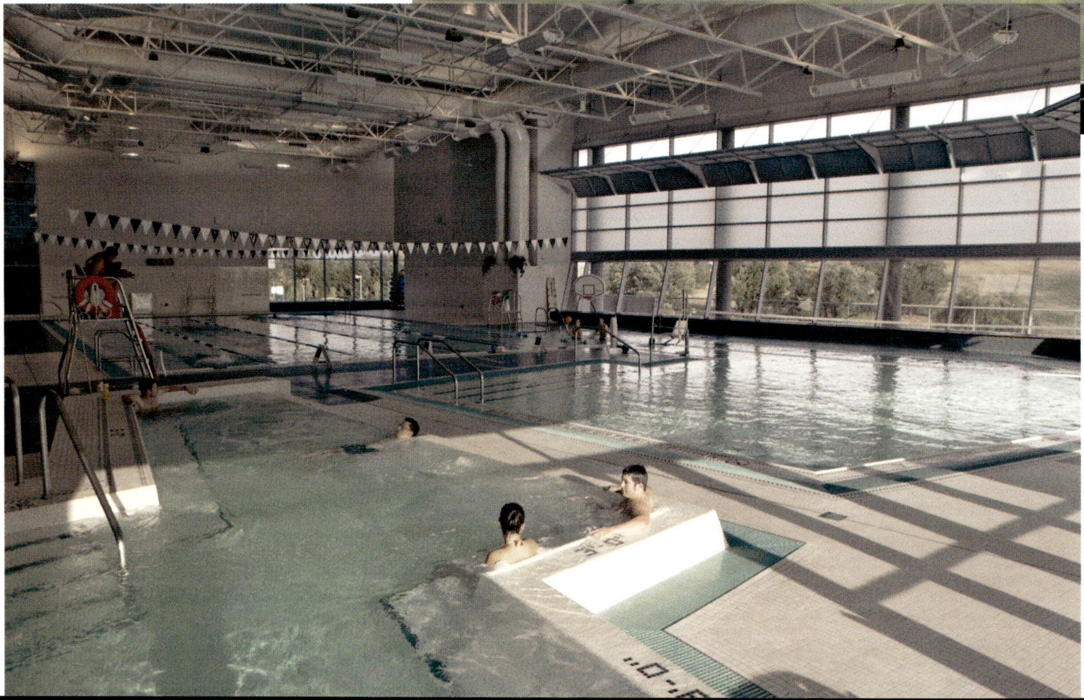

The 53-person hot tub (left foreground) and the swimming pool.

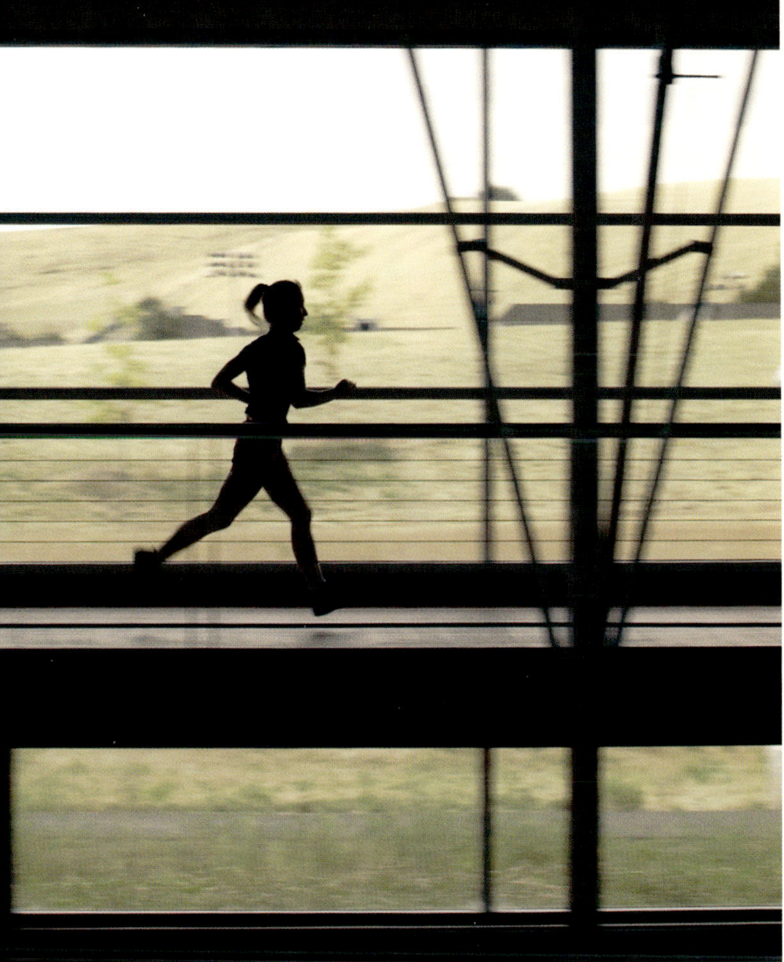

Runners on the 200-meter track.

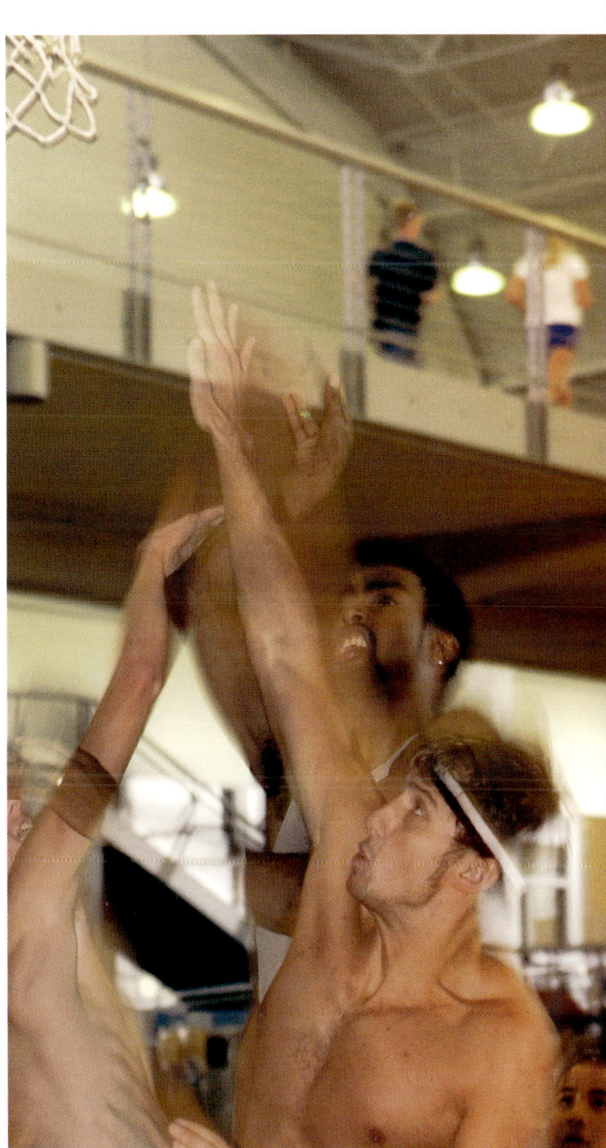

A blur of basketball activity, while joggers
pass by on the overhead track.

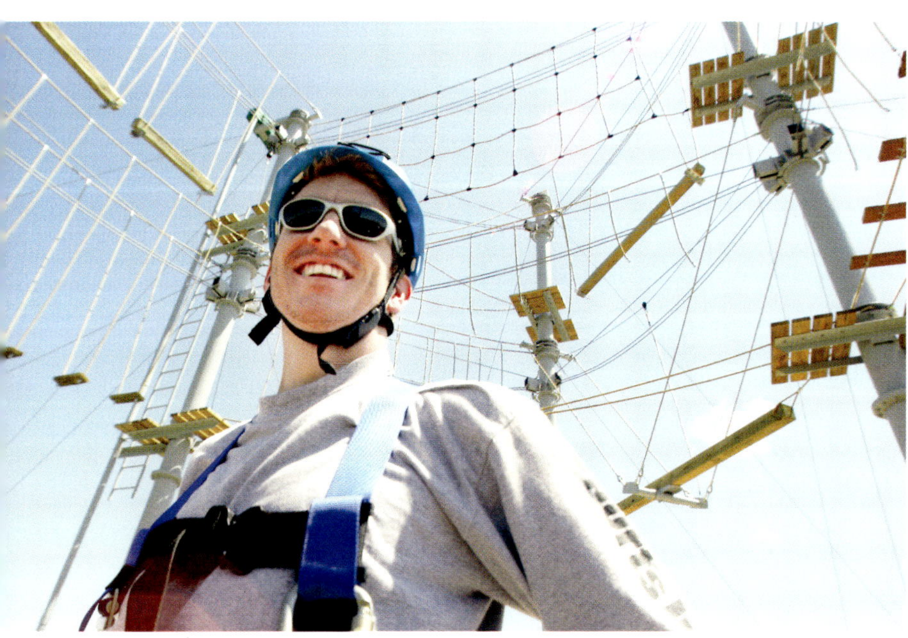

Challenge Course in the SRC's backyard, where teamwork and determination are required in Low and High challenge programs.

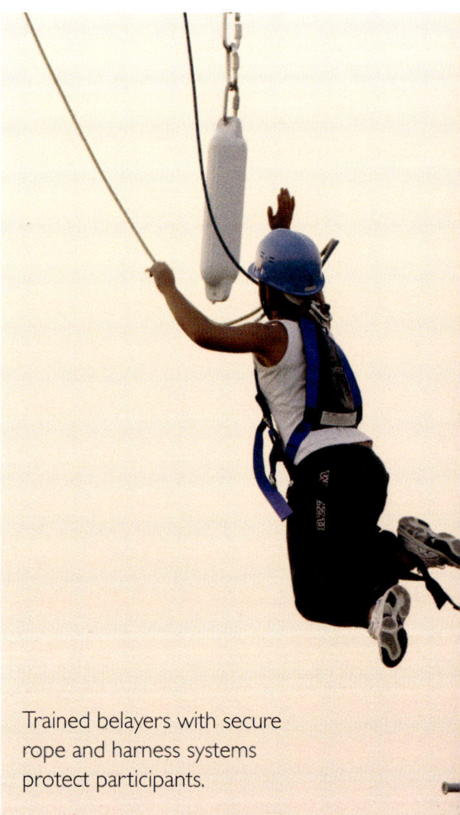

Trained belayers with secure rope and harness systems protect participants.

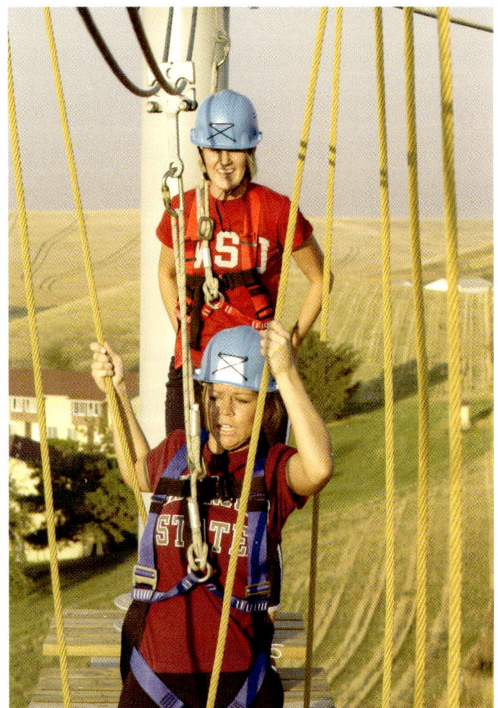

The High Challenge—17 to 32 feet above the ground.

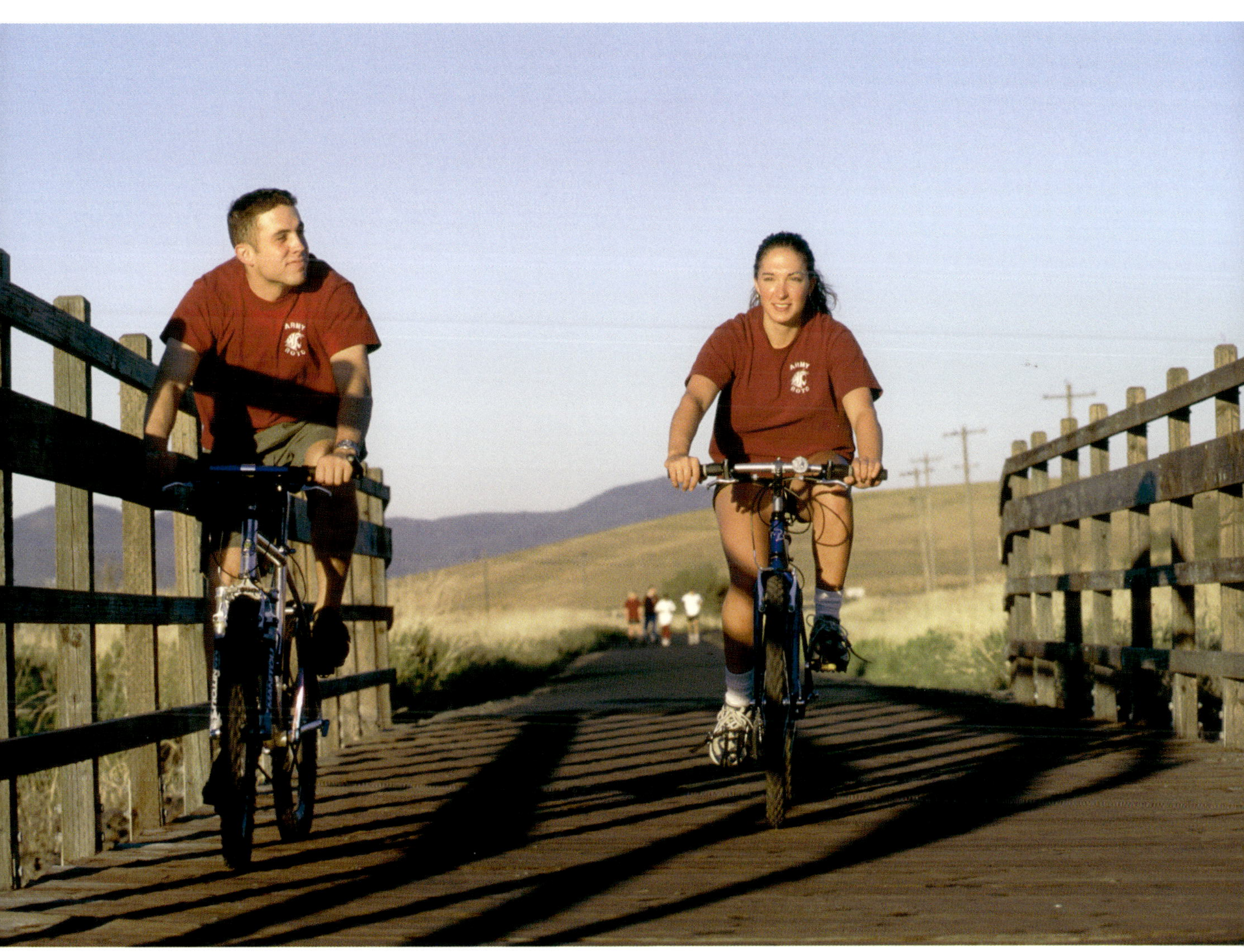

A seven-mile stretch of the Chipman Trail connects the WSU community with the University of Idaho in Moscow, Idaho. The route follows an abandoned Union Pacific rail line.

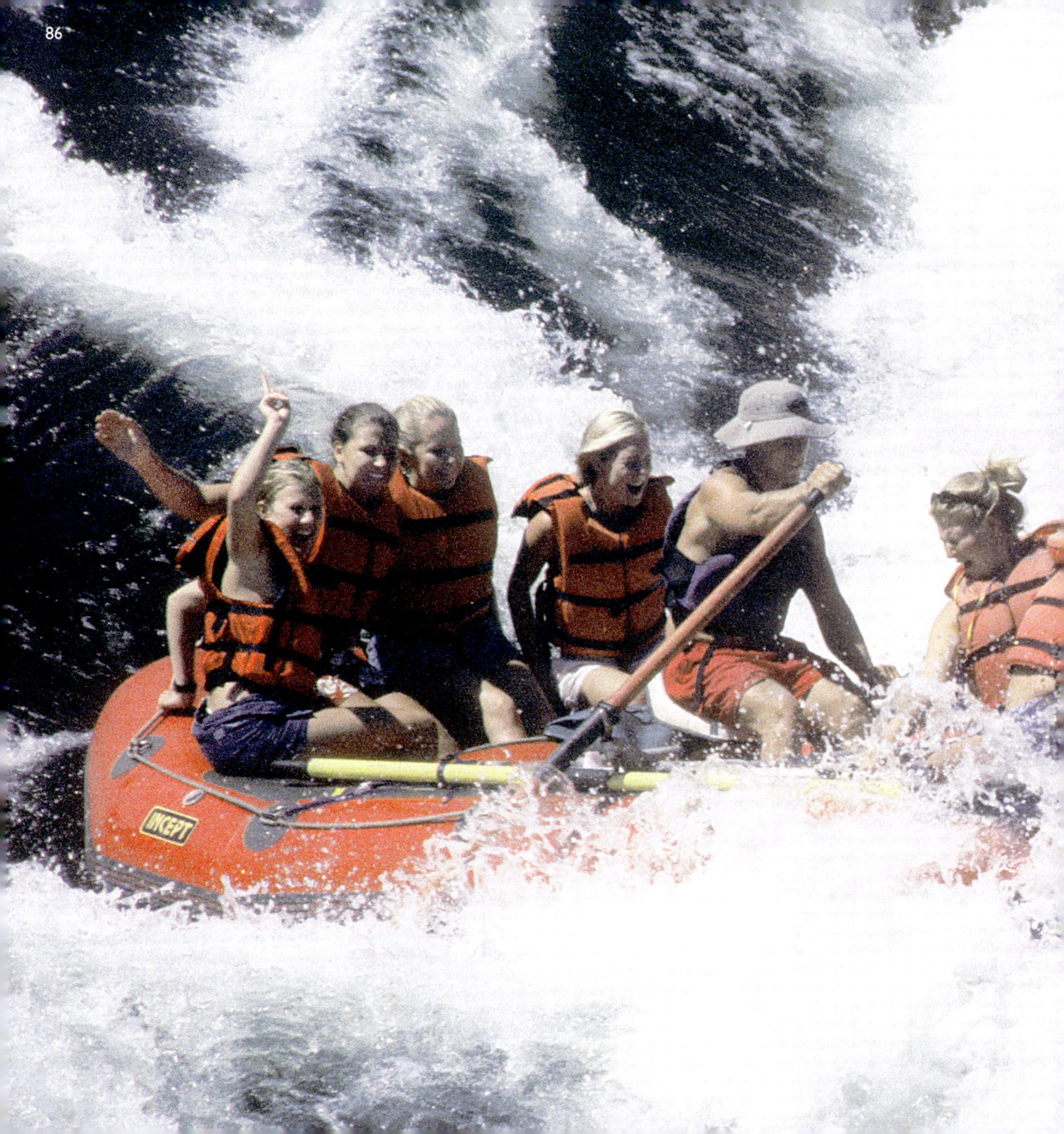
INCEPT

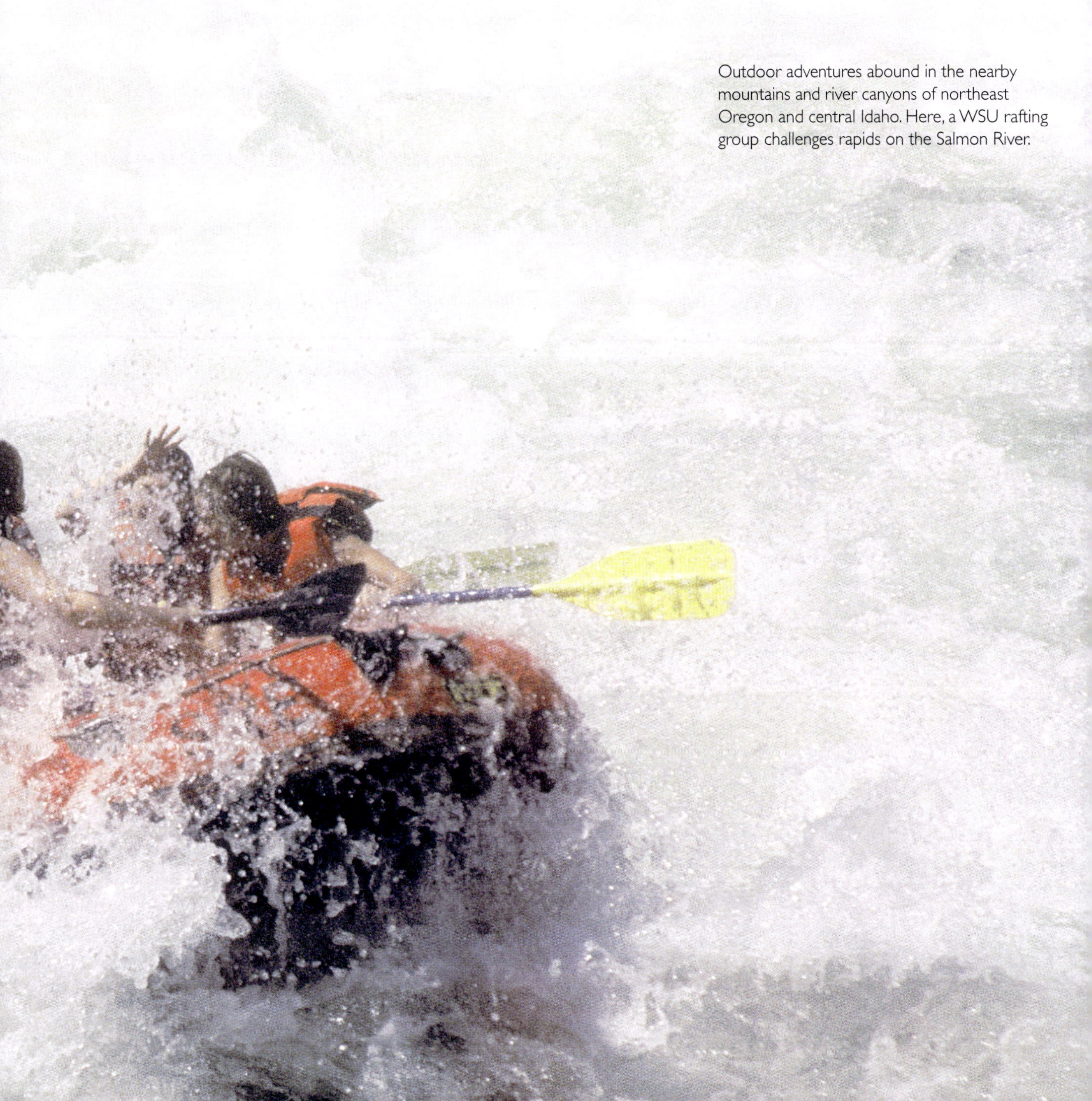

Outdoor adventures abound in the nearby mountains and river canyons of northeast Oregon and central Idaho. Here, a WSU rafting group challenges rapids on the Salmon River.

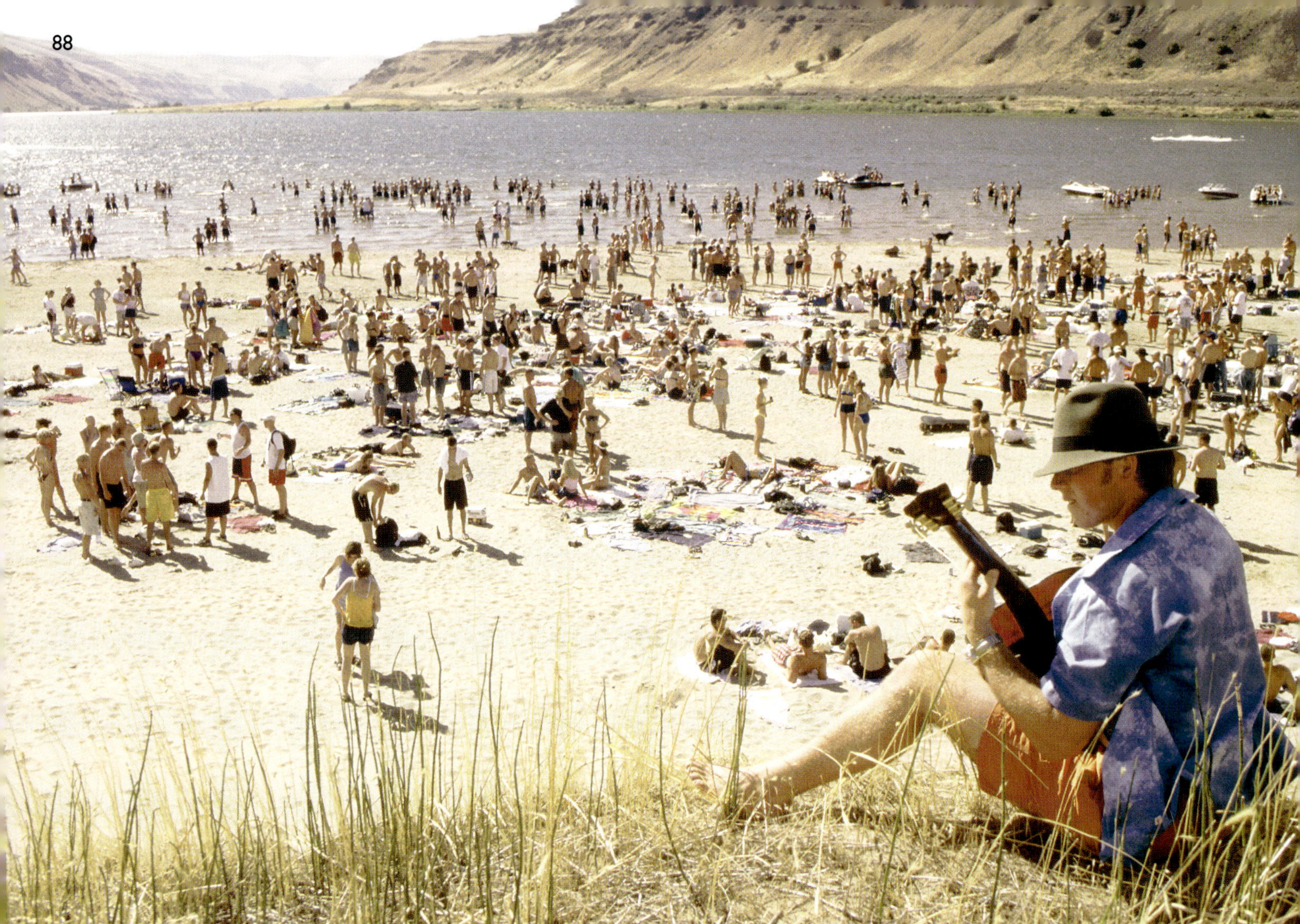

Sand, water, and sun at "The Dunes" on
the Snake River, southwest of Pullman.

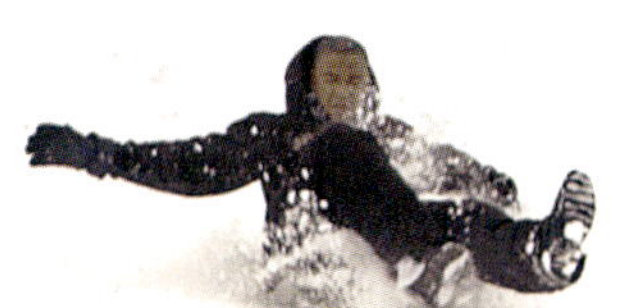

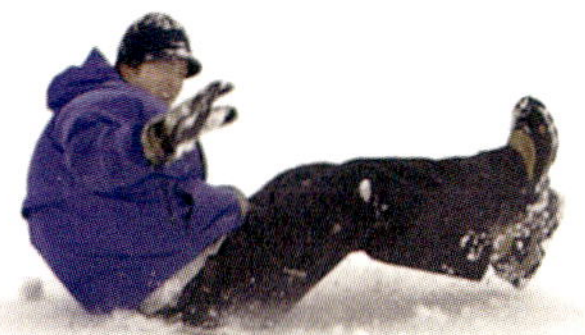

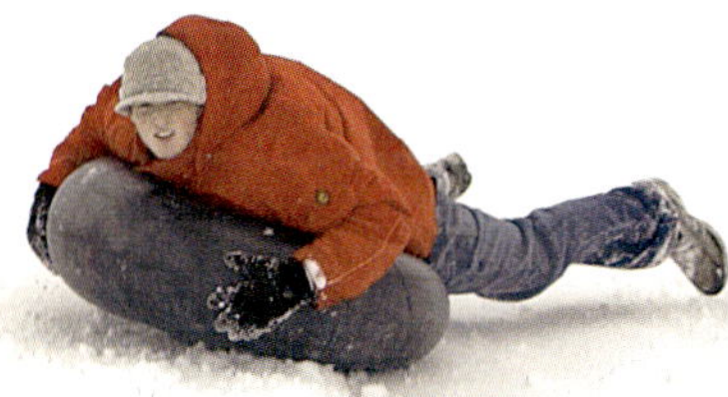

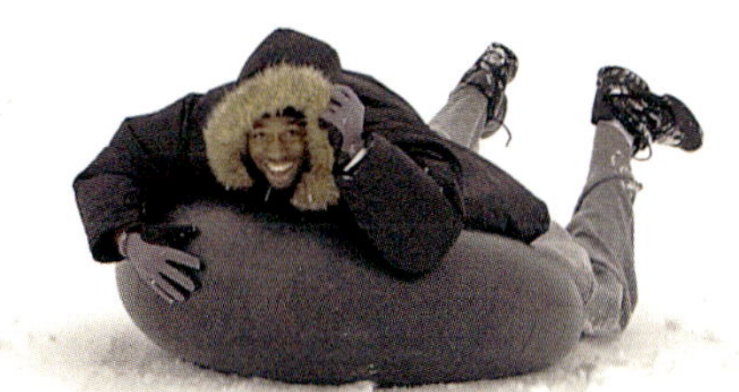

Fun in the snow on campus. Students can visit a half-dozen ski resorts within a two or three hour drive from Pullman. Snowshoeing and cross-country skiing also are popular activities in the nearby mountains.

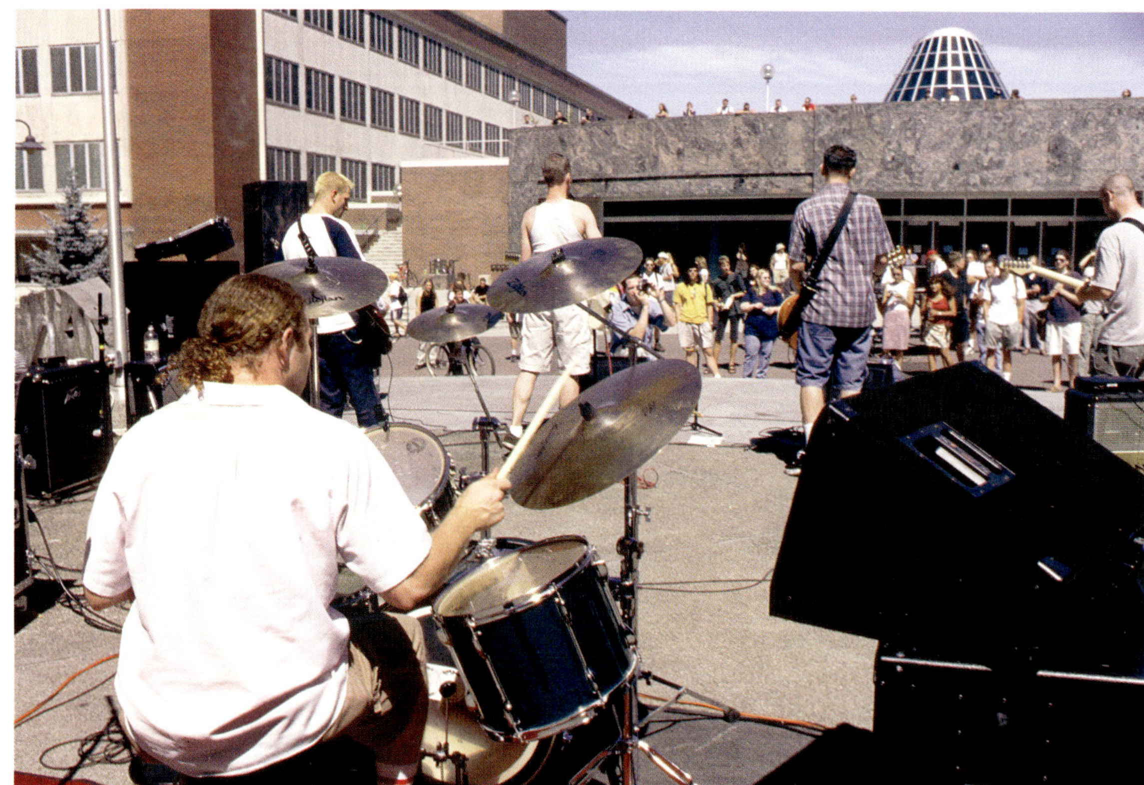

Bands and other entertainment groups frequently perform on the Glenn Terrell Friendship Mall, the hub of campus activity. The mall is named for the University's seventh president (1967–85).

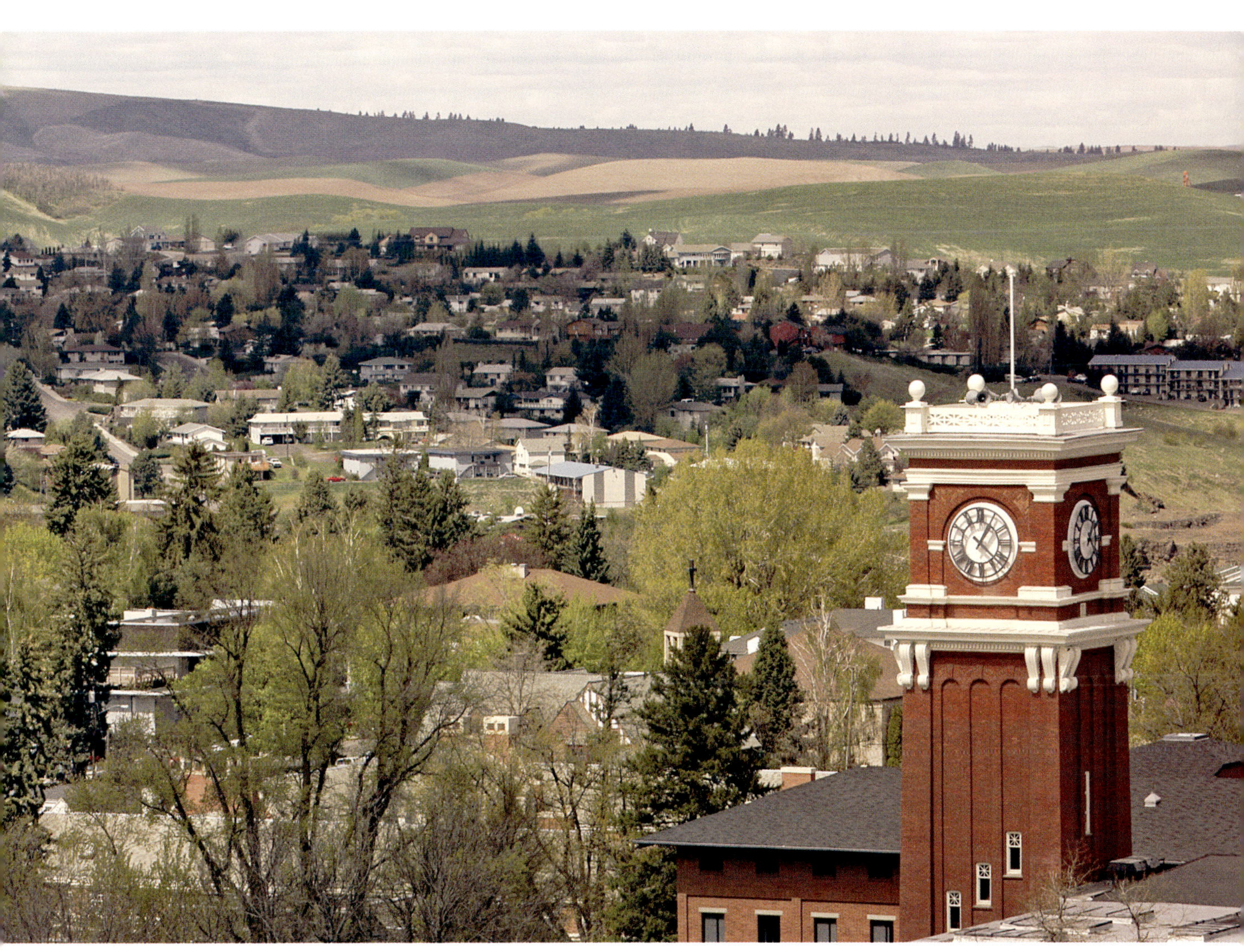

Town view, looking north from campus.

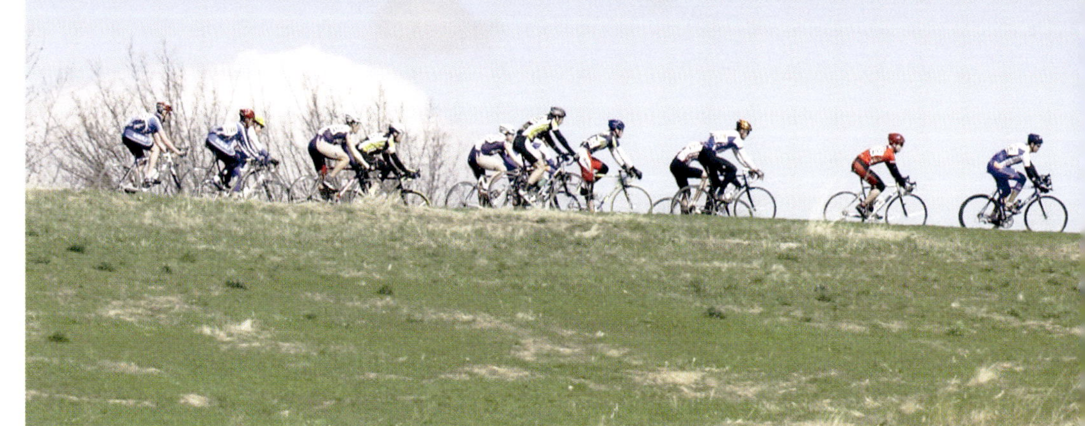

Women's rugby club.

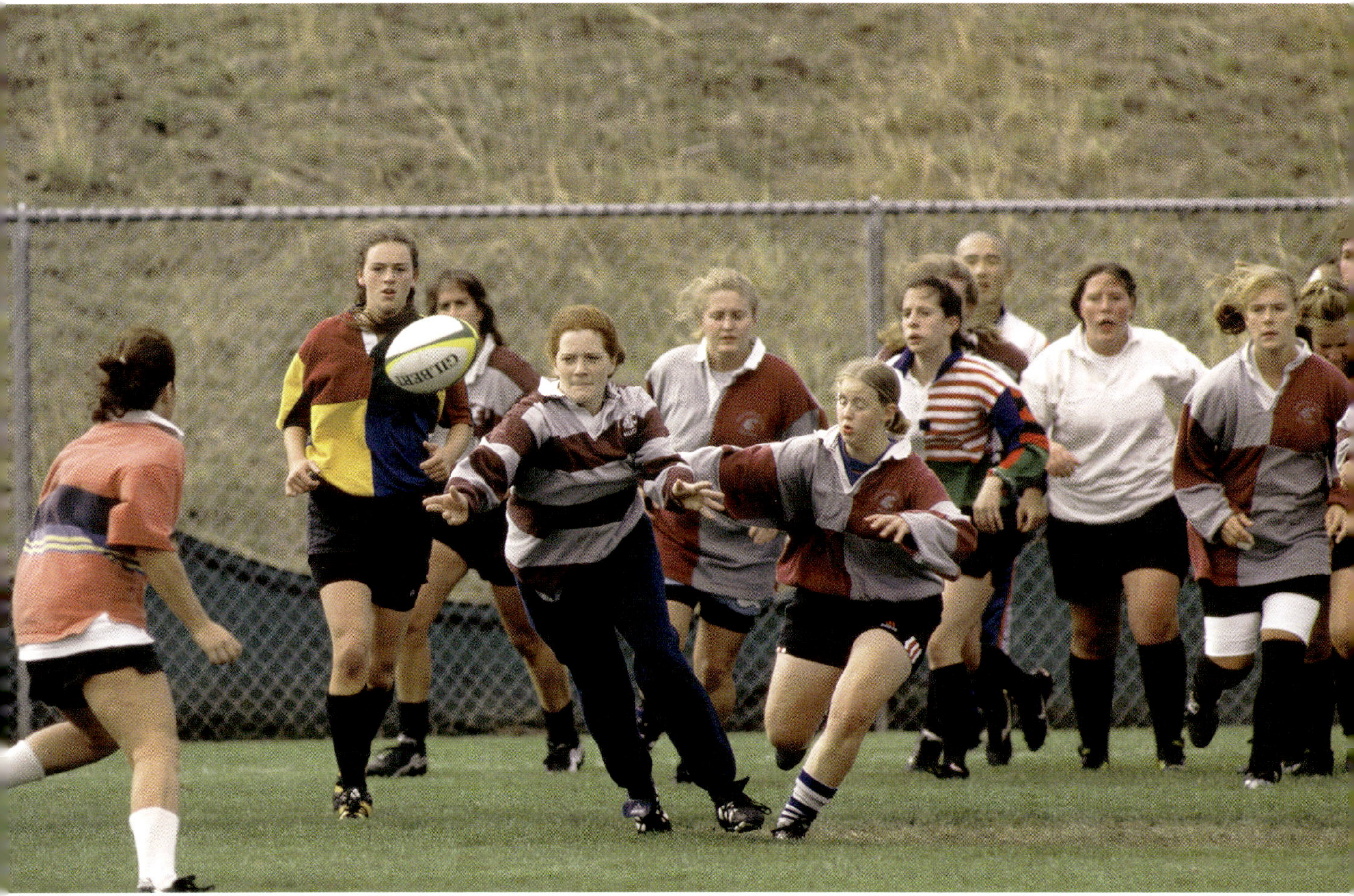

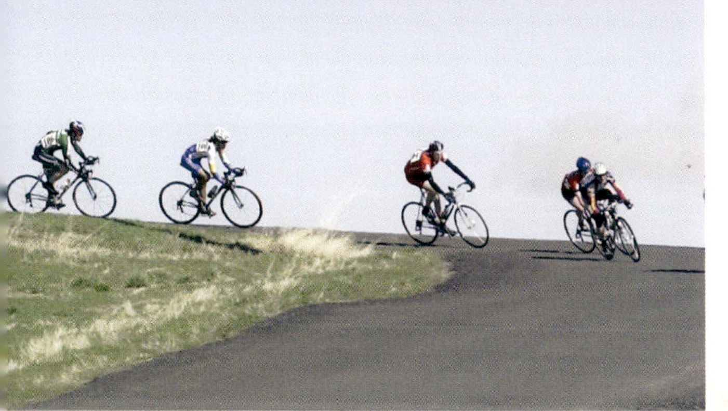

Men's cycling club
in a team race.

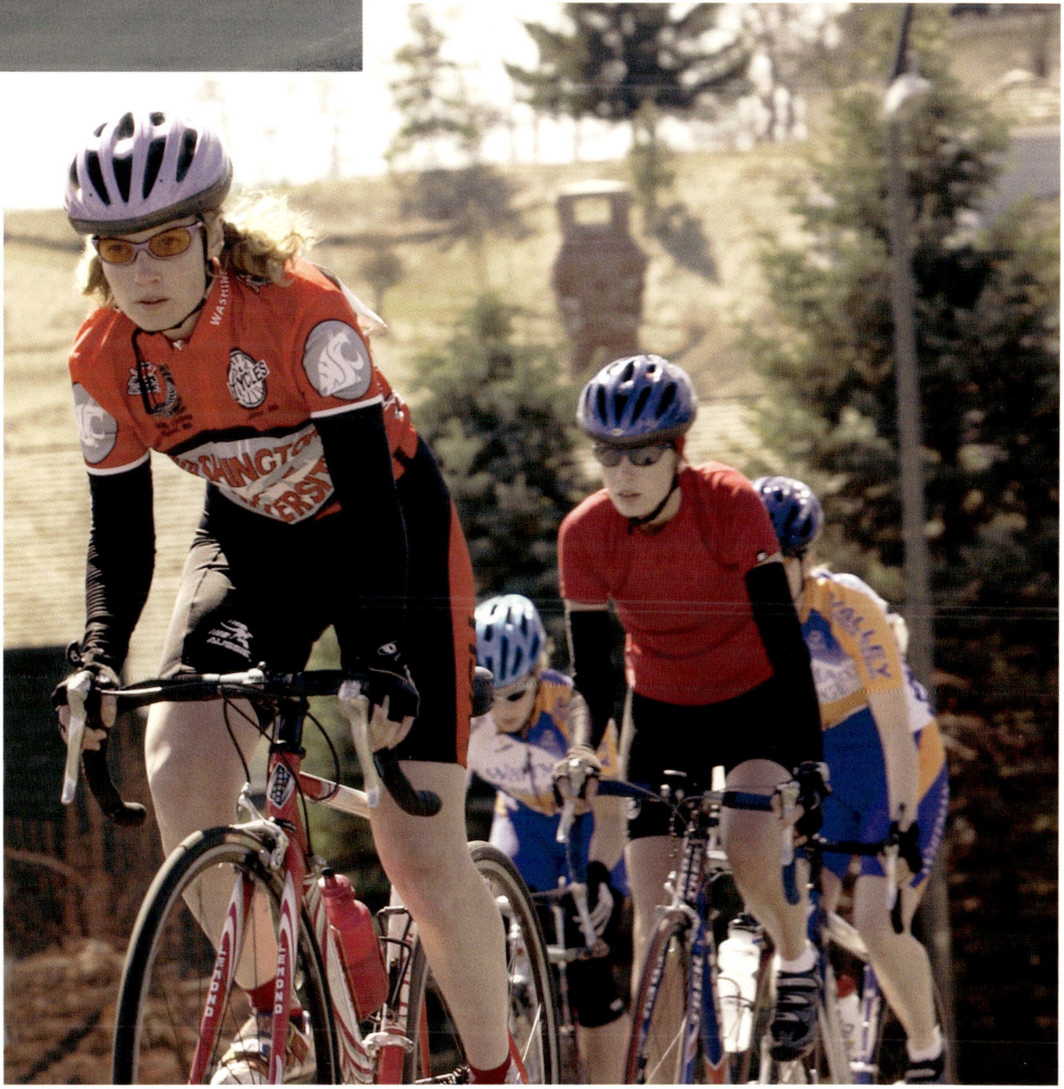

A WSU cyclist in
competition near the
Lewis Alumni Centre.

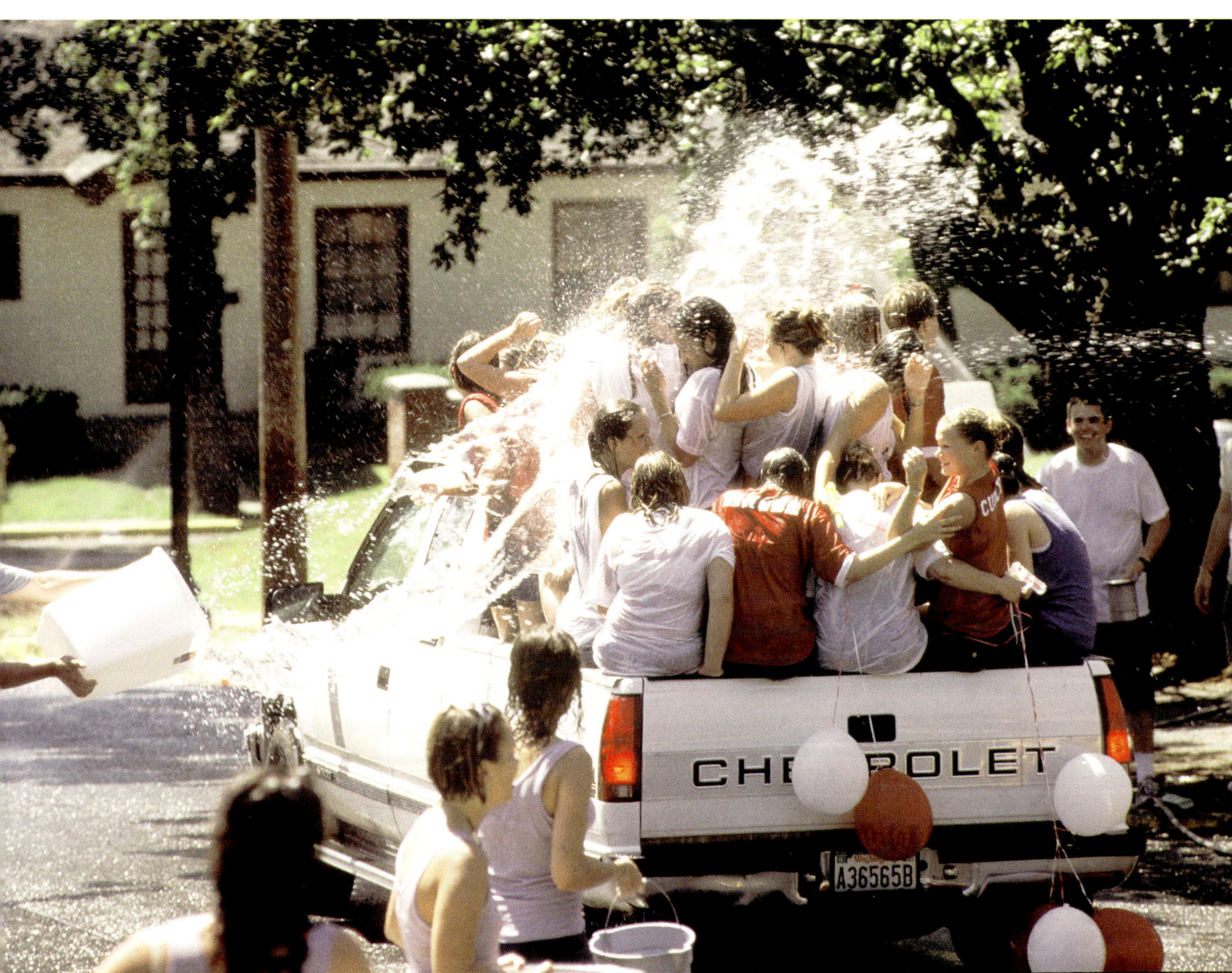

Greek Row water fight during ''Rush.''

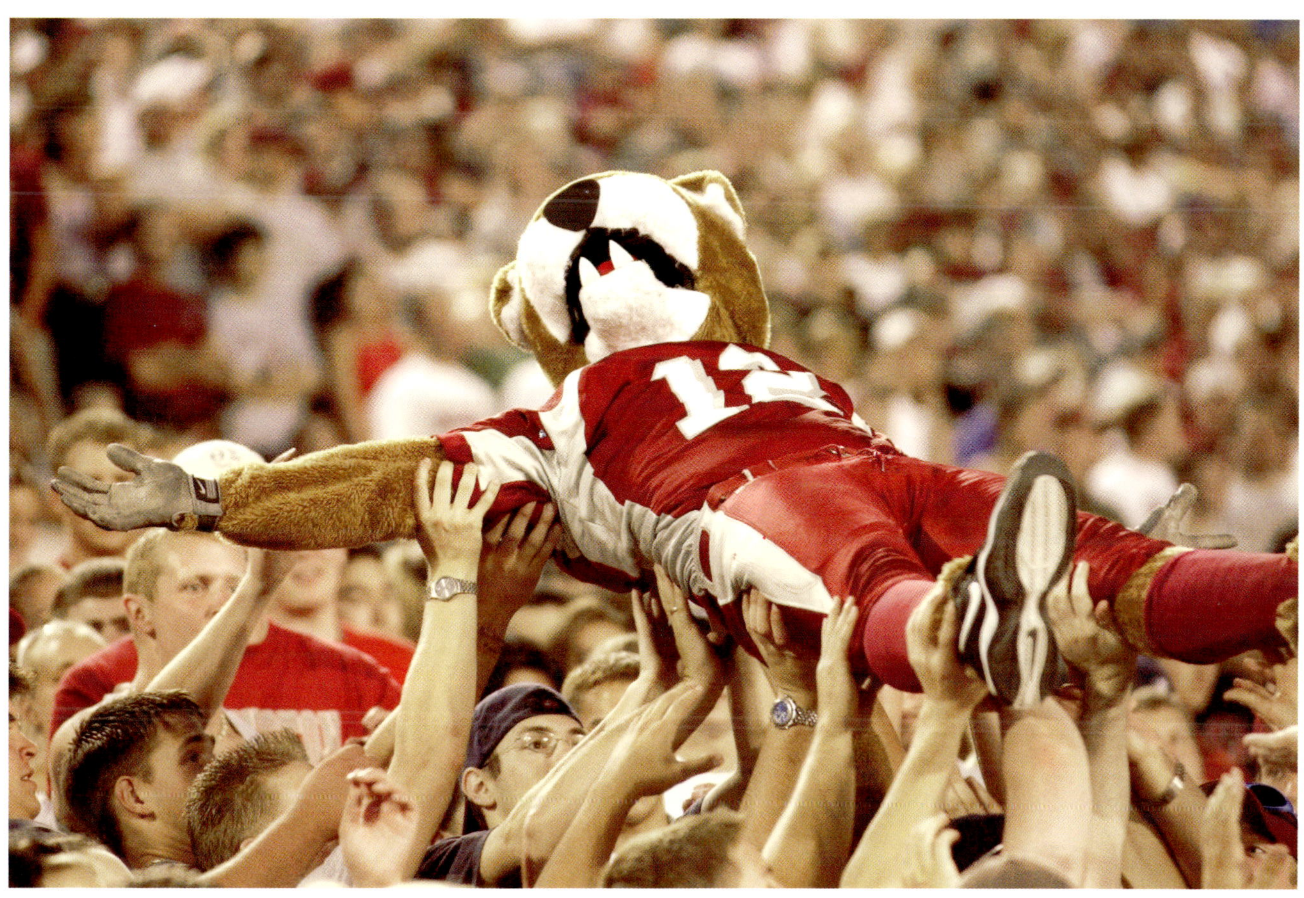

Butch goes crowd surfing
at a football game.

Overleaf:
Long shadows begin stretching
across Martin Stadium during
an afternoon game.

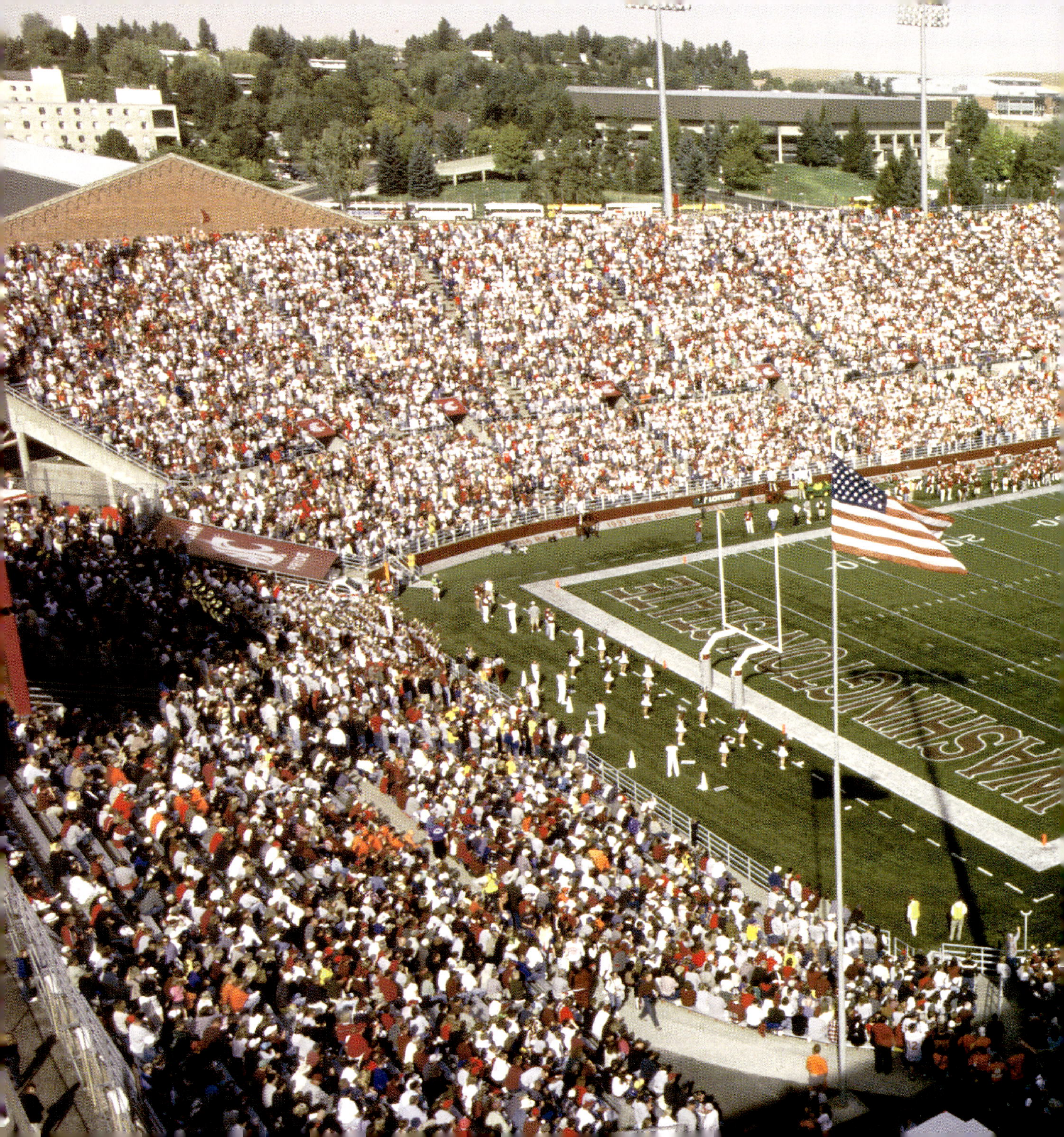

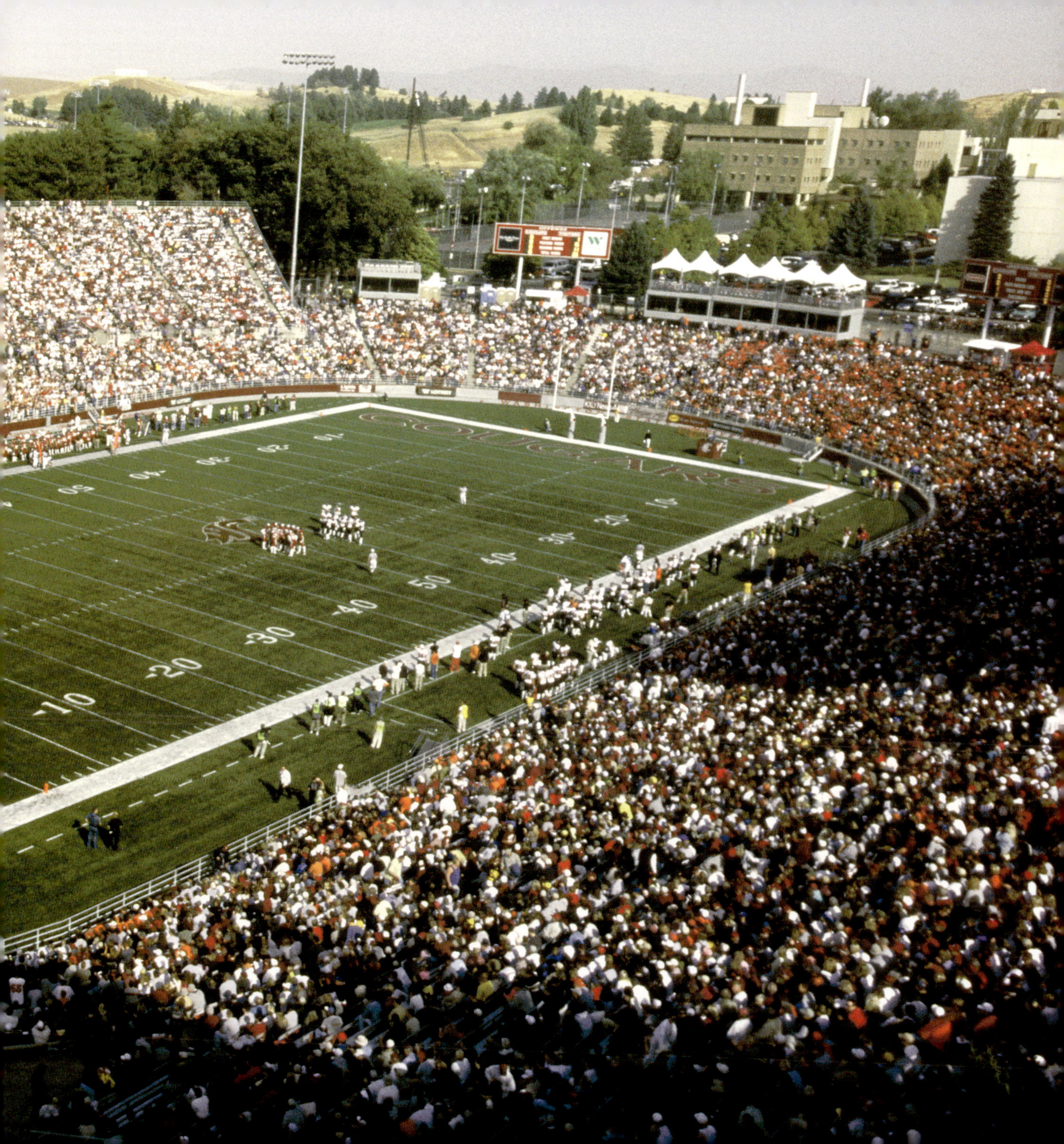

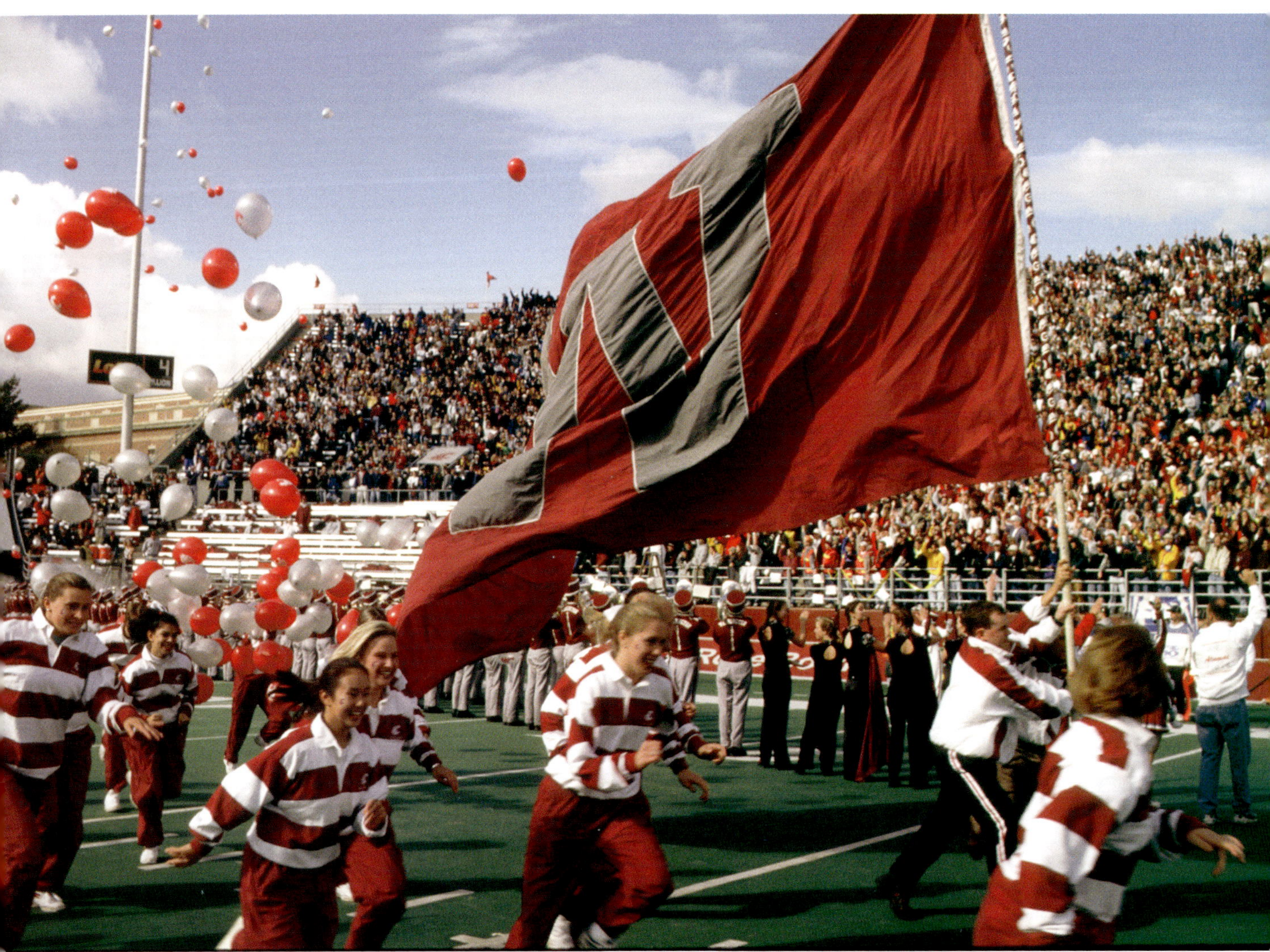

Rally squad and cheerleaders charge ahead of the team's entrance onto the gridiron.

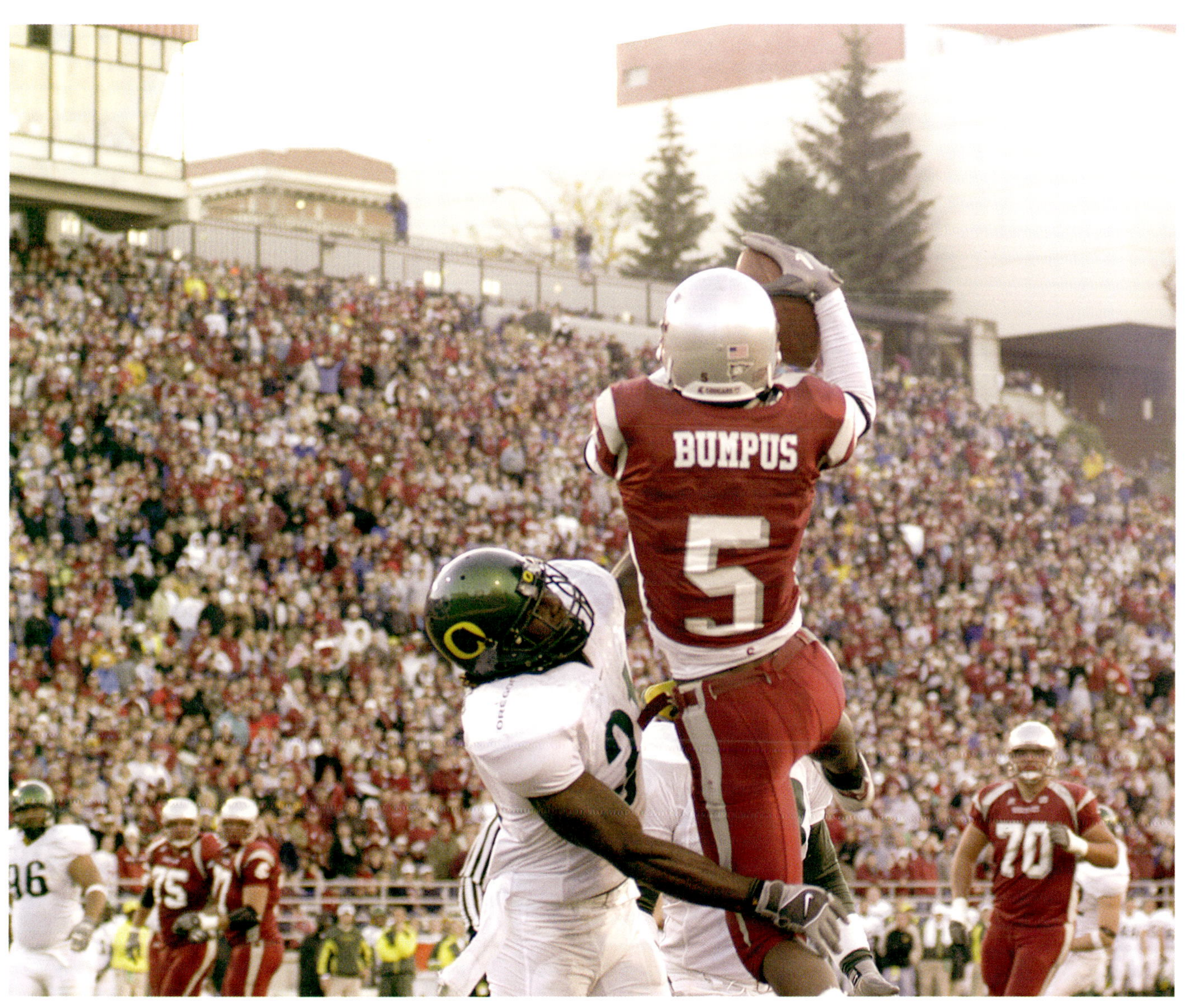

A Cougar wide receiver catches
a pass near the end zone.

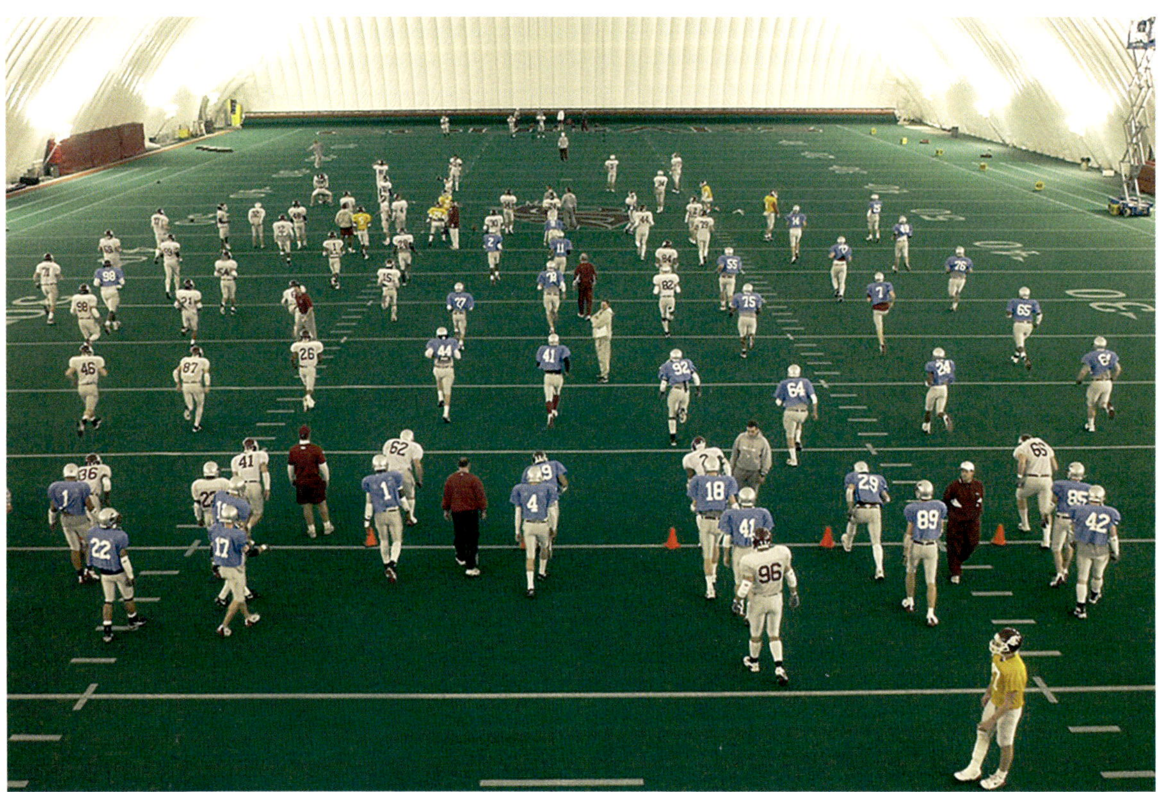

Running drill on the full sized football/soccer field in the Indoor Practice Facility. For track and field, the Astro-Turf surface rolls up, exposing a 200-meter track for training and indoor meets.

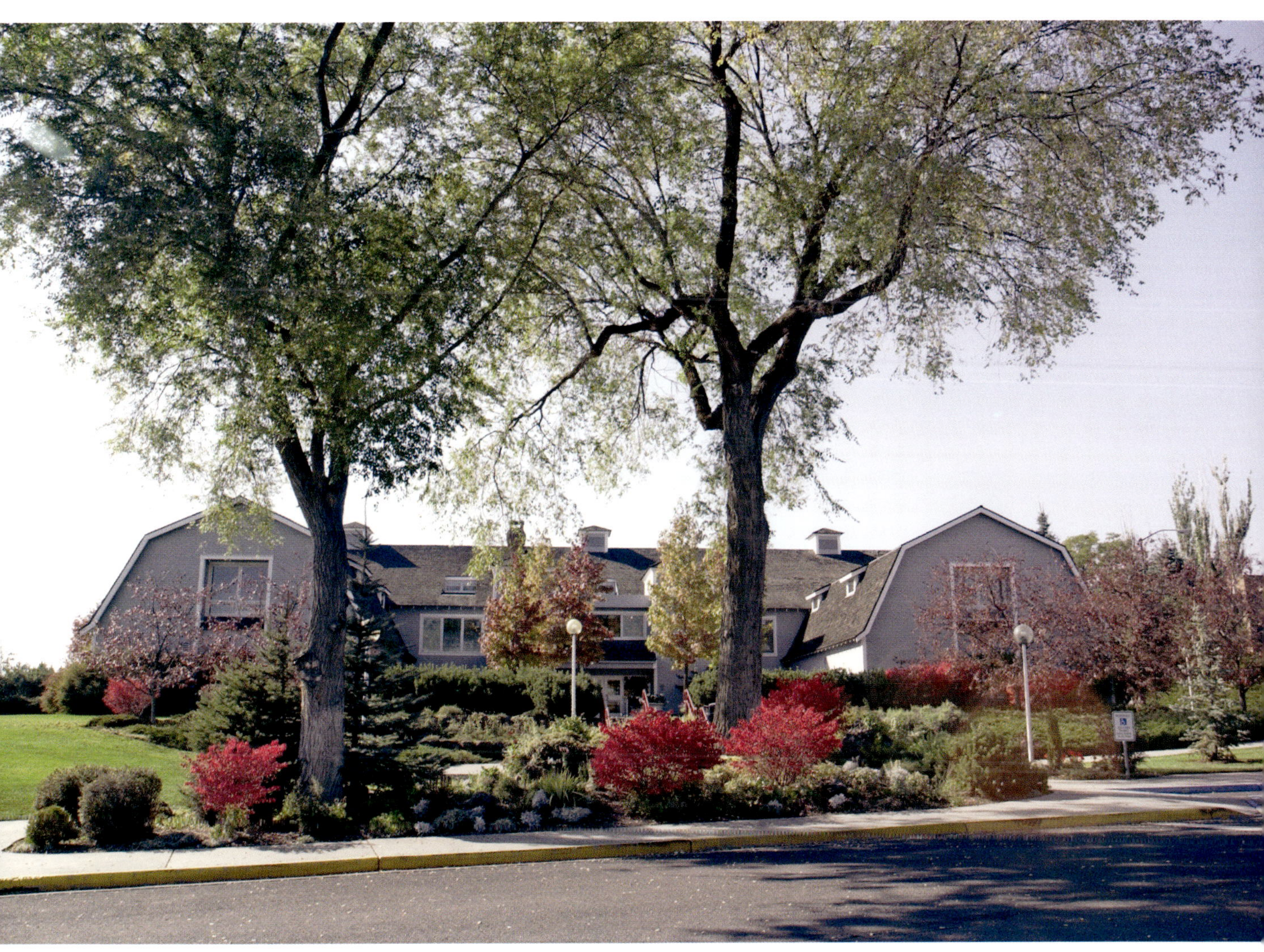

East side view of the Lewis Alumni Centre, a popular gathering place for visiting grads. In 1989, WSU alumni and friends remodeled the 1922 agricultural building into the "living room of the campus."

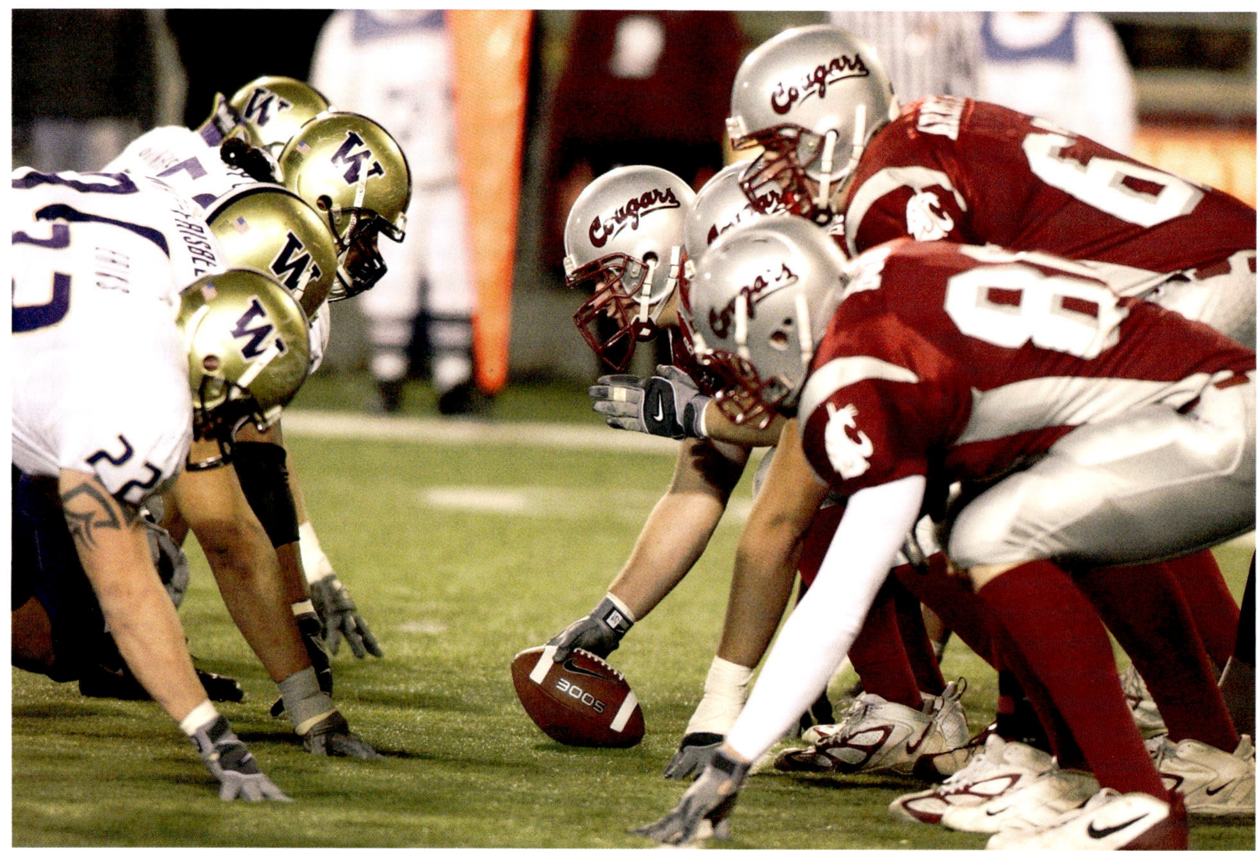

The annual football contest with the University of Washington became known as the Apple Cup in 1962. Formerly, it was the Governor's Cup. The gridiron rivalry dates back to 1900.

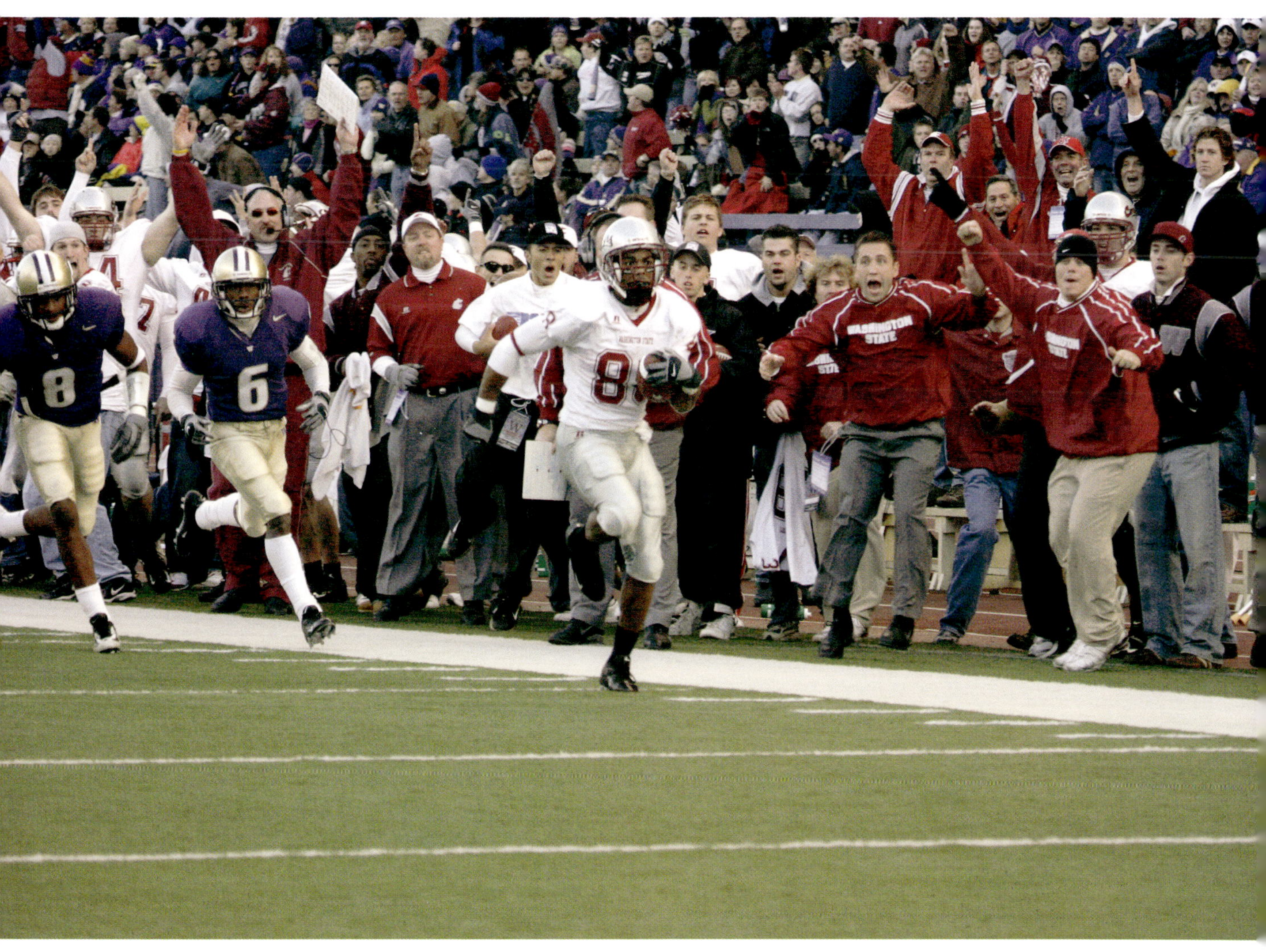

Touchdown WSU!

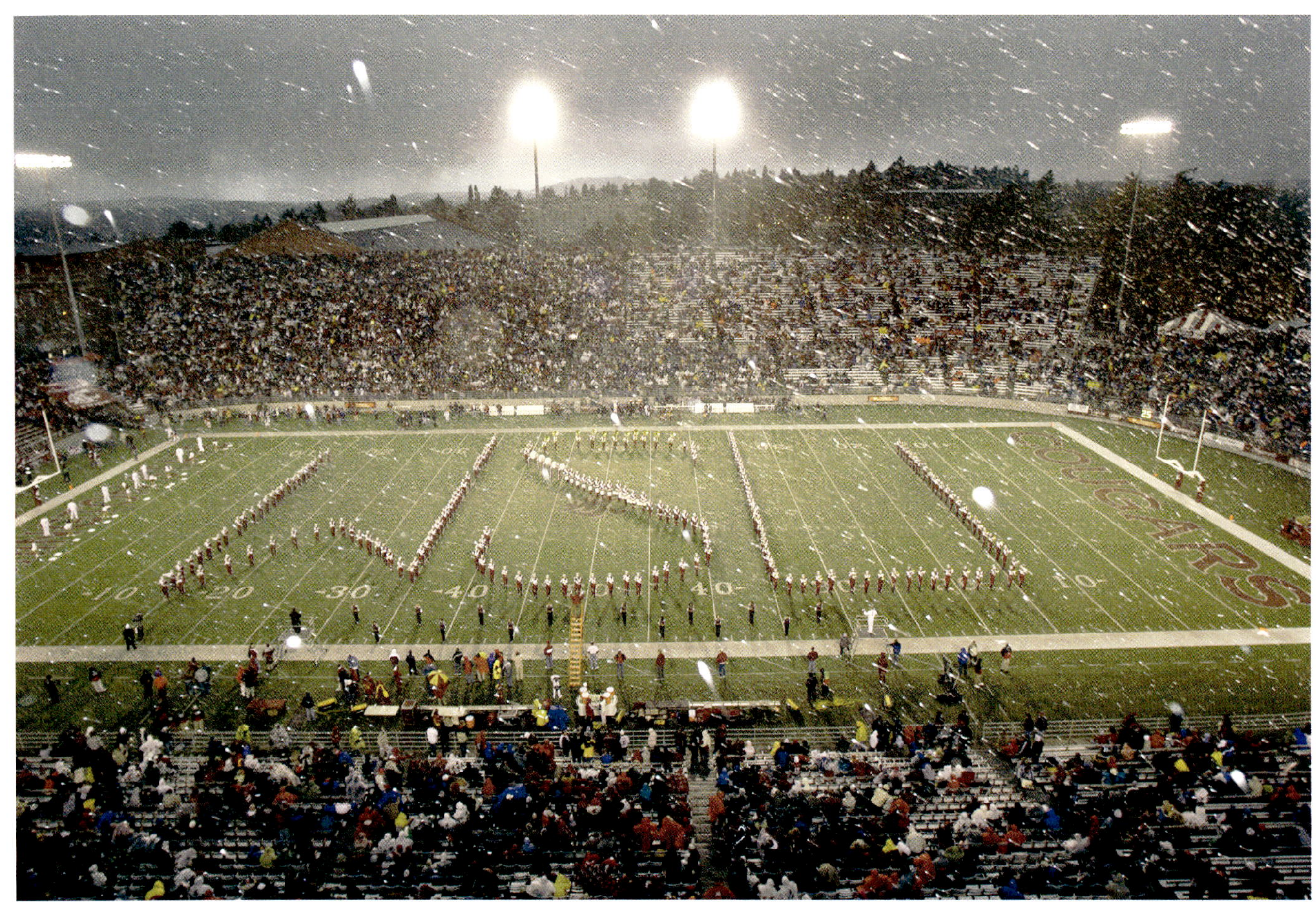

Cougars rejoice and opponents
despair when storm flurries
strike Martin Stadium.

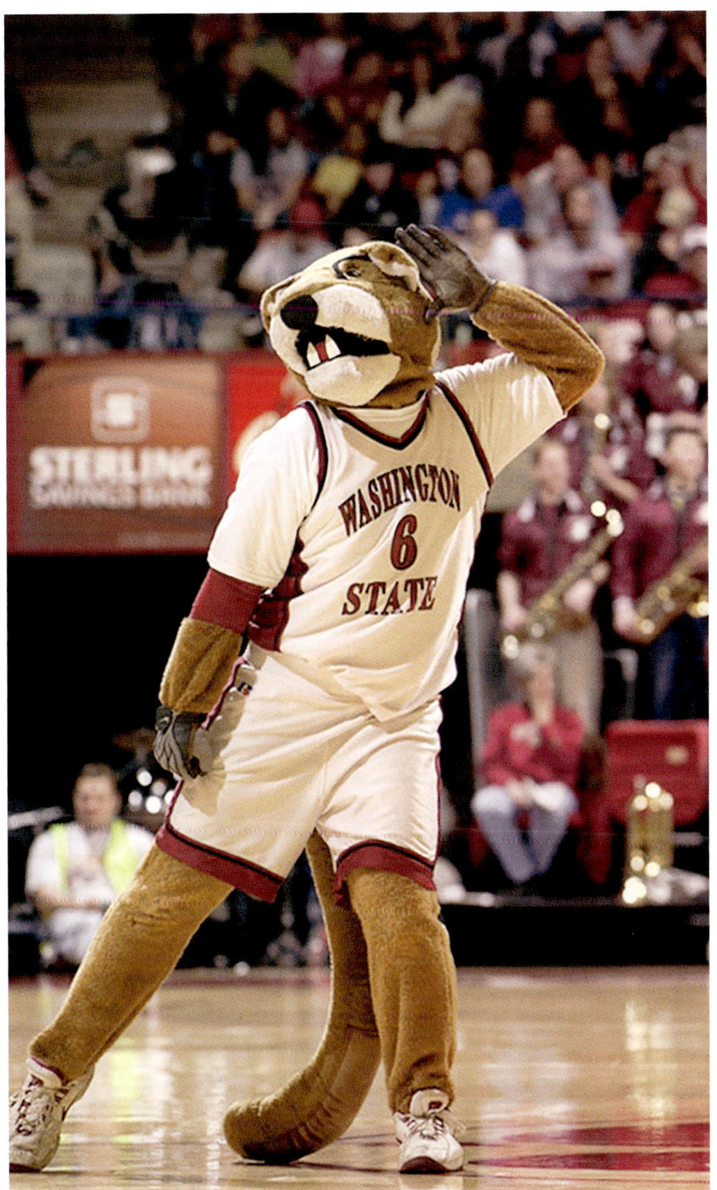

Ever silent but ever active, Butch T. Cougar inspires crowds at athletic contests and other events. The identity of the student playing the role of Butch remains a secret until the end of a two-year commitment.

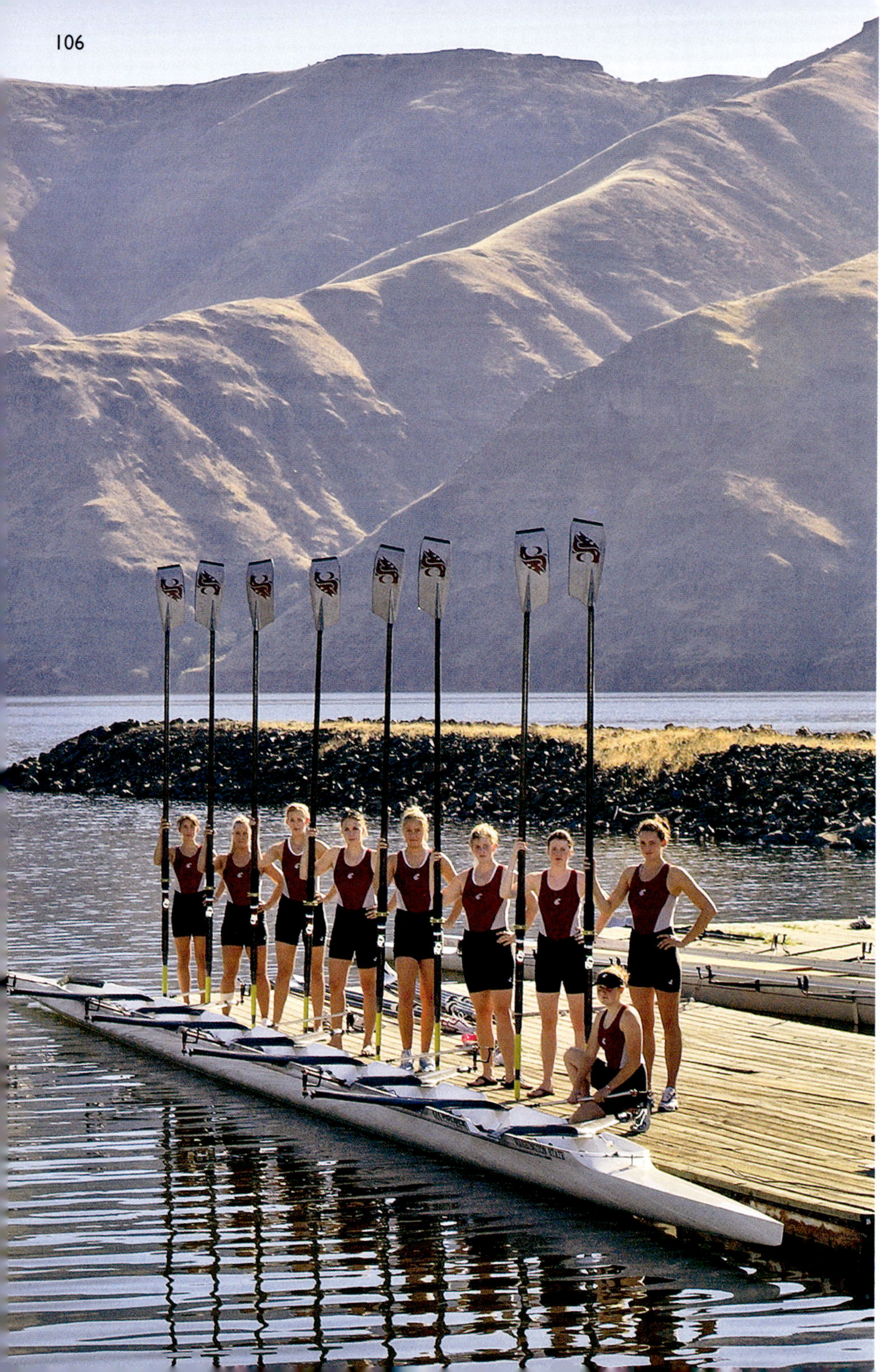

Women's rowing team at Wawawai Landing on the Snake River reservoir, 20 miles southwest of Pullman—one of the most spectacular rowing courses in the country.

More than 1.8 million fans have watched basketball action at Friel Court since Beasley Coliseum opened in 1973. The court is named for legendary coach Jack Friel, who guided the Washington State team to the national title game in 1941.

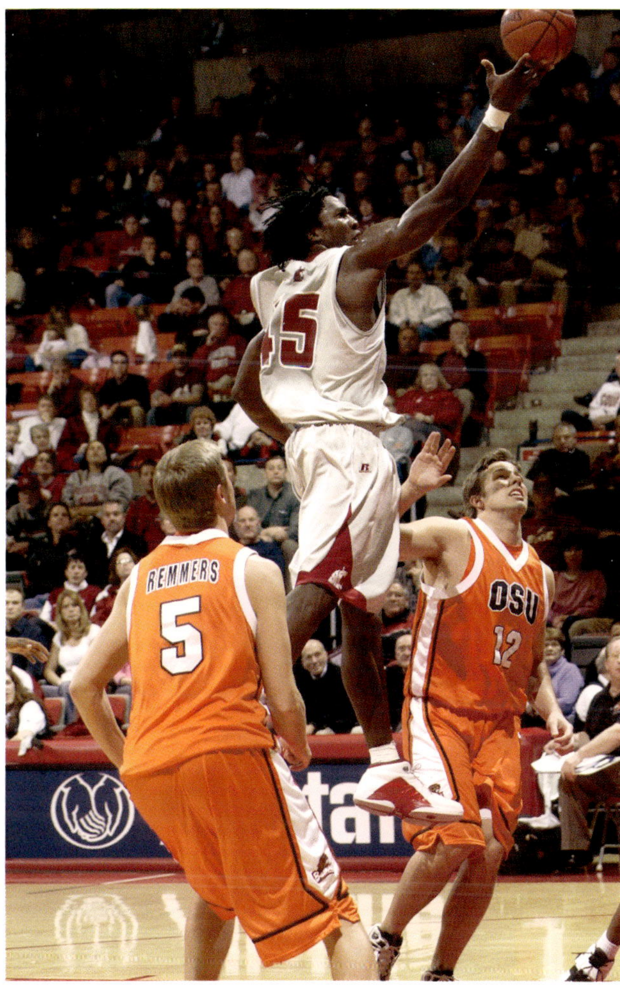

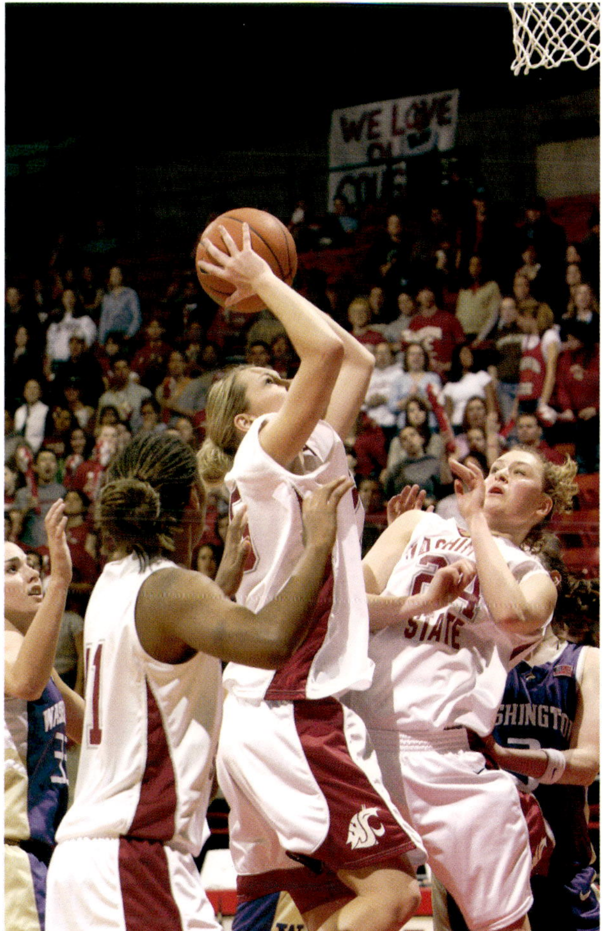

Contests between the Cougars and Huskies always arouse a higher level of intensity for athletes and spectators alike.

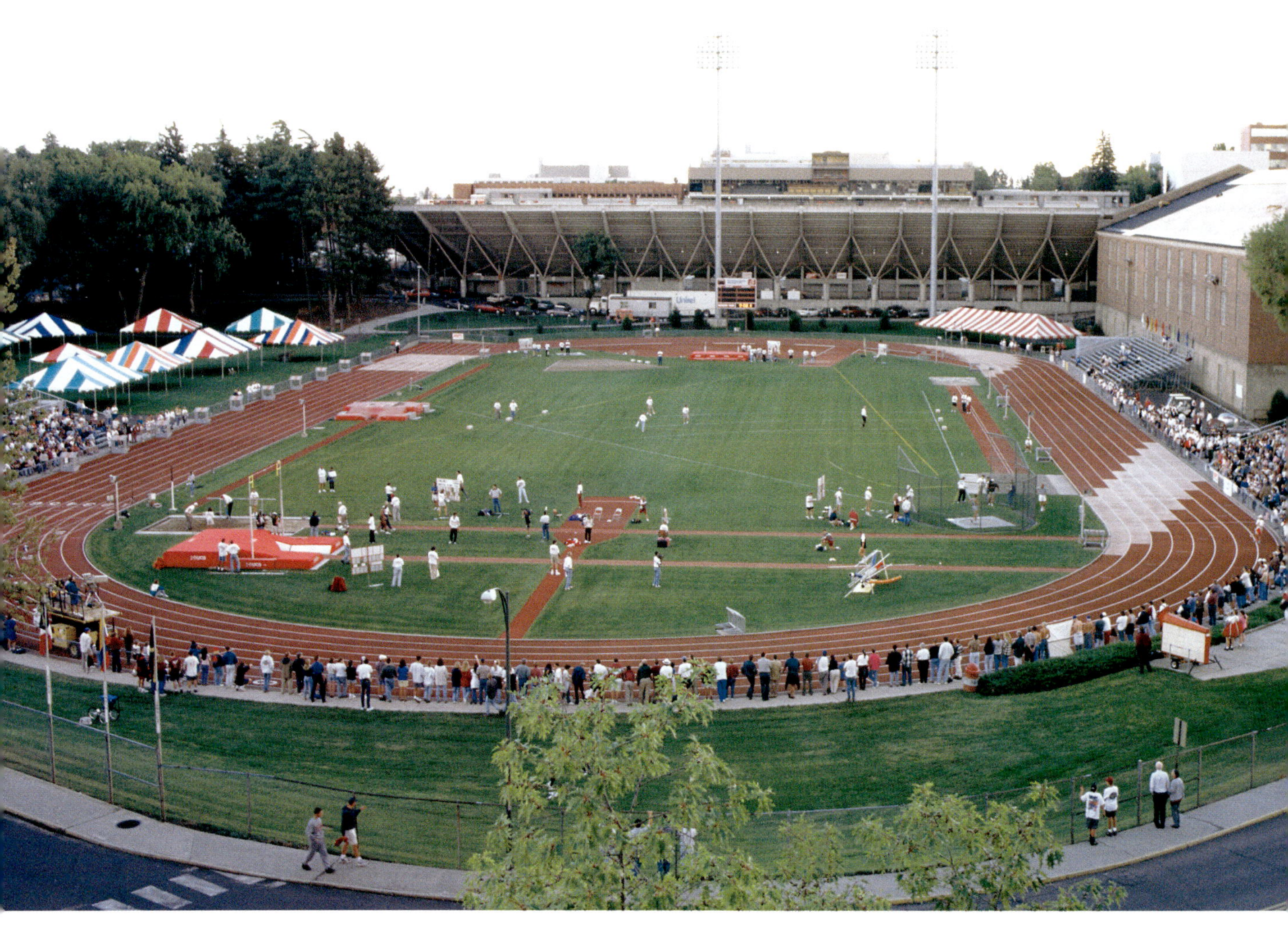

Jack Mooberry Track (1981) honors the Cougars' coach from 1945 to 1973. Running events began in June 1892, when students cut a track in an oat field where Martin Stadium stands today.

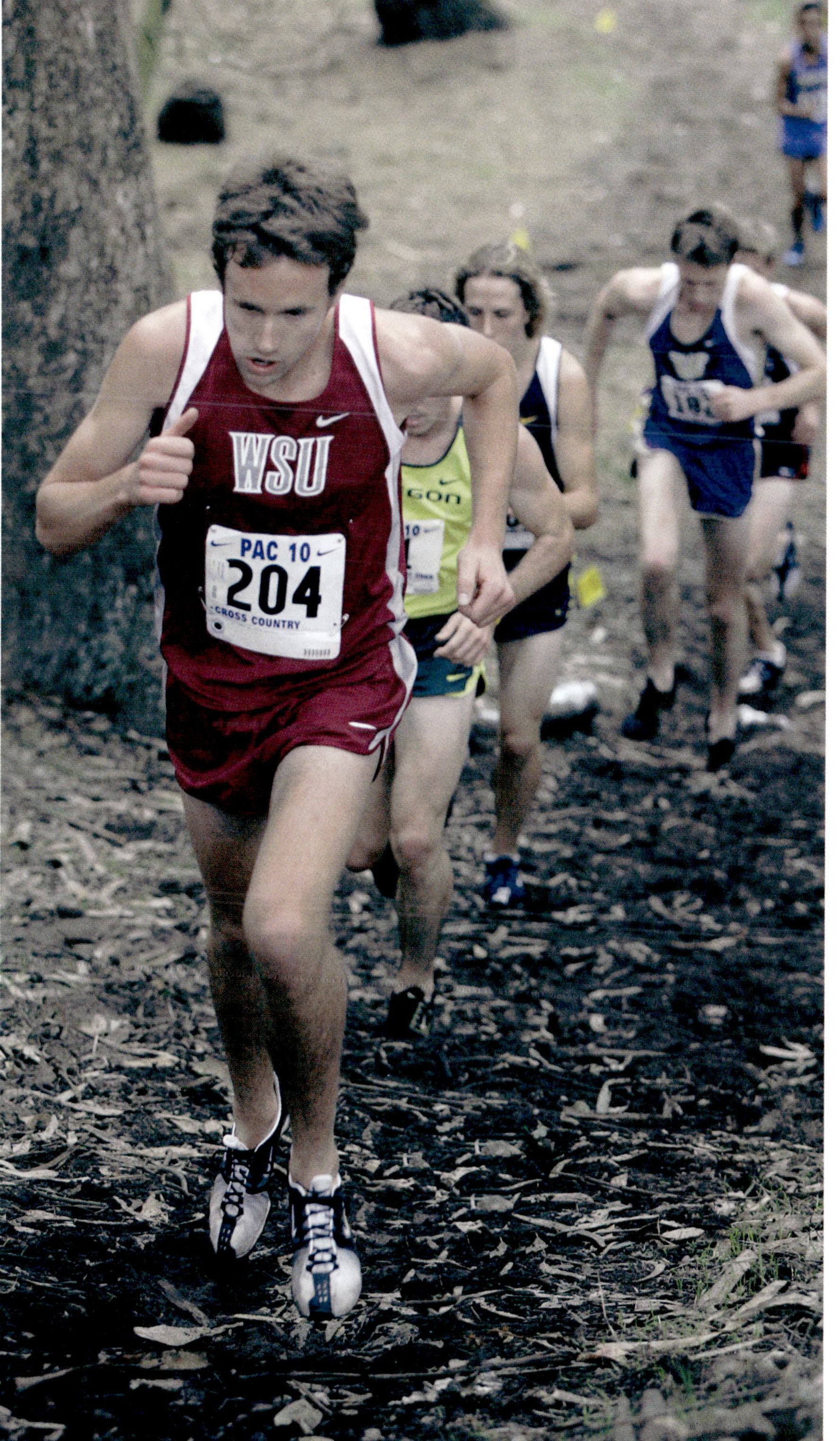

WSU hosted
the PAC-10
Cross Country
Championships on
November 1, 2003.

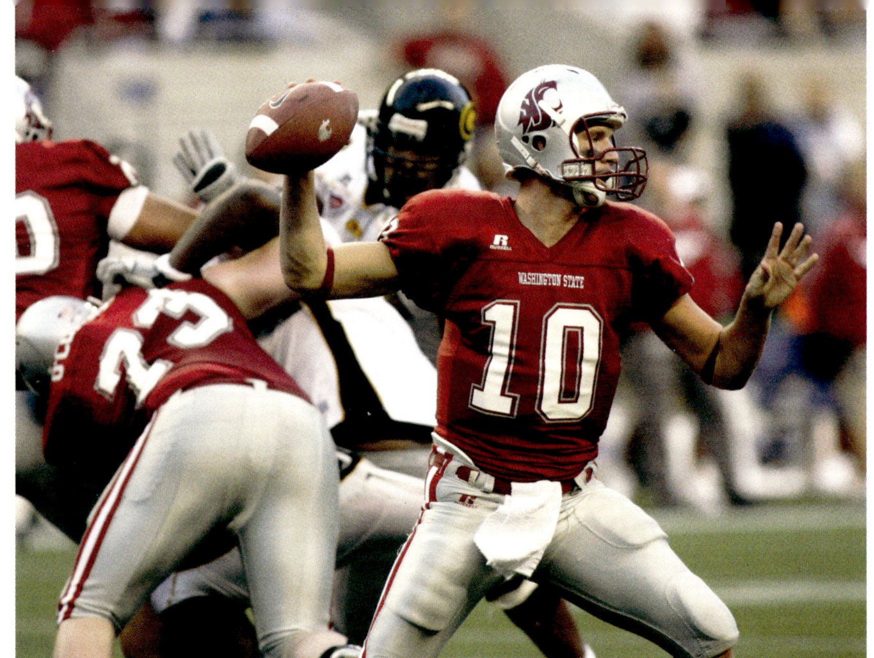

Cougars playing Grambling State at Qwest Field, September 17, 2005. An annual game in Seattle against a non-conference opponent is popular with thousands of "west-side" alumni.

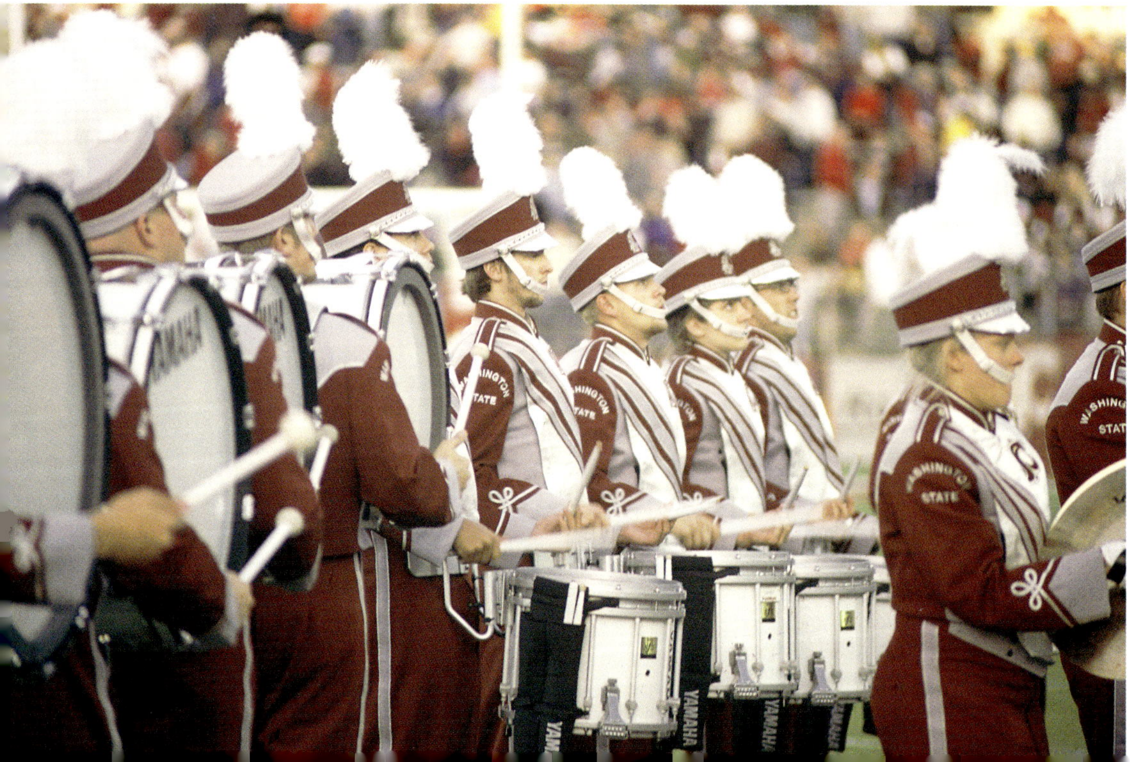

WSU Marching Band's percussion line.

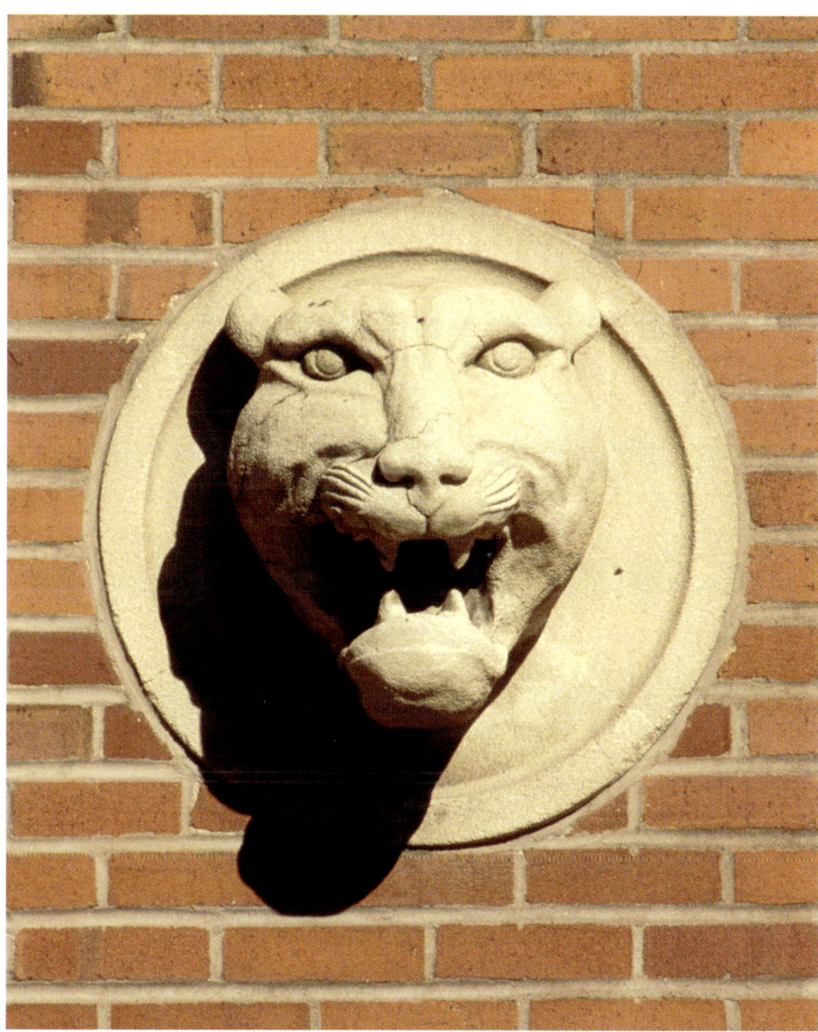

Cougar bust on Bohler Gym, dating from 1928.

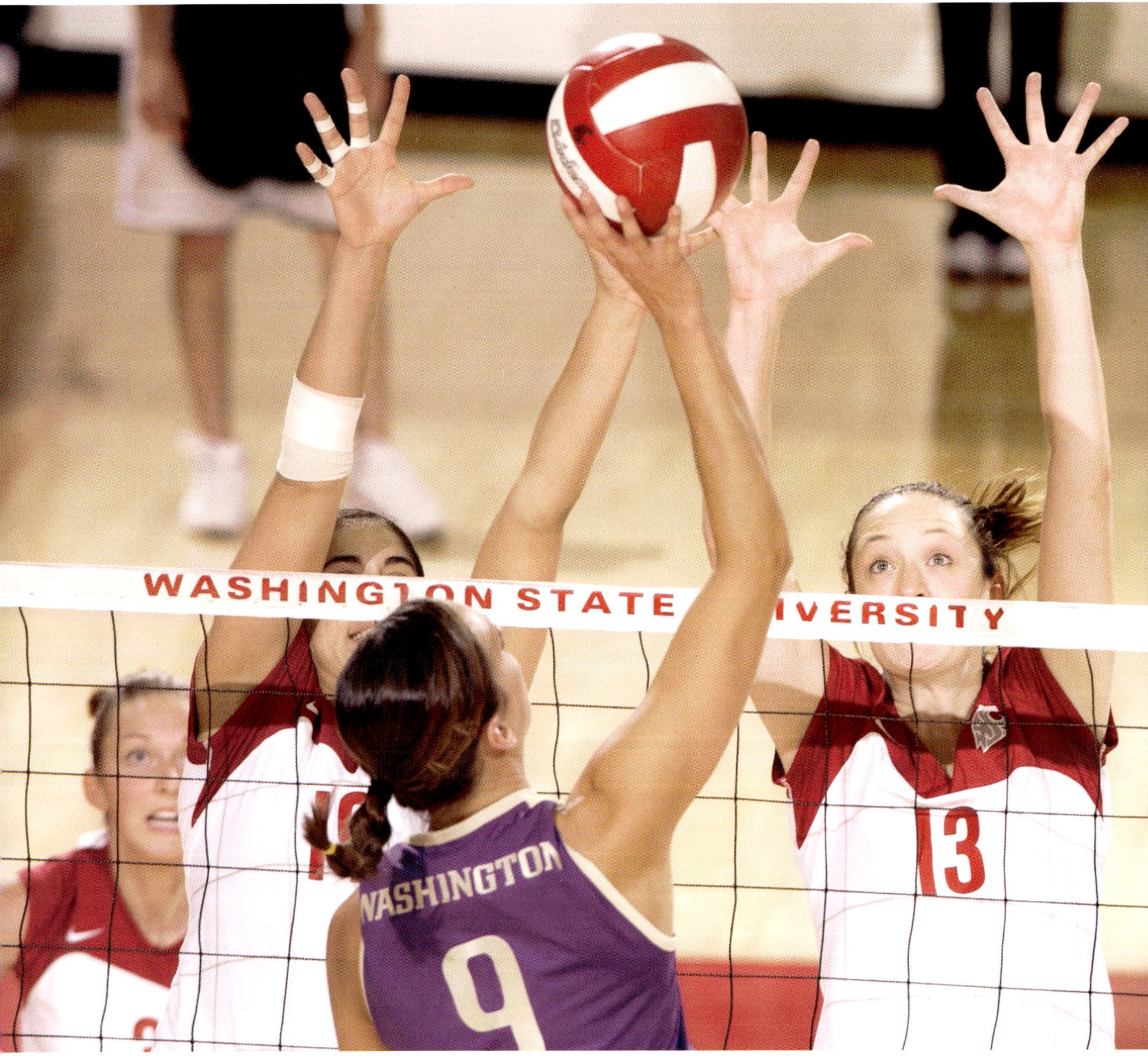
WASHINGTON STATE UNIVERSITY
WASHINGTON
9
13

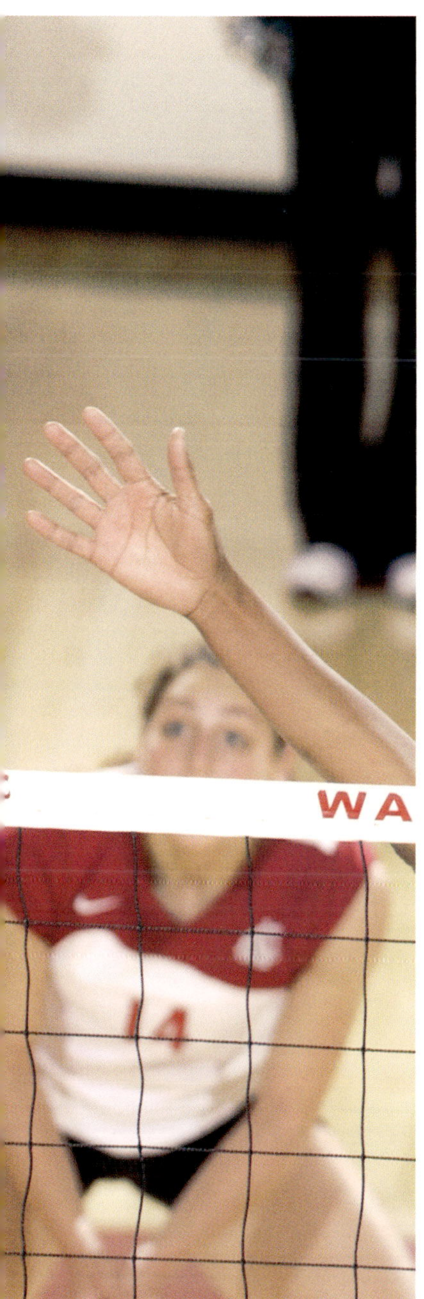

Bohler Gym hosts intense volleyball action in the highly competitive PAC-10 Conference.

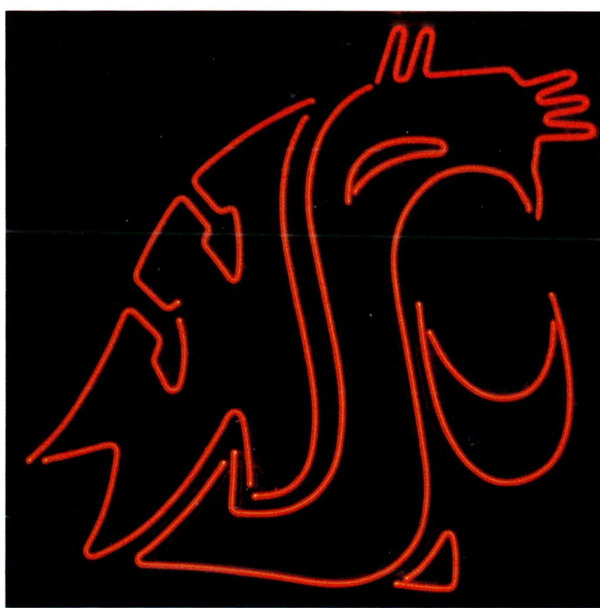

Designed in 1936 by undergraduate Randall Johnson (class of 1938) and slightly modified over the years, the Cougar monogram is one of the most widely recognized sports emblems in college ranks.

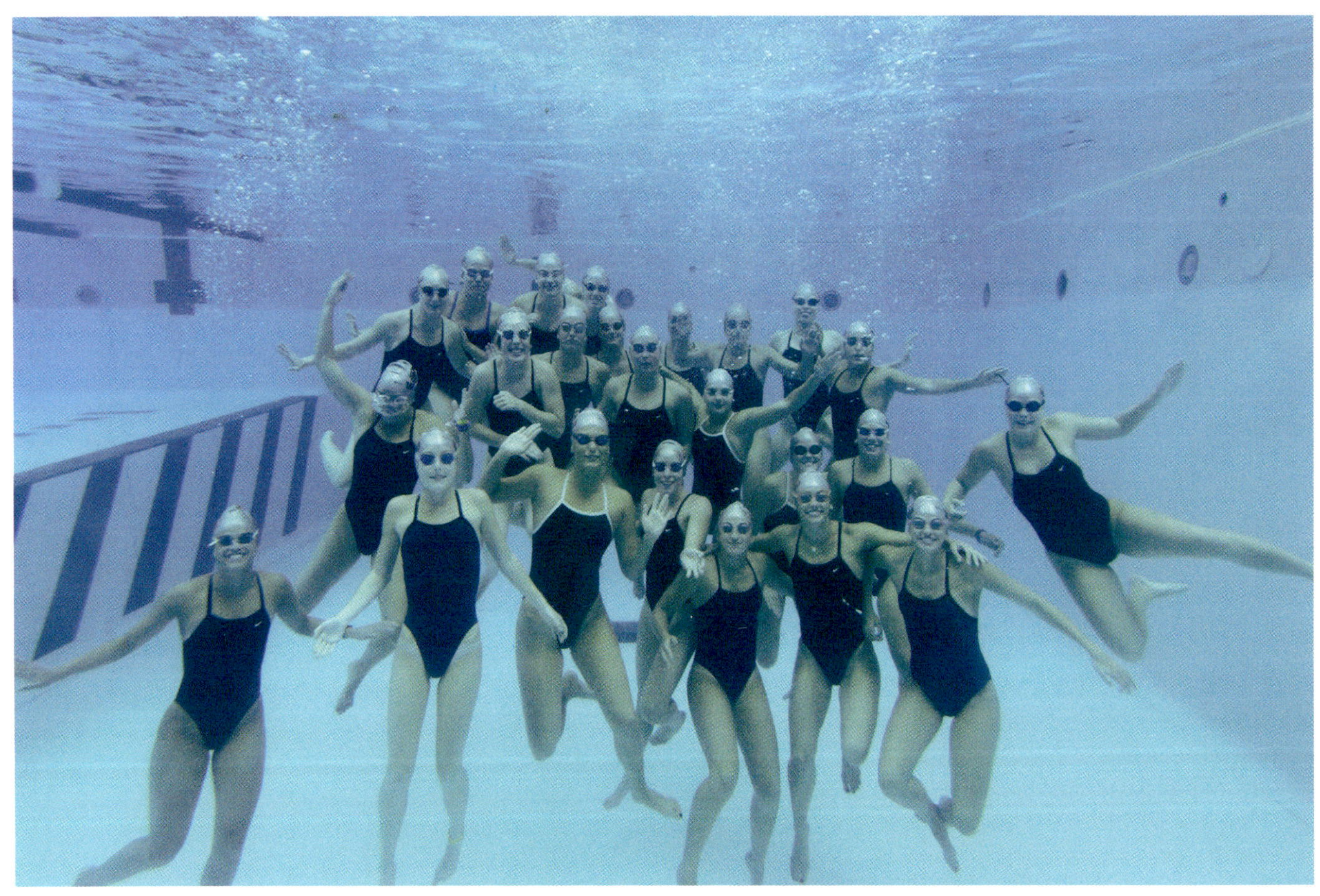

Women's swimming
team in Gibb Pool.

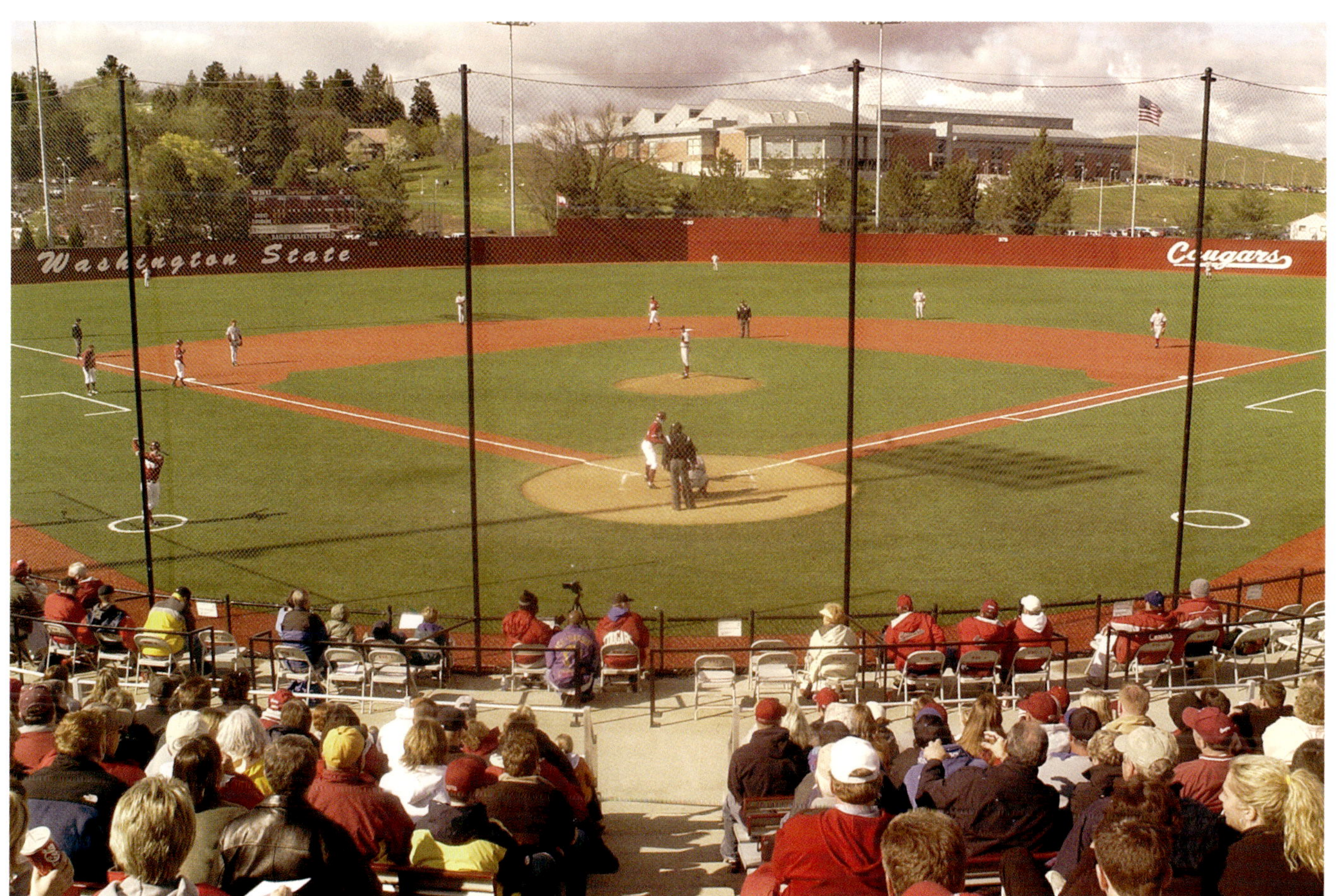

Bailey-Brayton Field seats 3,500. Lighting added in 1984 made it one of the few NCAA college-owned facilities in the nation with illumination for night games. The Student Recreation Center sits on the brow of a hill to the north.

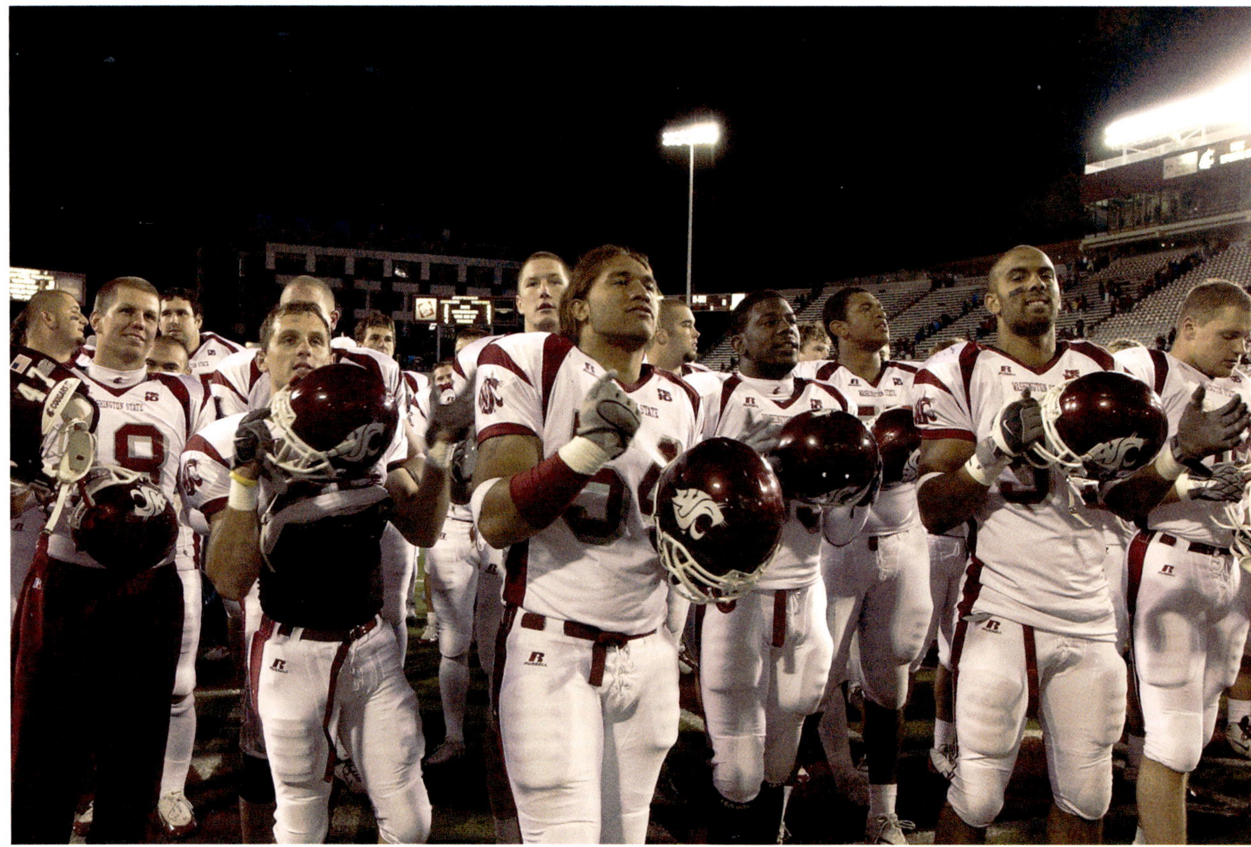

The Cougars sing the WSU
Fight Song following a Martin
Stadium game against the
University of Idaho.

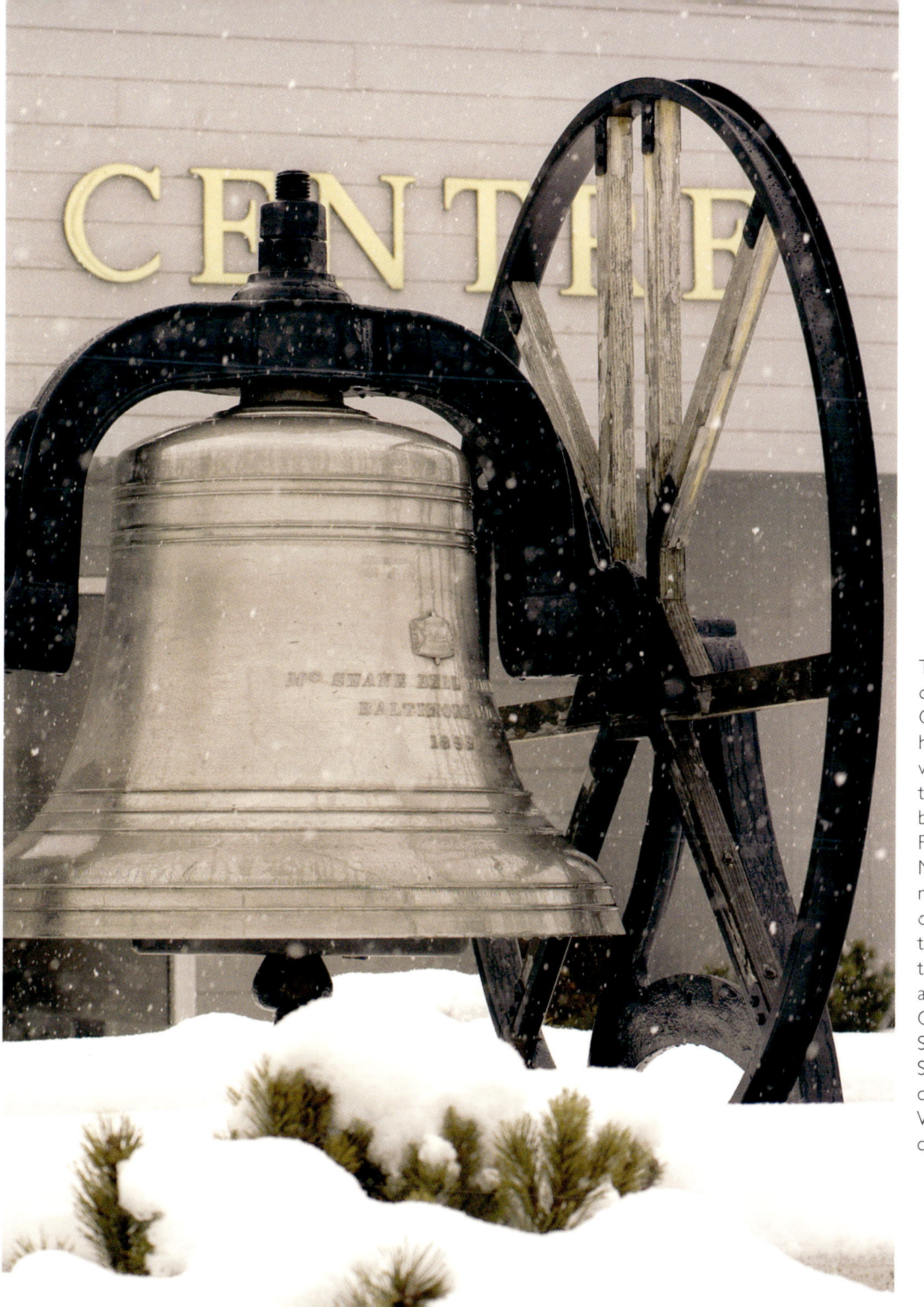

The Victory Bell in front of the Lewis Alumni Centre is rung following home-game football wins. Cast more than a century ago by the McShane Bell Foundry of Baltimore, Maryland, it remains mounted on the original frame. Initially, the bell announced the changing of classes after the Agricultural College, Experiment Station and School of Science of the State of Washington (now WSU) opened its doors in 1892.

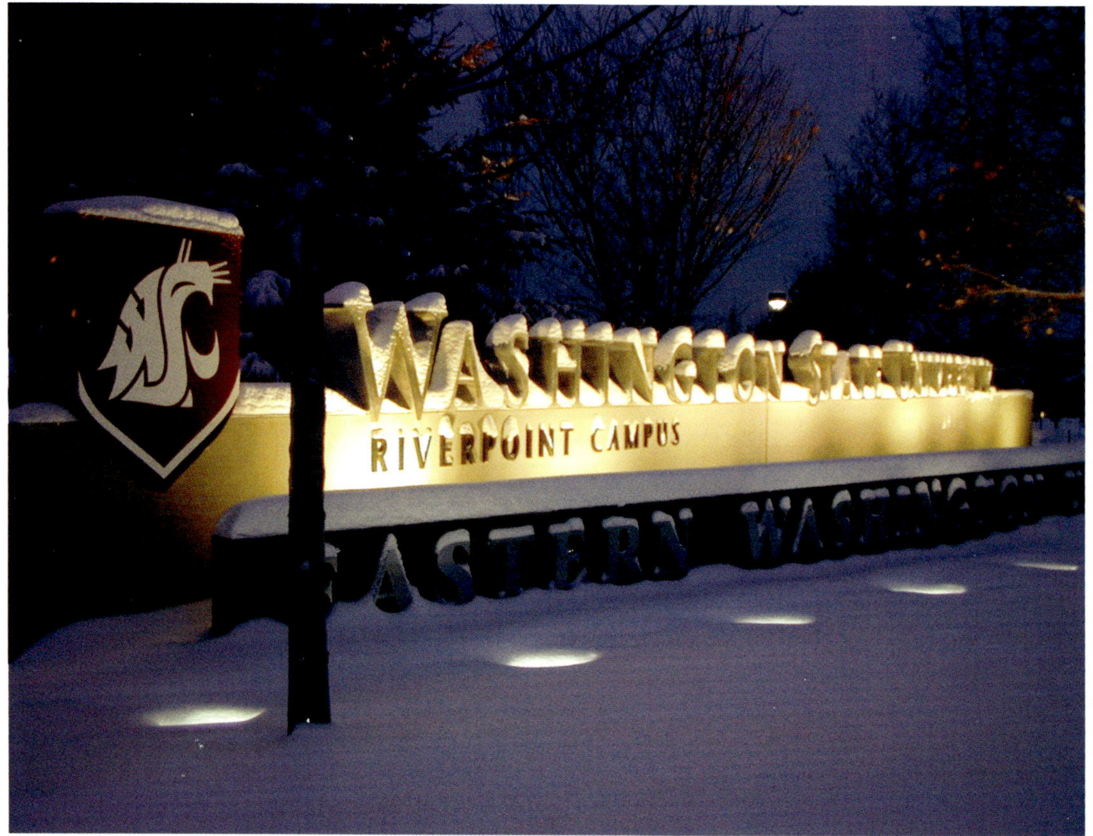

WSU Spokane at the state-of-the-art Riverpoint Campus—established in 1989 in the downtown area as a cooperative venture with Eastern Washington University.

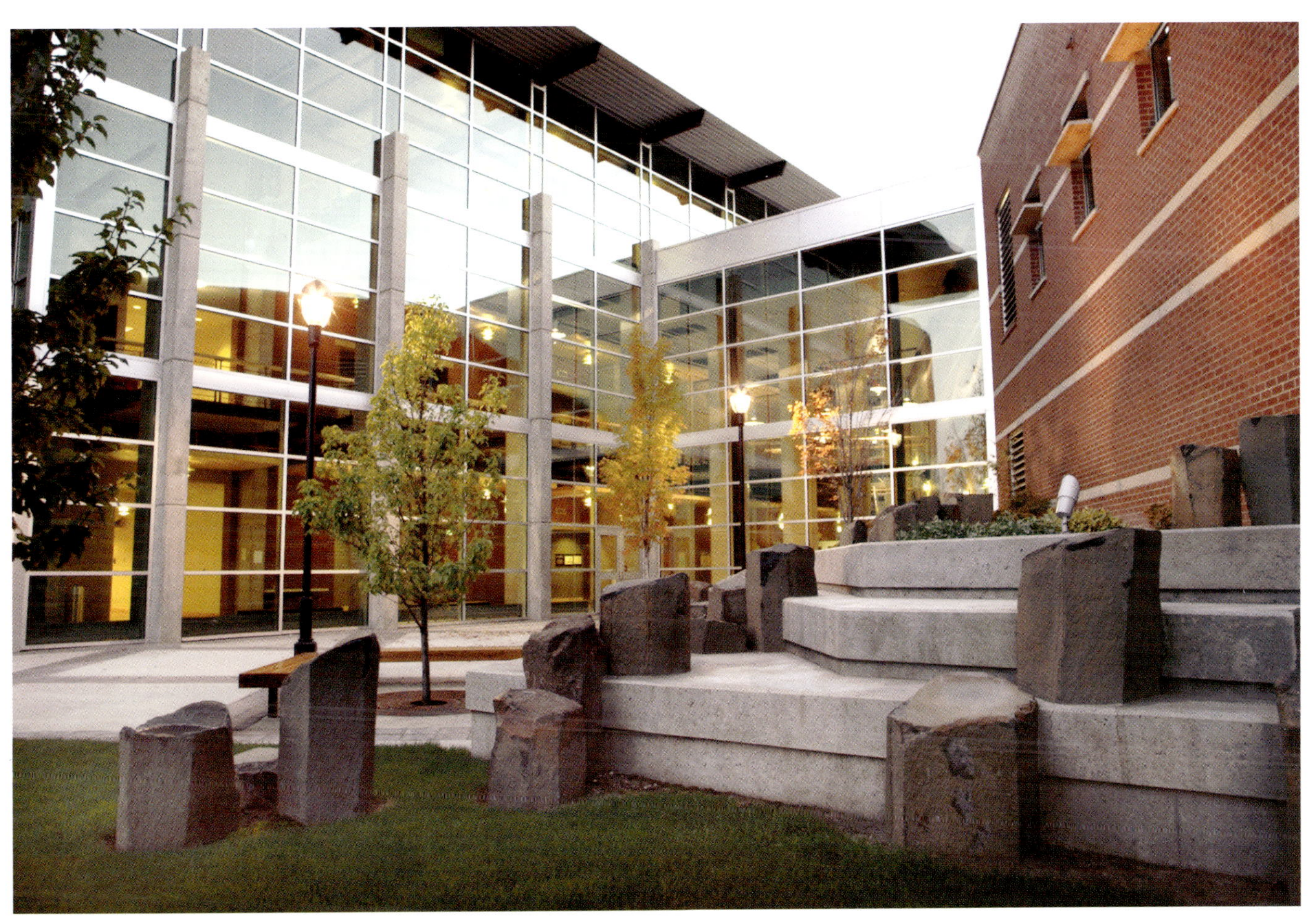

Nearly 900 students are enrolled at the Riverpoint Campus in a variety of academic and research programs. Seen here is the Health Sciences Building.

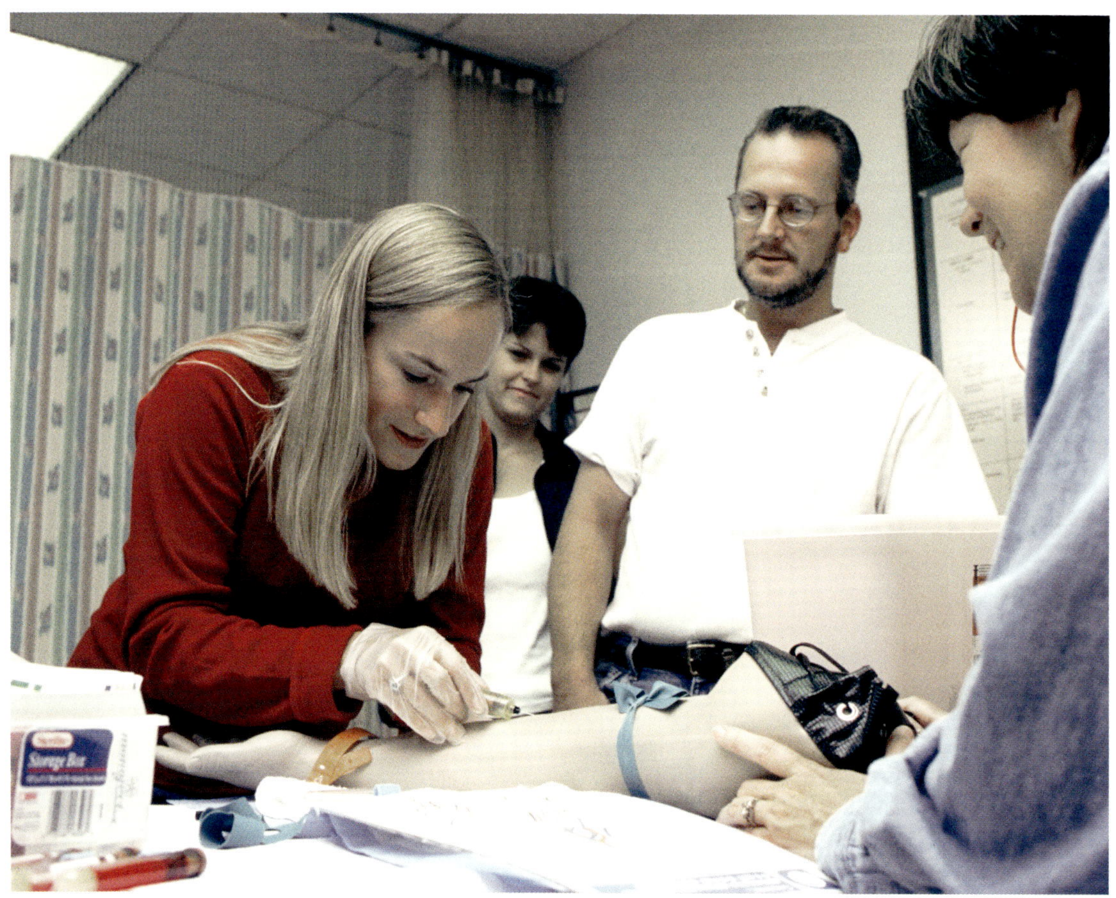

A student in training at the Intercollegiate College of Nursing (founded in 1968) on the Fort George Wright Drive campus in west Spokane. With more than 500 students in attendance, the ICN consortium includes WSU, Eastern Washington University, Gonzaga University, and Whitworth College.

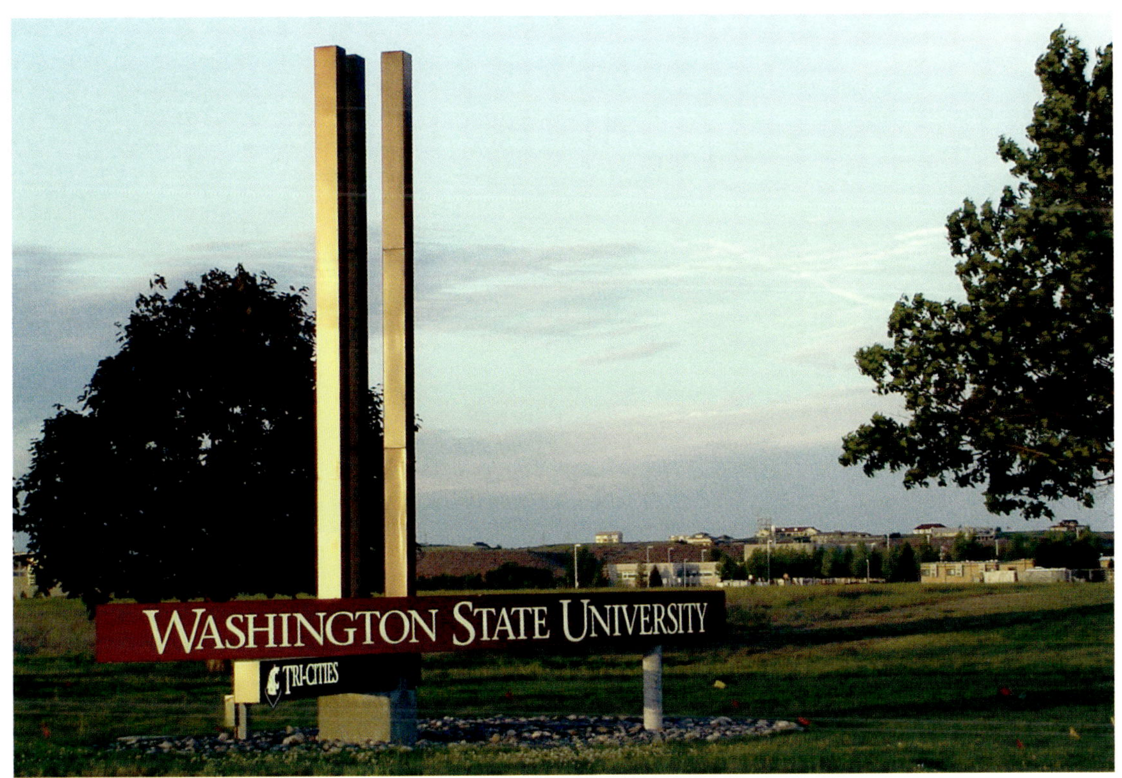

WSU Tri-Cities serves more than 1,300 students at its Richland campus and several branch units in other central Washington cities. Most classes are offered during evening hours to accommodate working adults. Other students are community college transfers who attend full time. In 2007, freshmen and sophomores will be admitted.

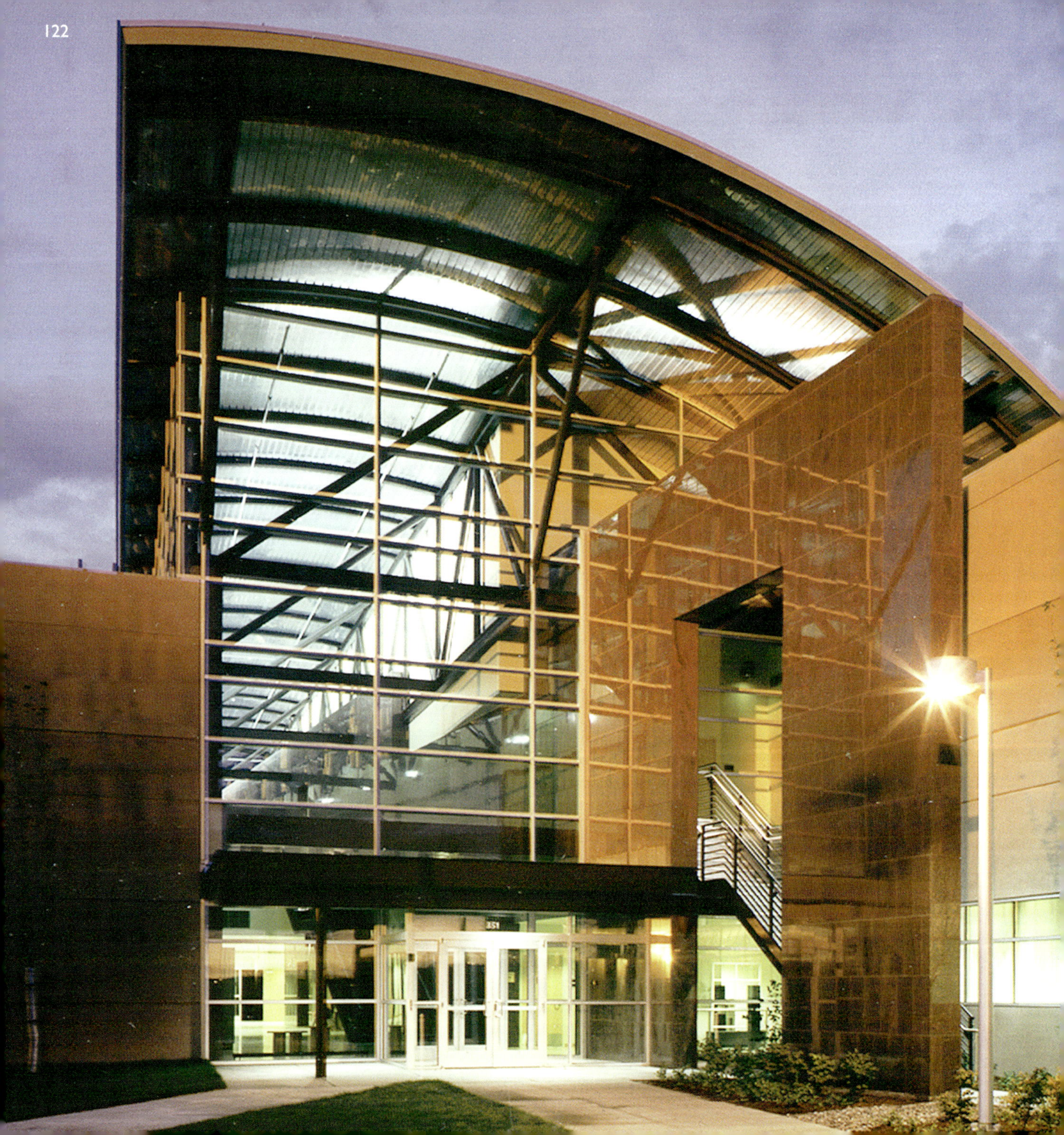

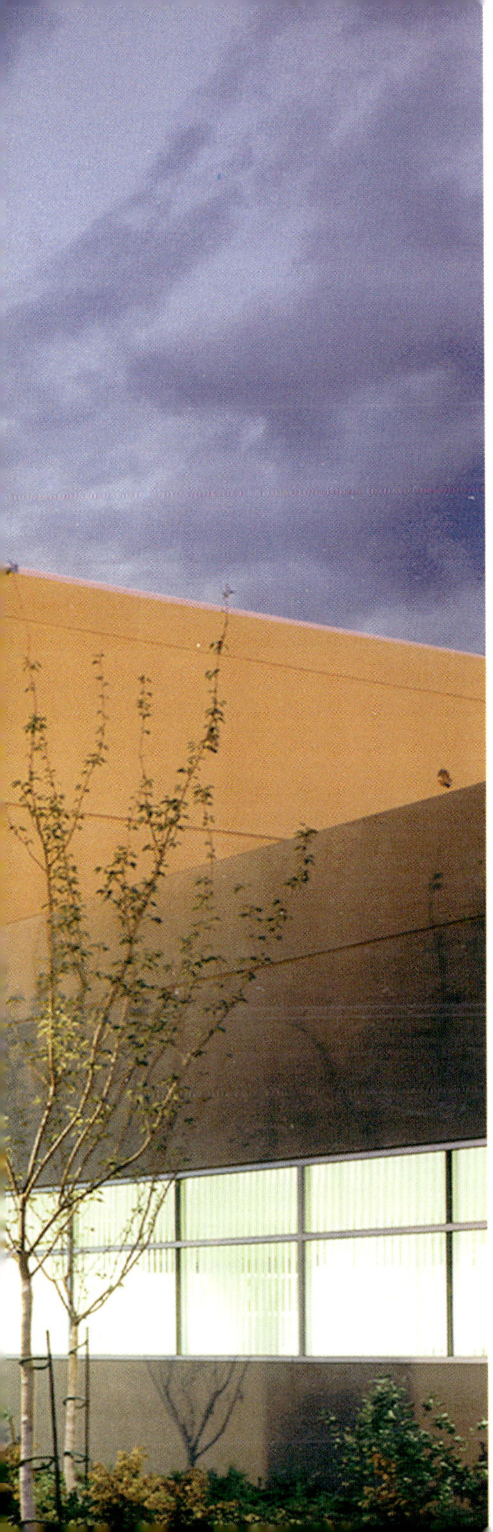

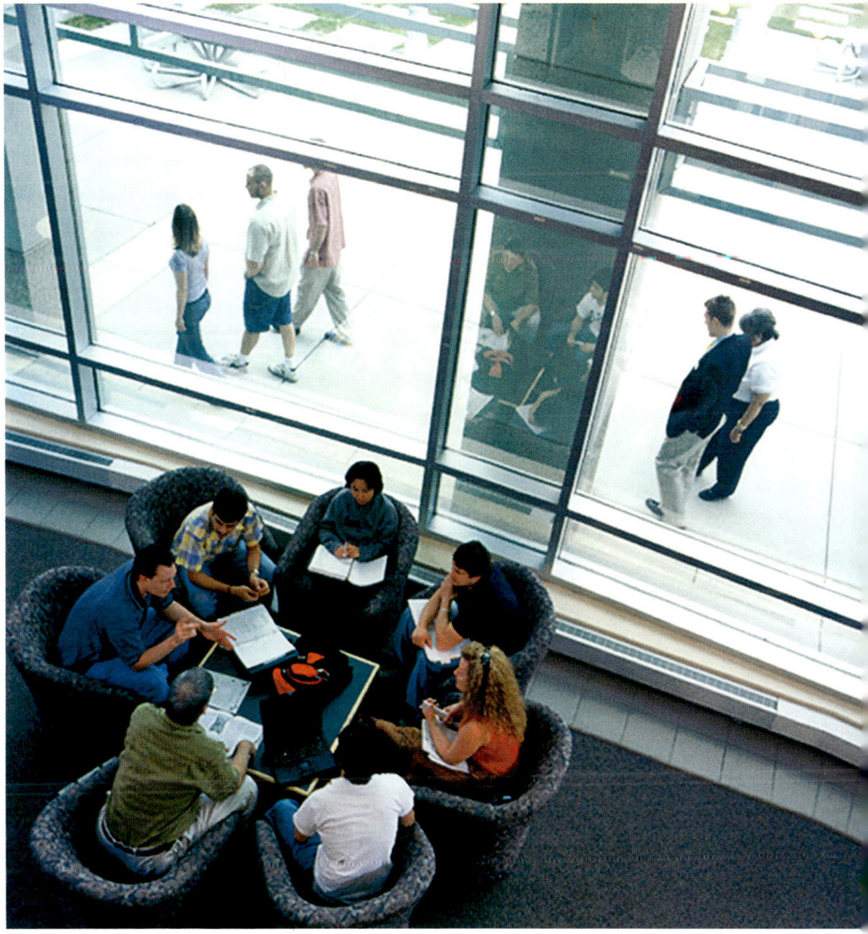

Funded by the State of Washington and the U.S. Department of Energy, the Consolidated Information Center opened its doors on the Richland campus in June 1997.

At WSU Tri-Cities, students complete bachelor's or earn master's degrees in an array of programs—from business to science, nursing to agriculture, humanities to engineering, and education to environmental science.

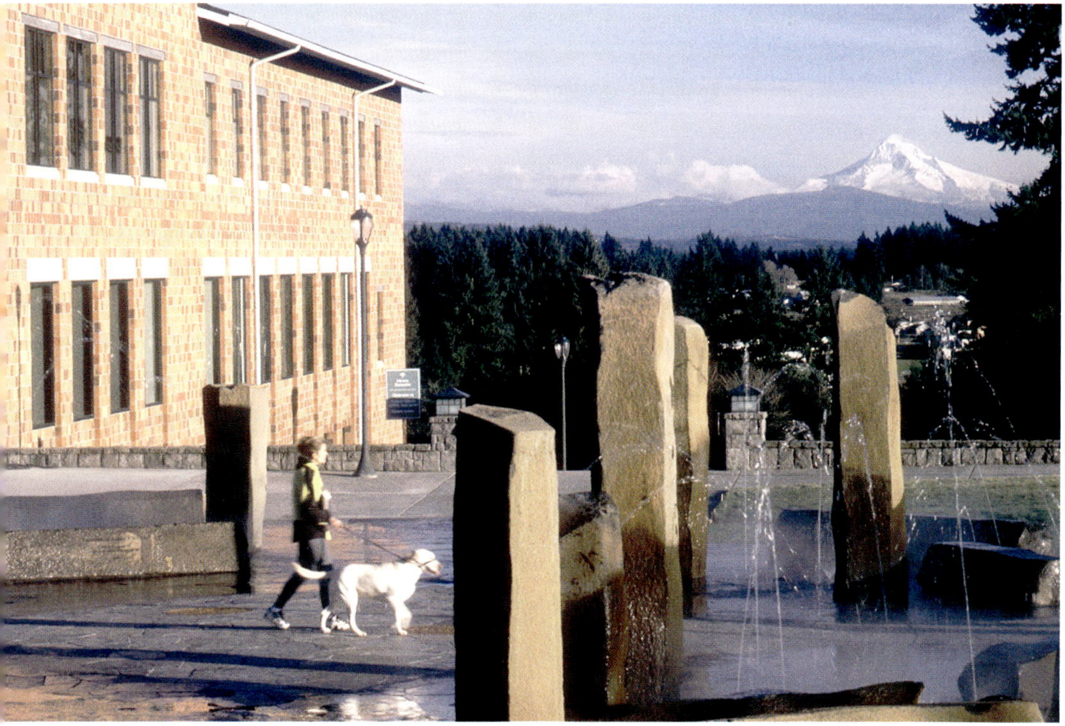

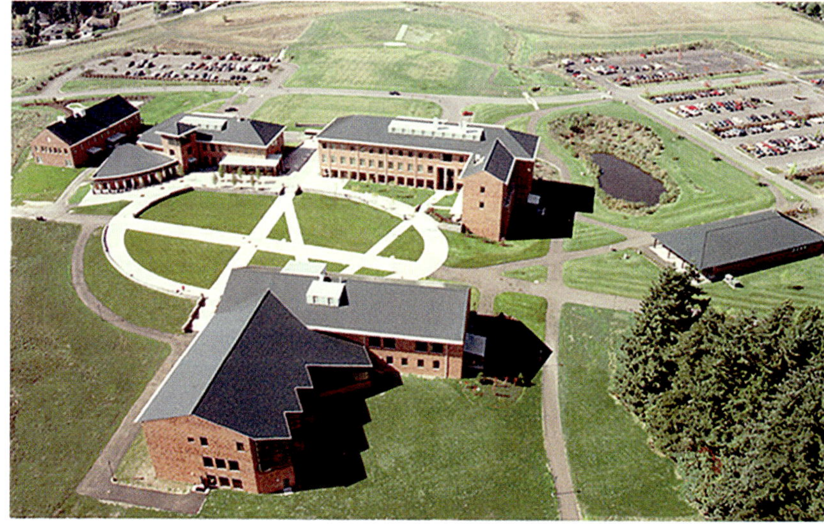

Firstenburg Fountain, the focal point of WSU Vancouver, with Oregon's Mount Hood in the distance.

WSU Vancouver in southwest Washington opened its Salmon Creek campus in 1996—with a bright future and plenty of room to grow. Today, more than 90 full-time faculty instruct 2,000 students in 15 bachelor's and 9 master's programs.

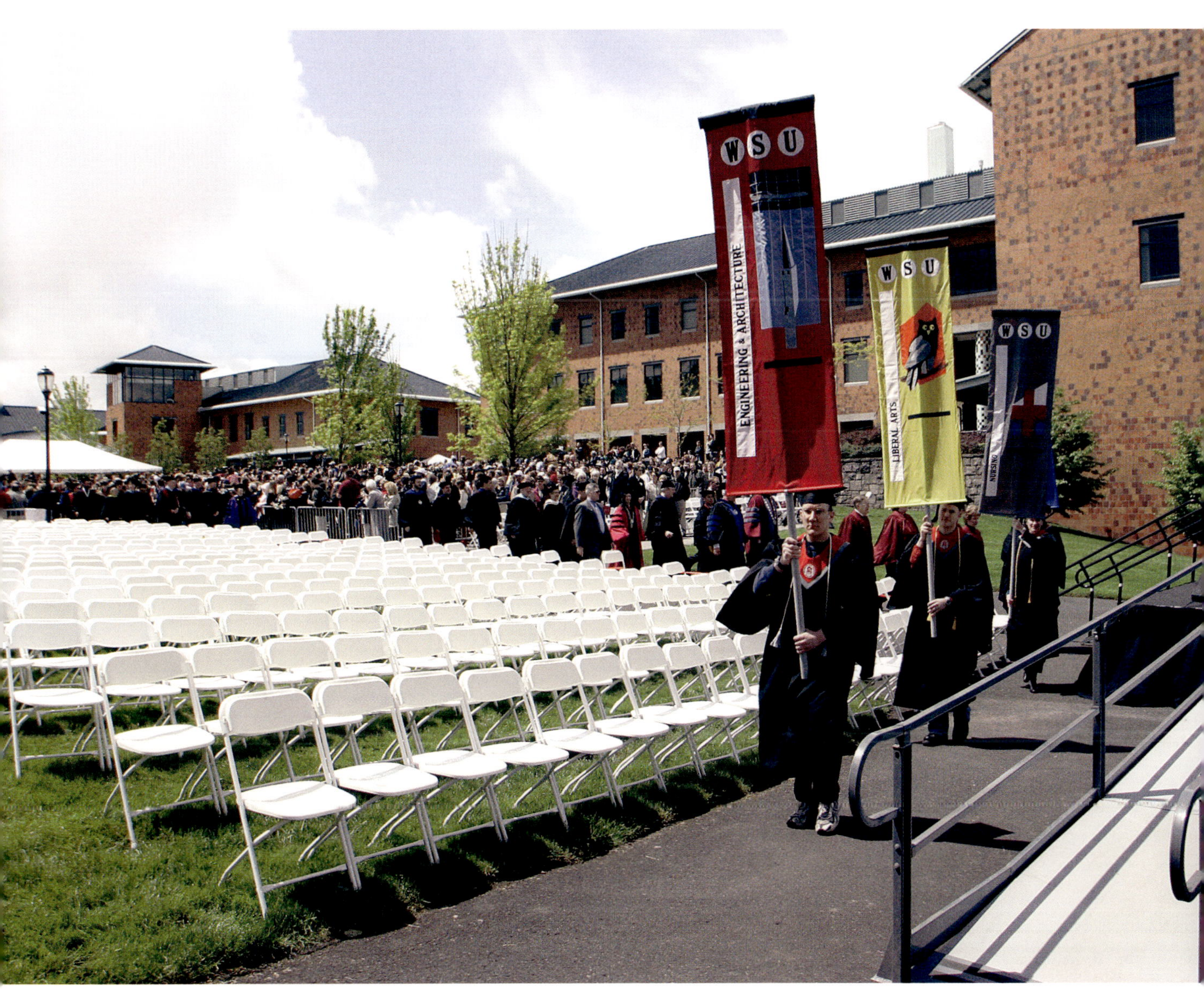

Commencement at WSU Vancouver.

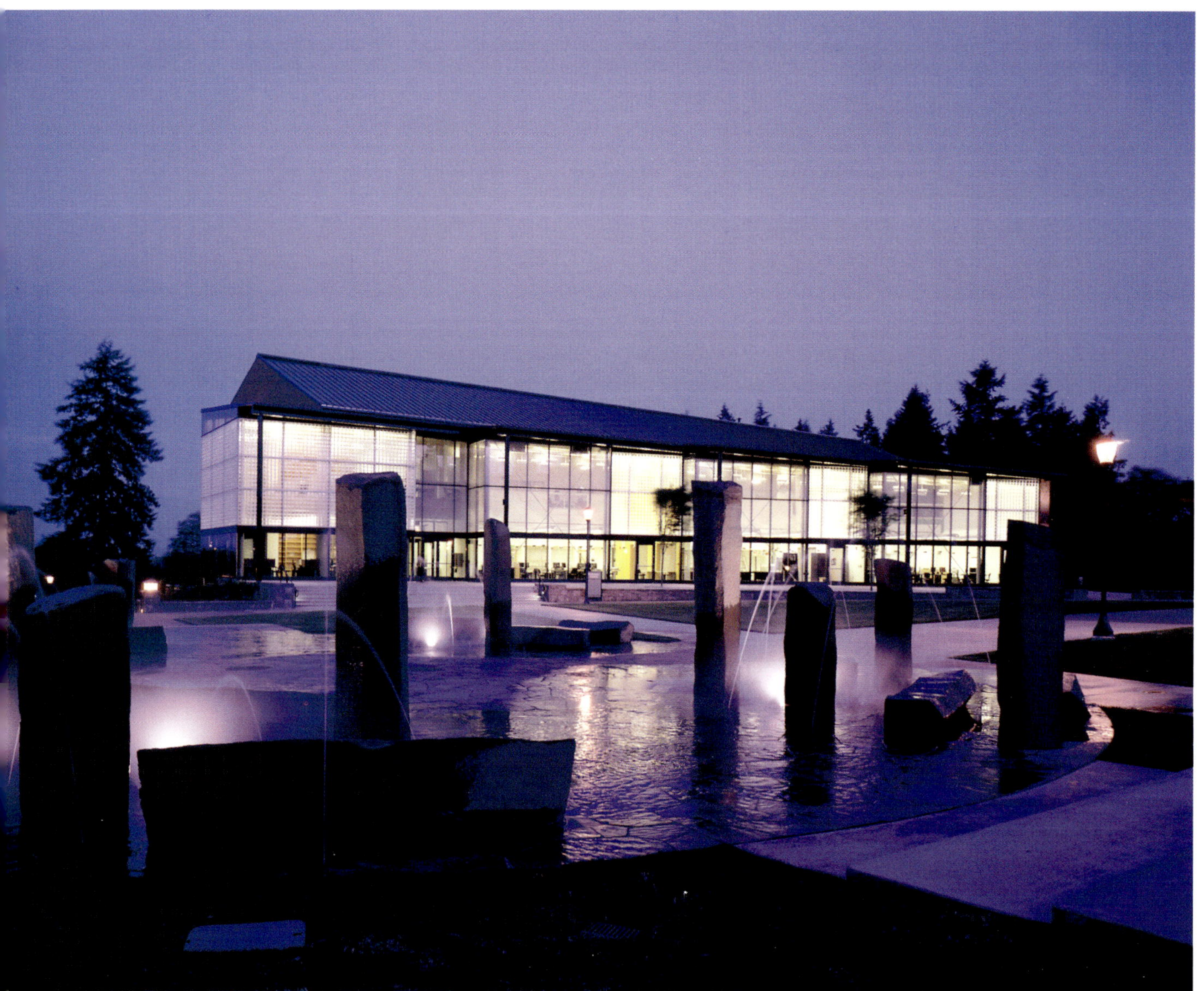

Multi-Media Classroom Building and the Firstenburg Fountain. In 2006, WSU Vancouver became a "four-year" institution, adding freshmen and sophomores to its normal transfer enrollment of juniors and seniors.

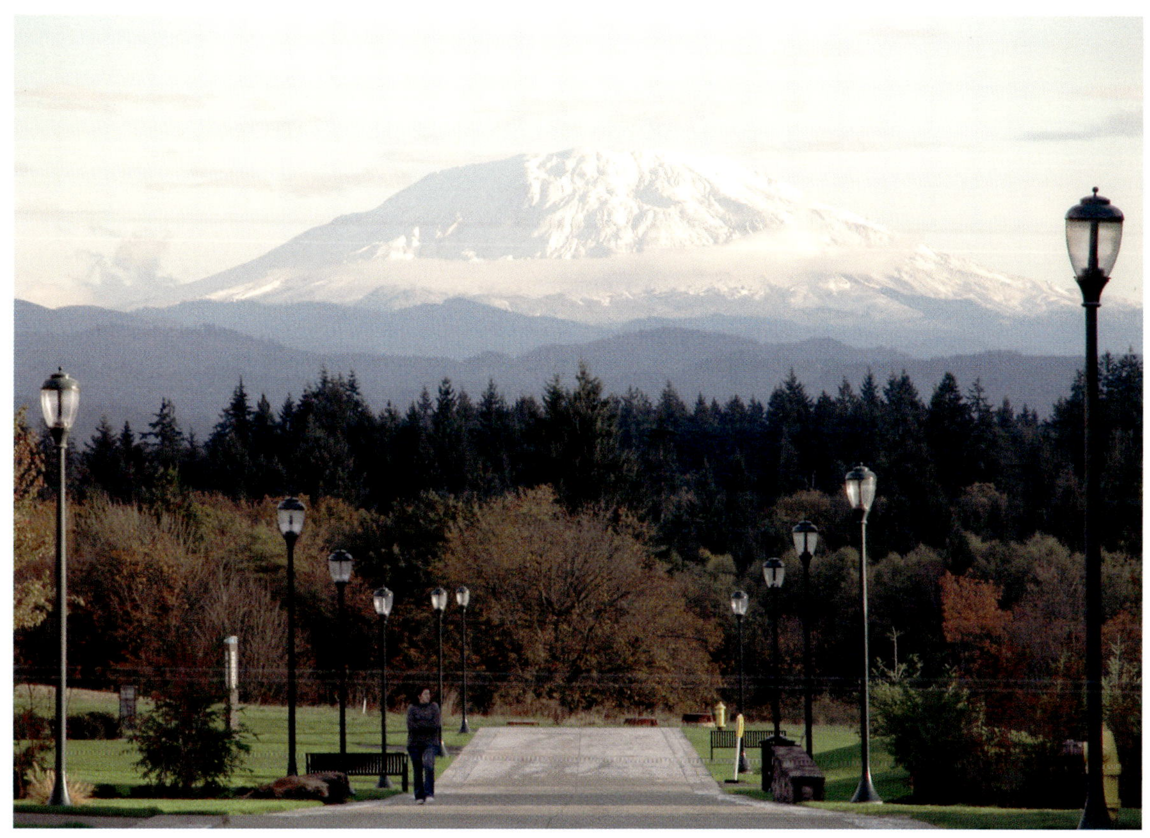

Situated on the north side of the City of Vancouver, the regional campus has an unparalleled view of Mount St. Helens.

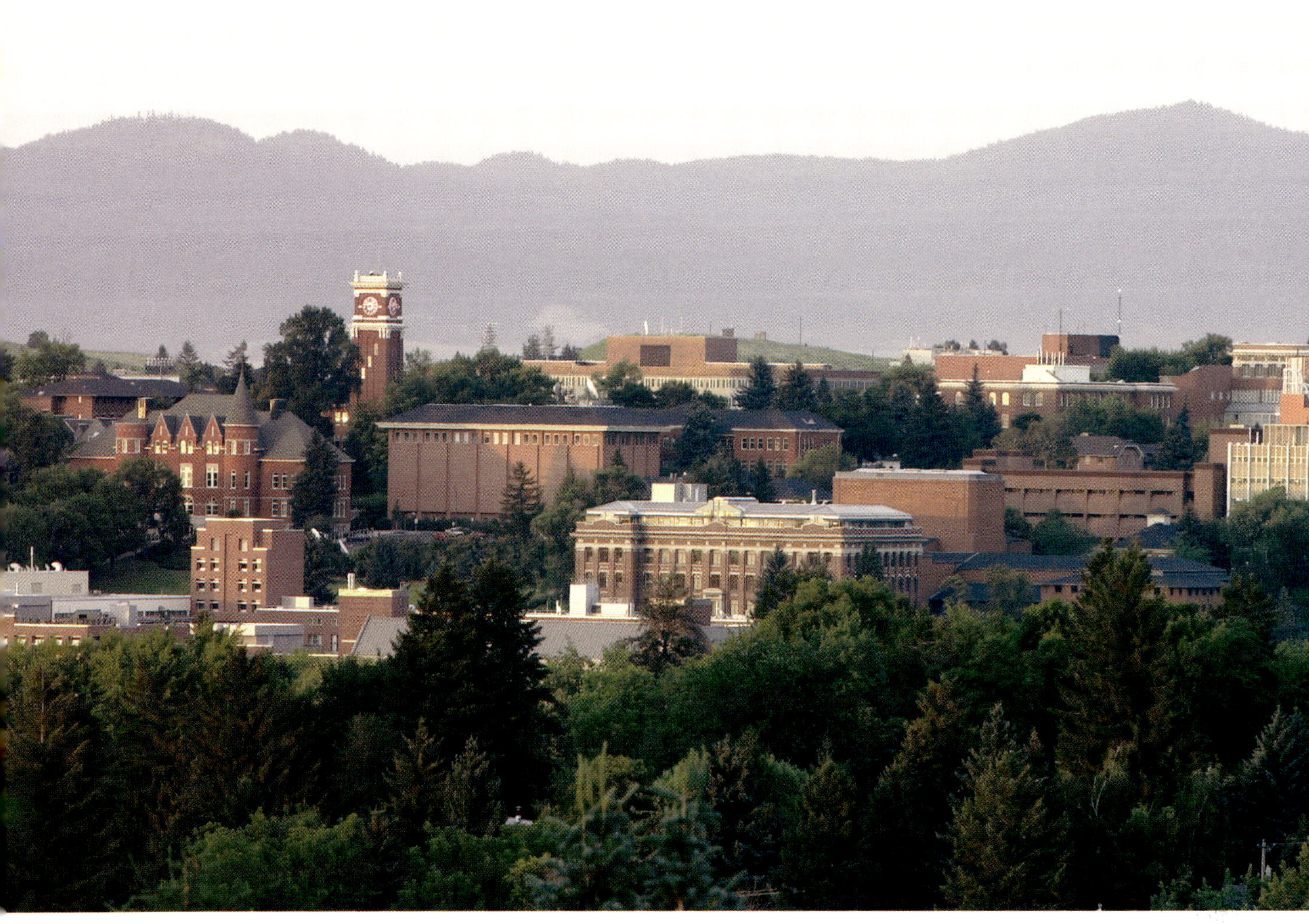

Looking east over the Pullman campus at sunset, with the familiar outline of Idaho's Moscow Mountain (4,988 ft.) in the distance.

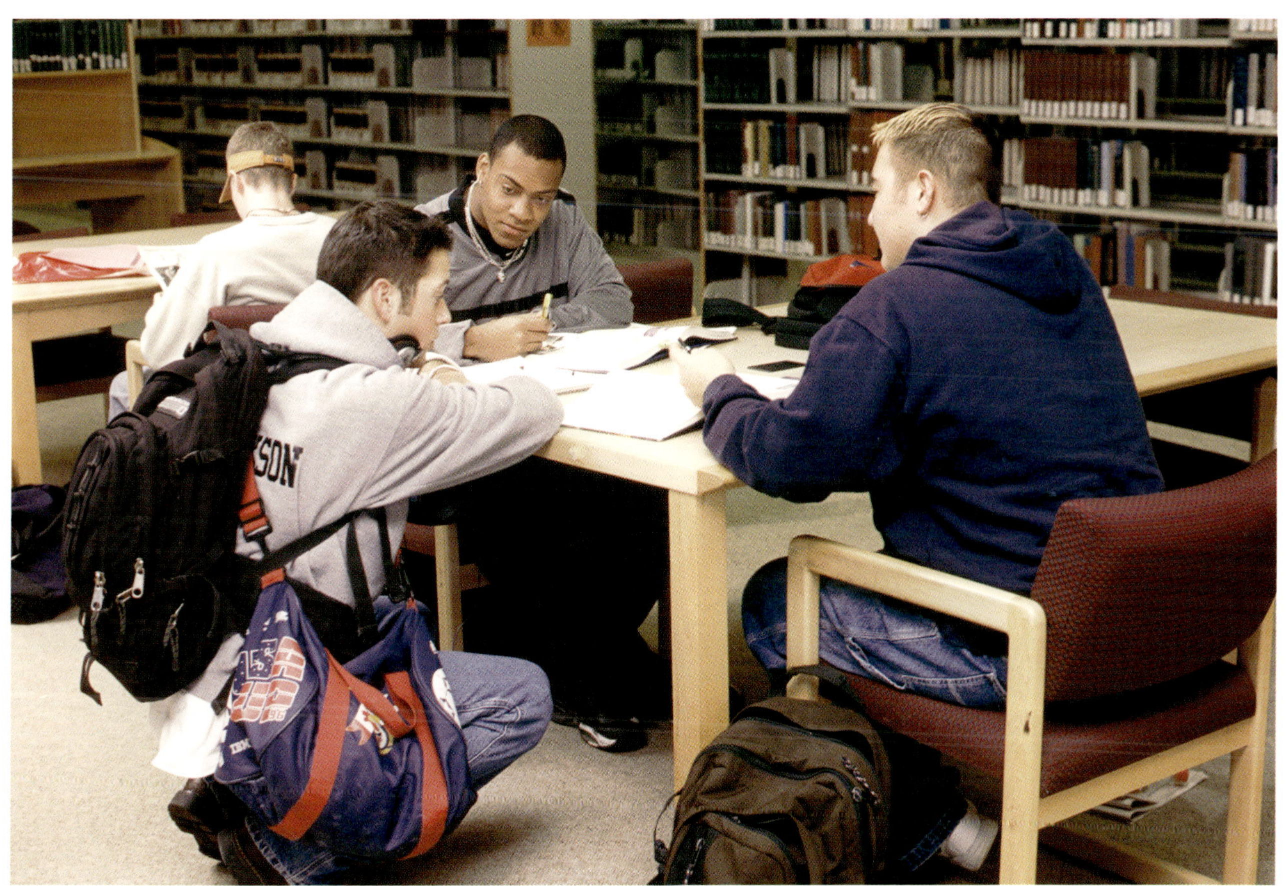

"How's it going?"—three students converse in Holland-Terrell Library.

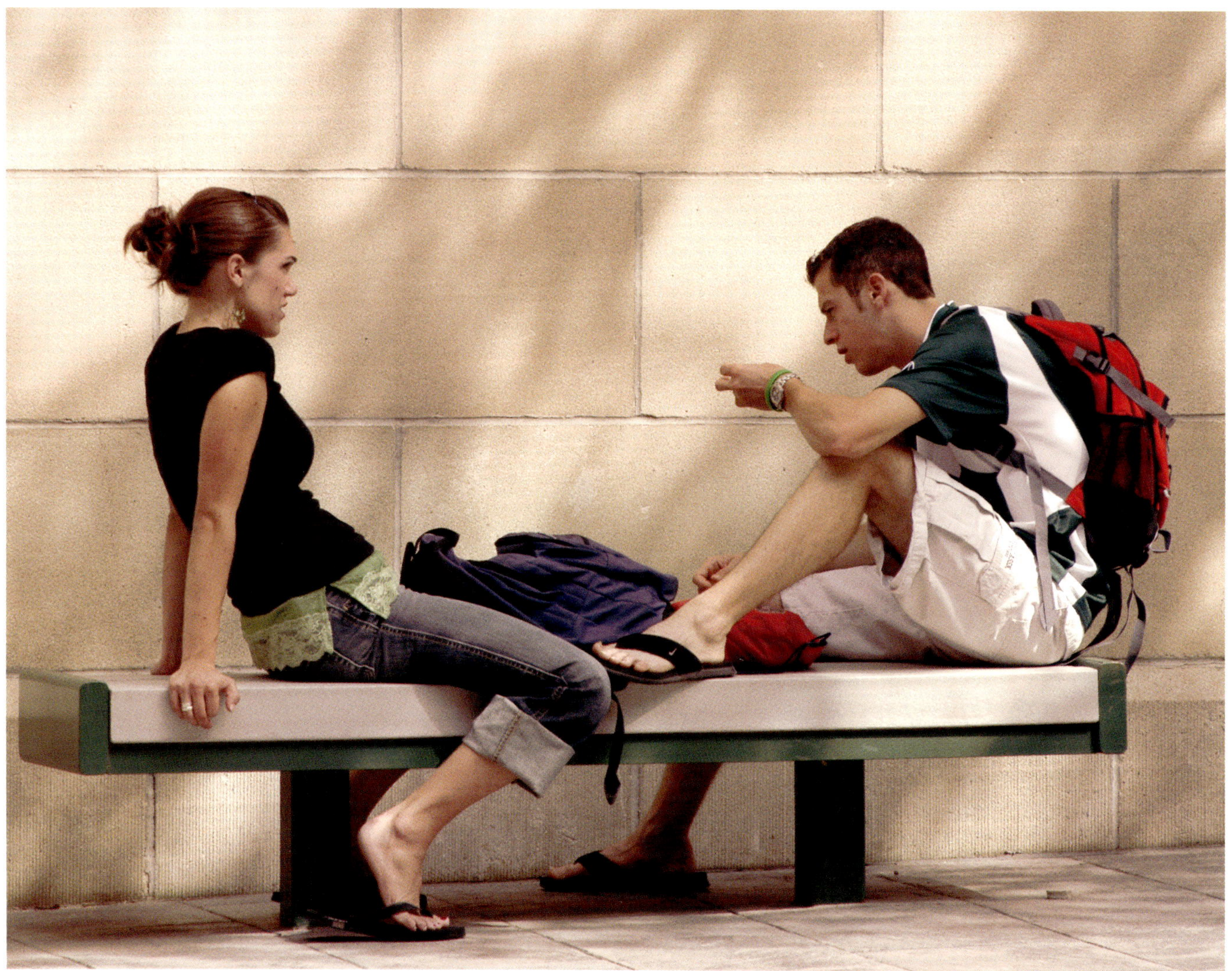

Private places for
conversation are
common across campus.

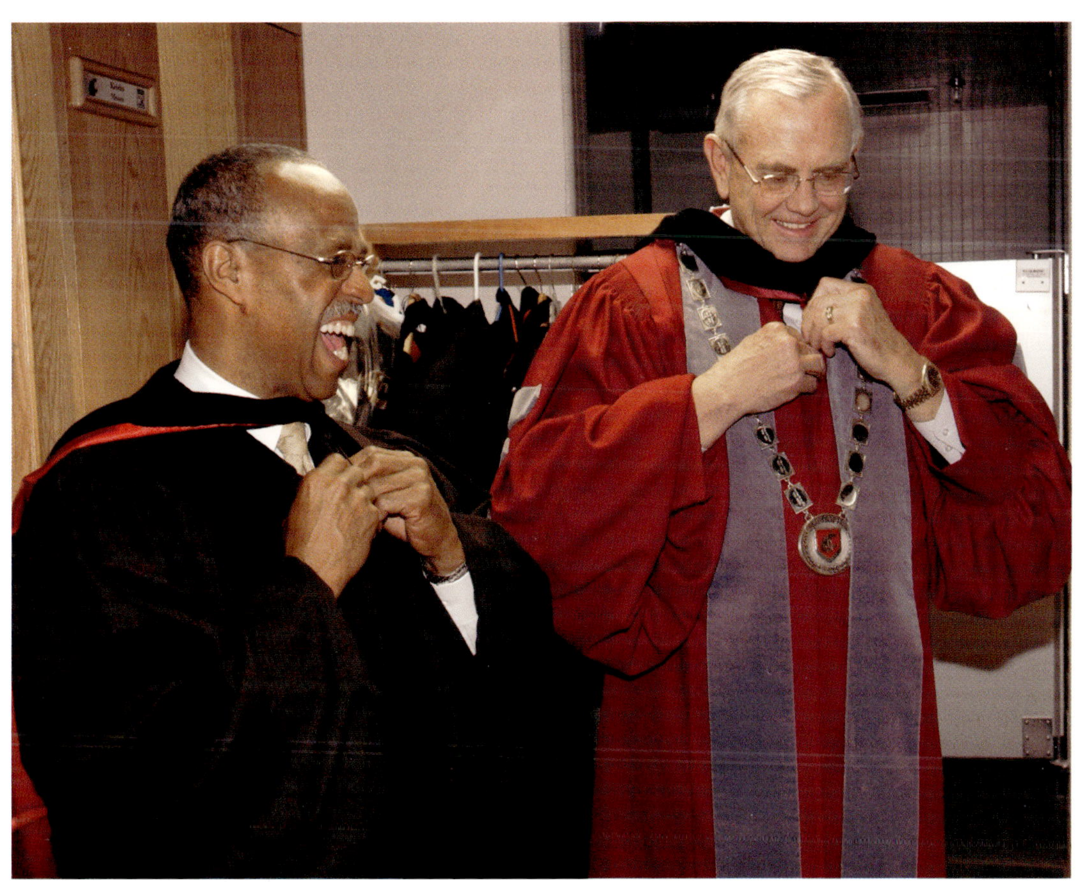

WSU President V. Lane Rawlins
and a regent prepare for the key
moment in the lives of hundreds
of students.

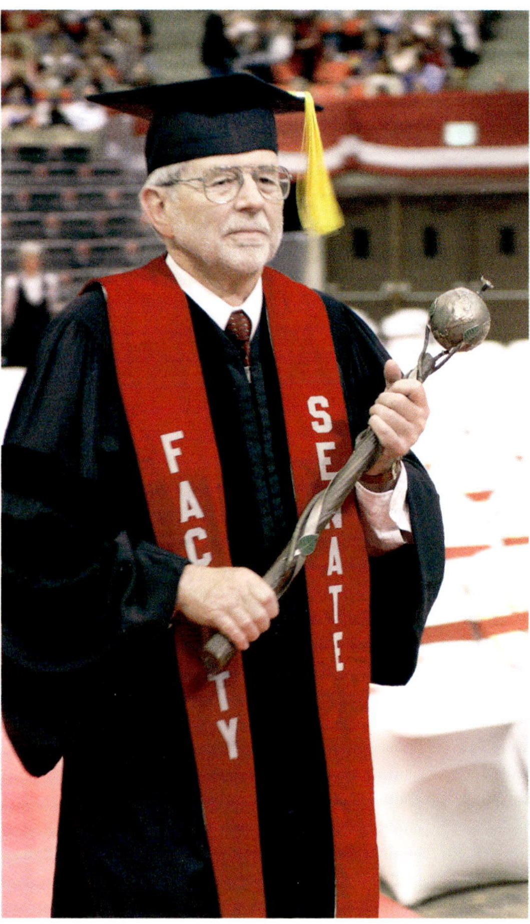

Chair of the Faculty Senate holding
the University Mace while leading
the academic procession at
Pullman's commencement.

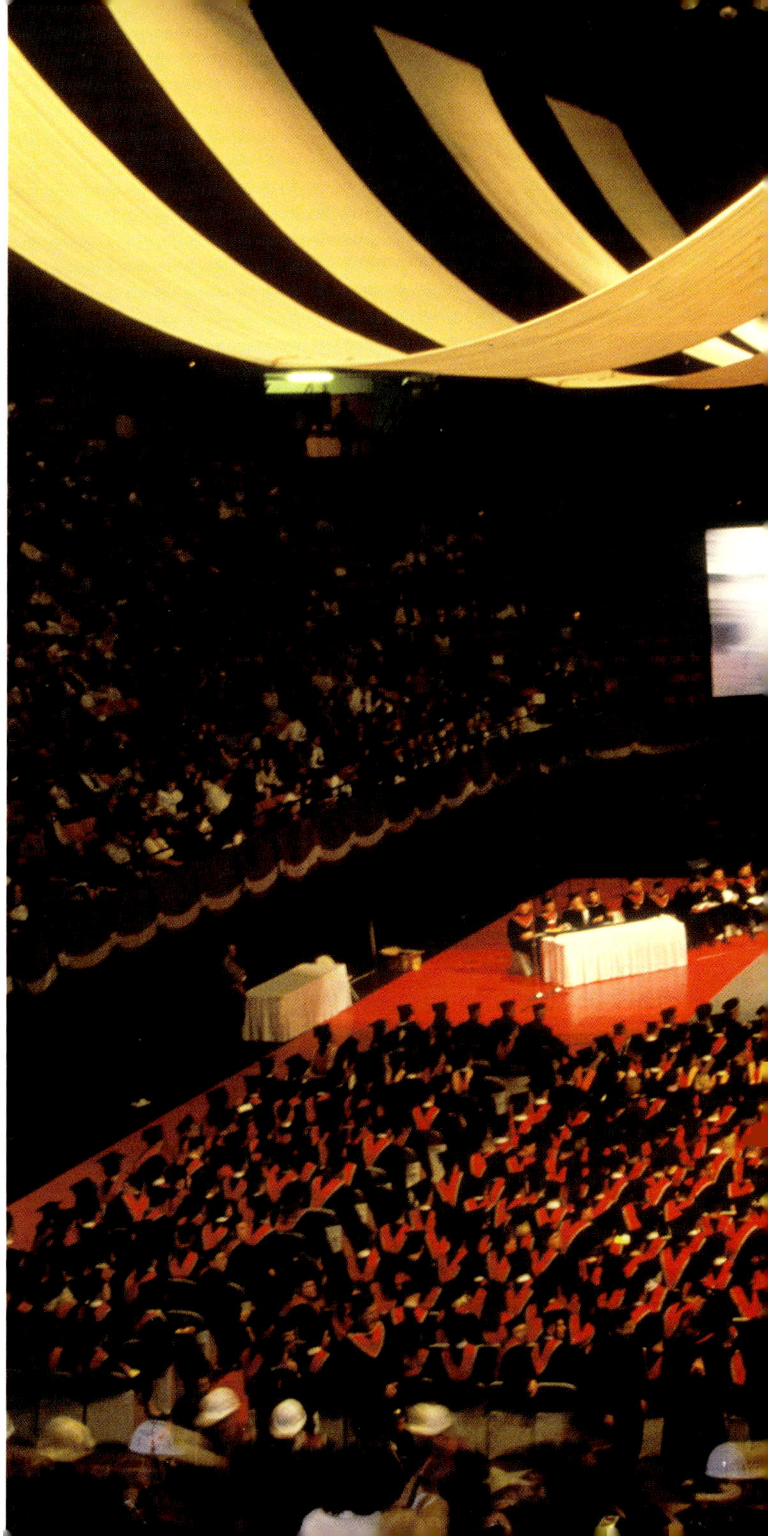

Graduation day in the
Beasley Performing Arts
Coliseum.

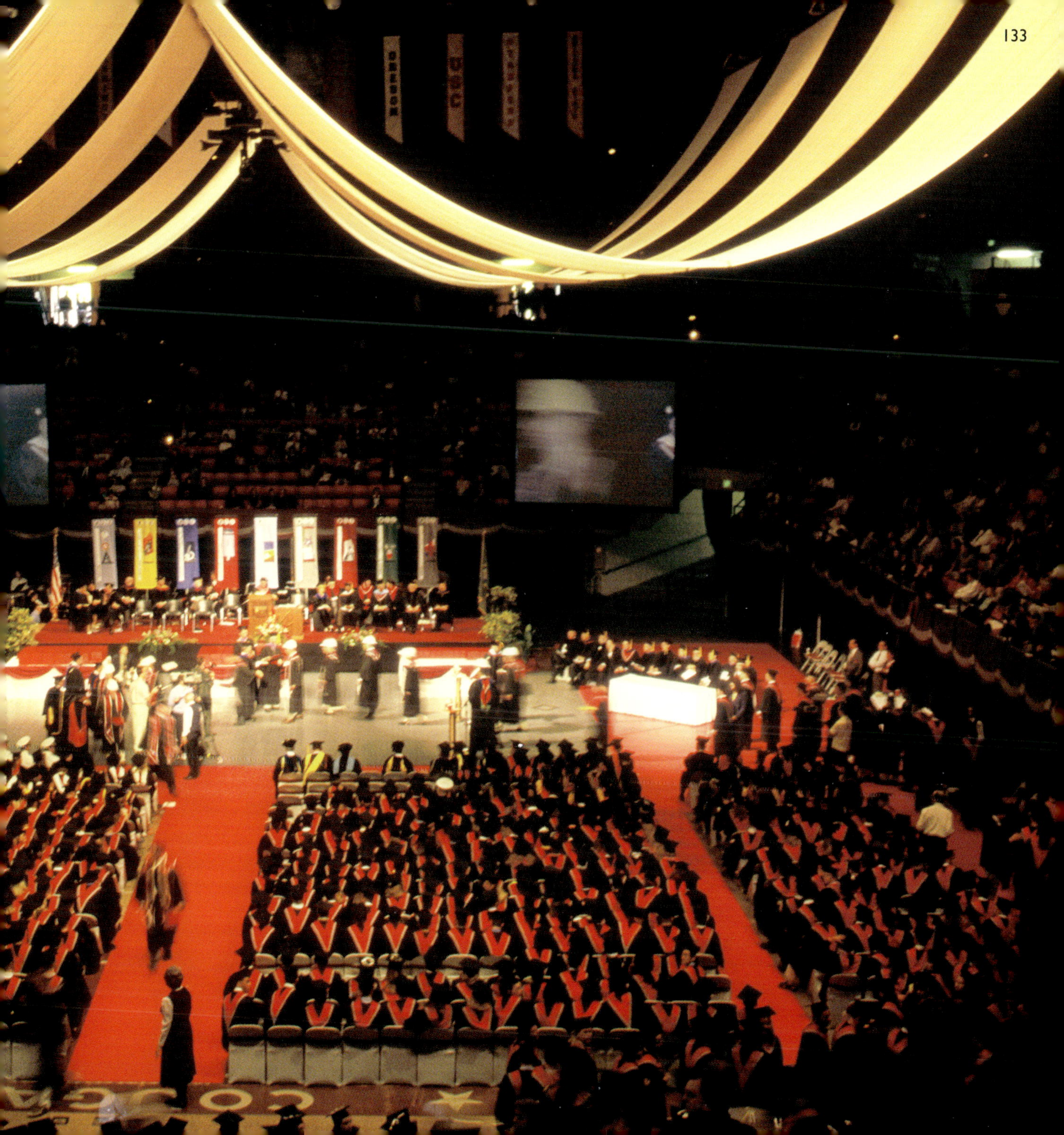

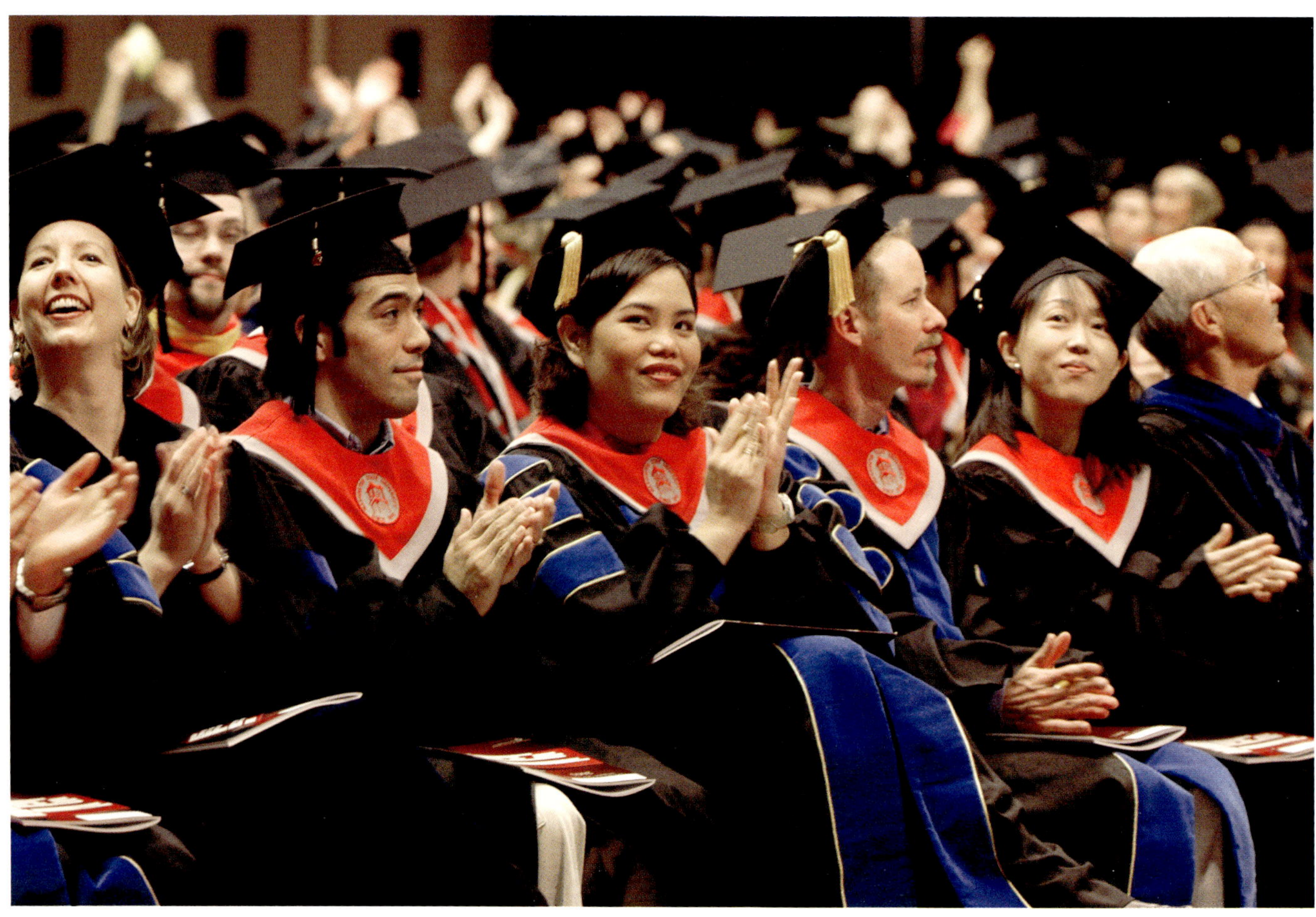

Graduate students await the
final culminating moment.

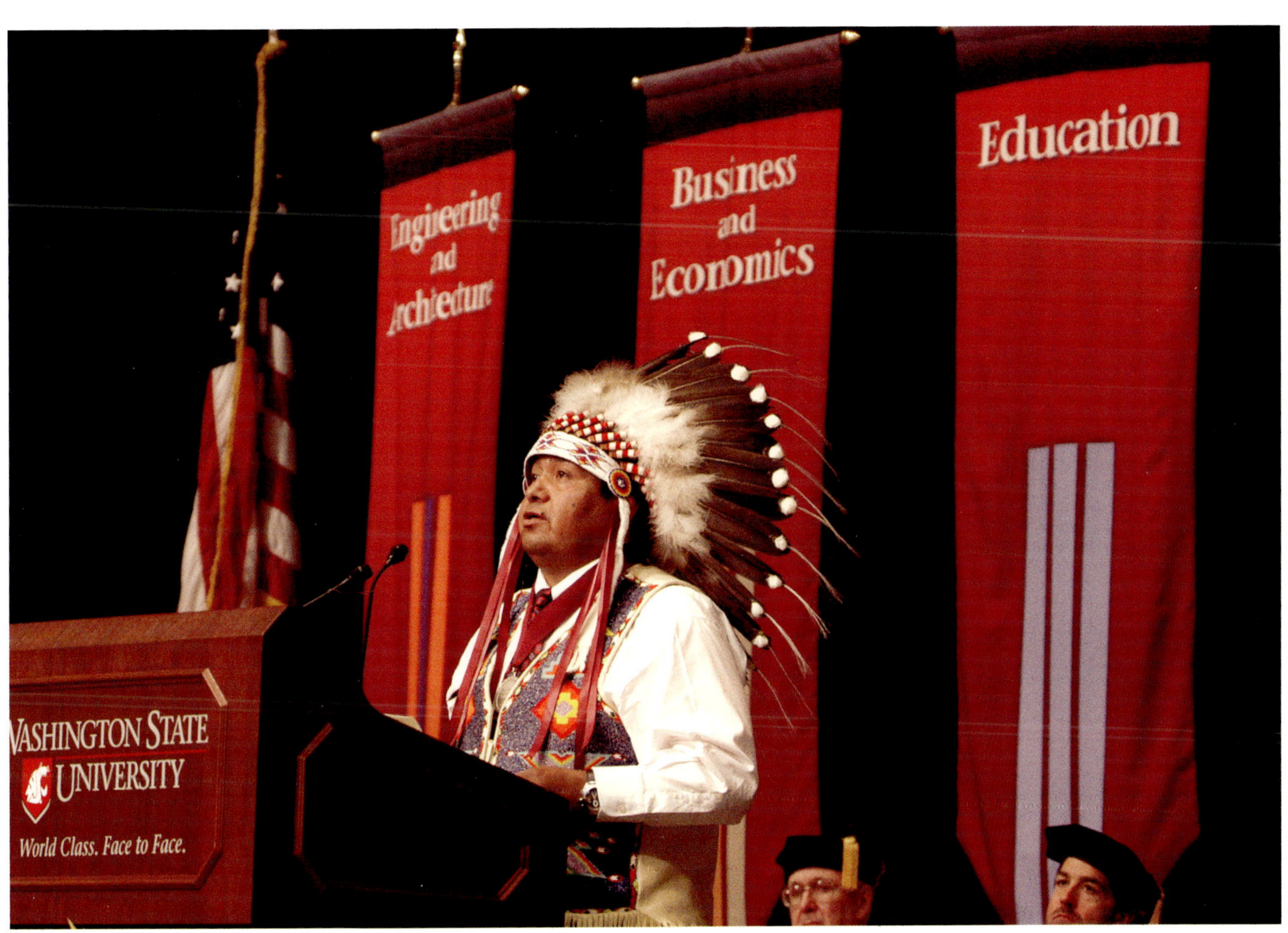

A WSU alumnus from the Warm Springs Confederated Tribes of Oregon addresses a commencement gathering.

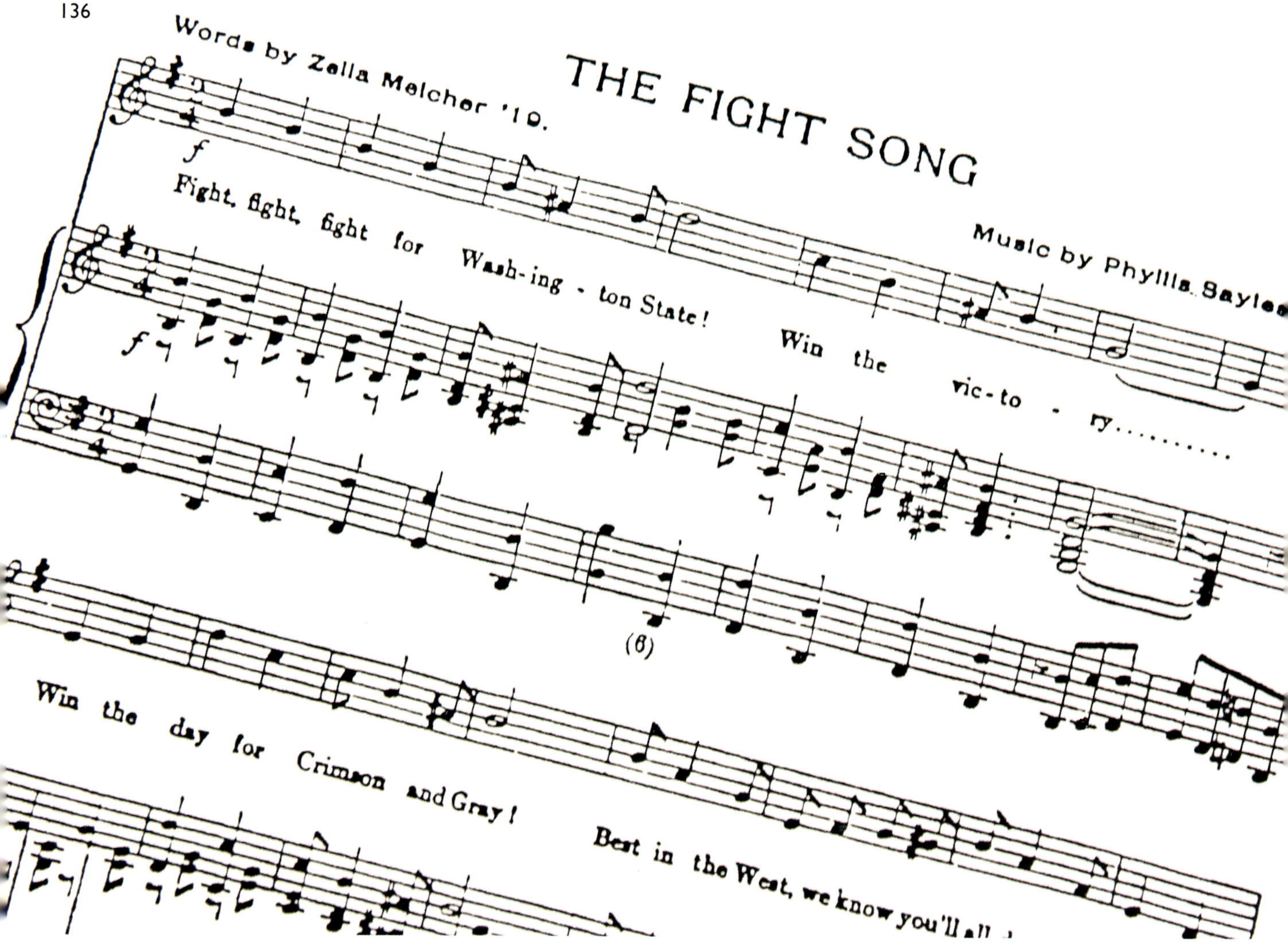

Words by Zella Melcher '10.

THE FIGHT SONG

Music by Phyllis Sayles

f

Fight, fight, fight for Wash-ing - ton State! Win the vic-to - ry........

(6)

Win the day for Crimson and Gray! Best in the West, we know you'll all...

Fight, fight, fight for Washington State! Win the Victory!
Win the day for Crimson and Gray! Best in the West,
*   we know you'll all do your best!*
So on, on, on, on! Fight to the end! Honor and glory
*   you must win!*
So fight, fight, fight for Washington State and victory!

The fight song was a class project in 1919 by music majors Zella Melcher (words) and Phyllis Sayles (music). The word "cougar" is not included as it was written six months prior to the selection of "Cougars" as the official mascot by the student body.

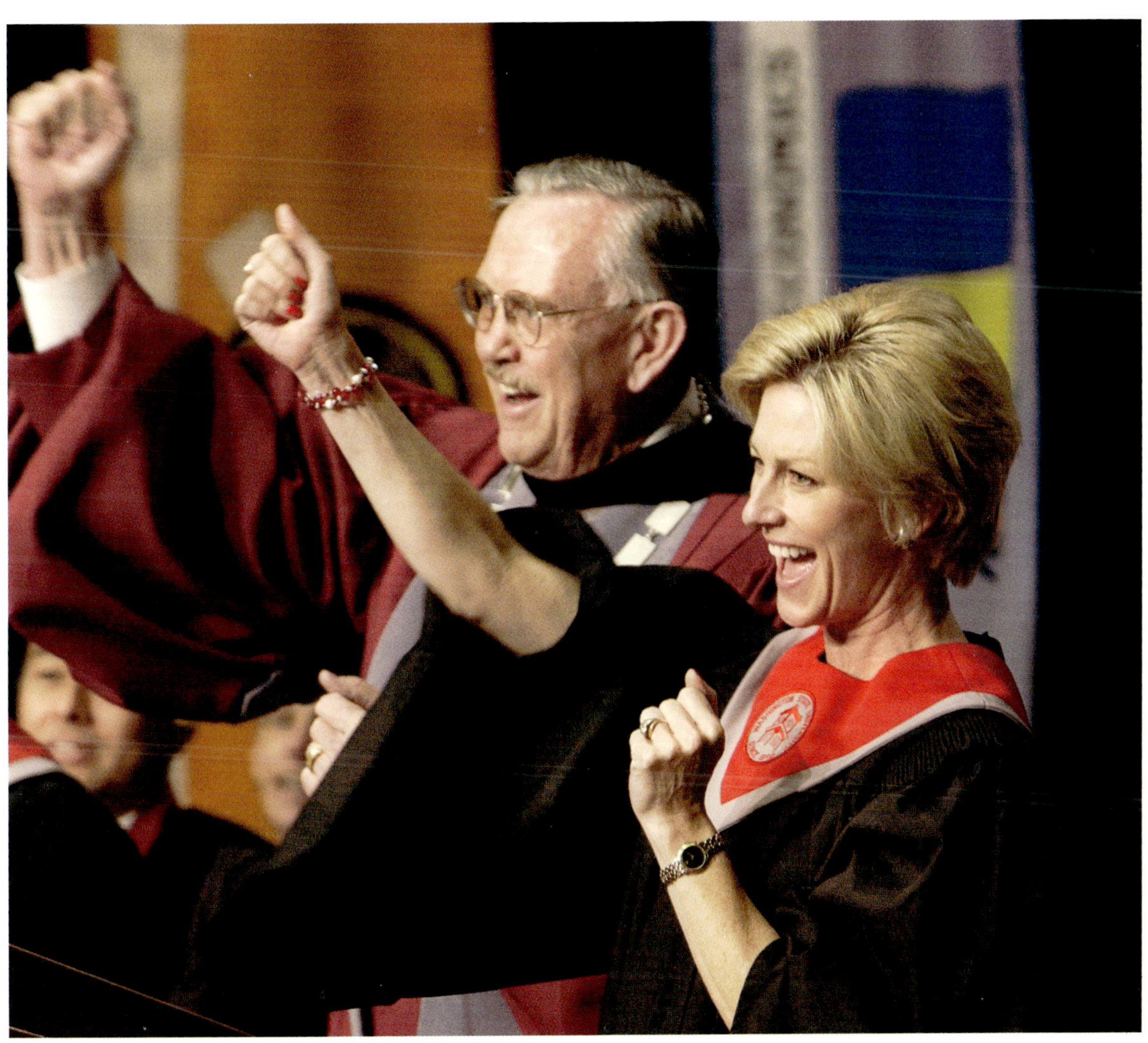

A broadcasting alumna and the WSU President lead the crowd in singing the WSU Fight Song.

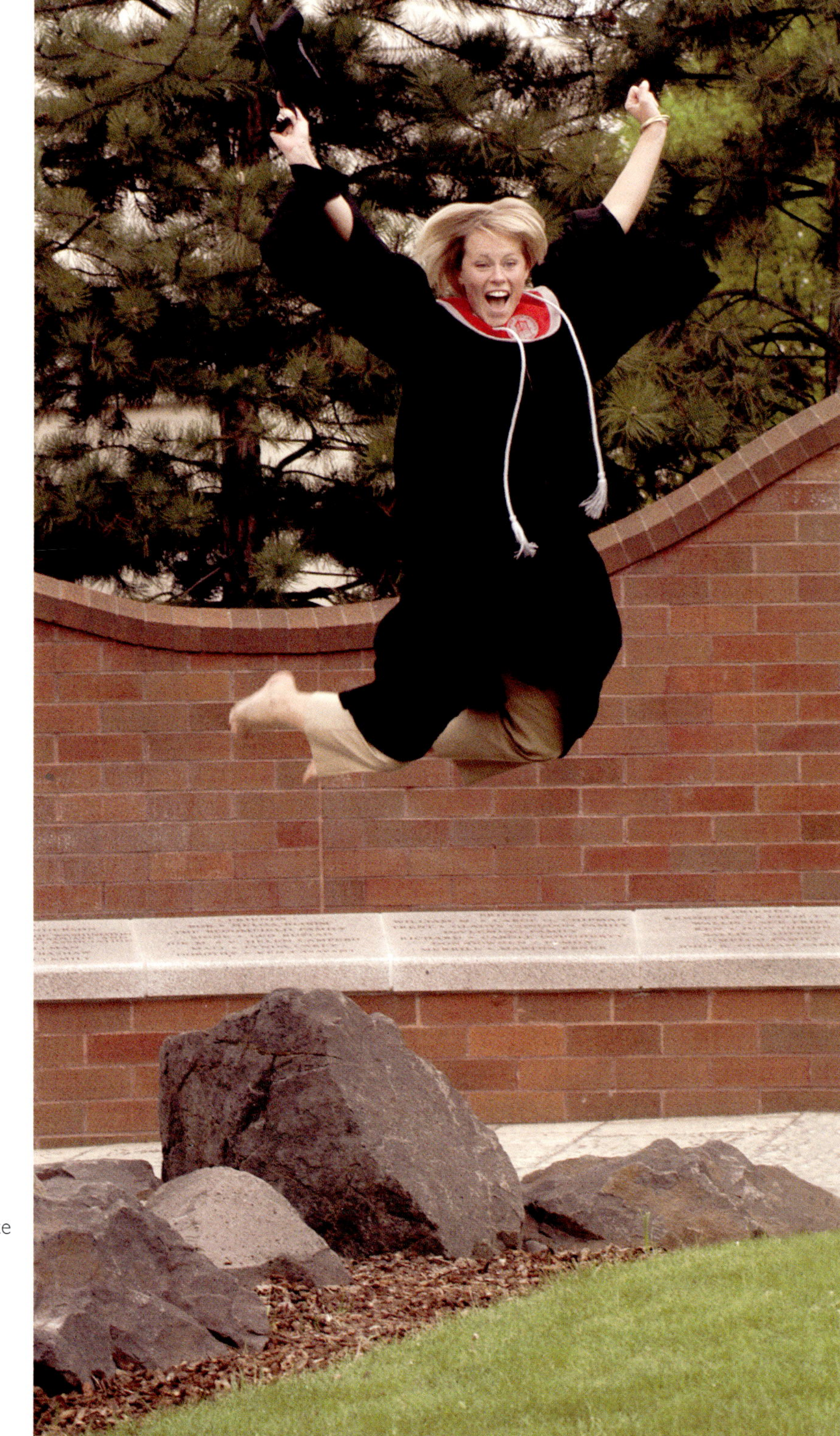

The exuberance
of graduation.

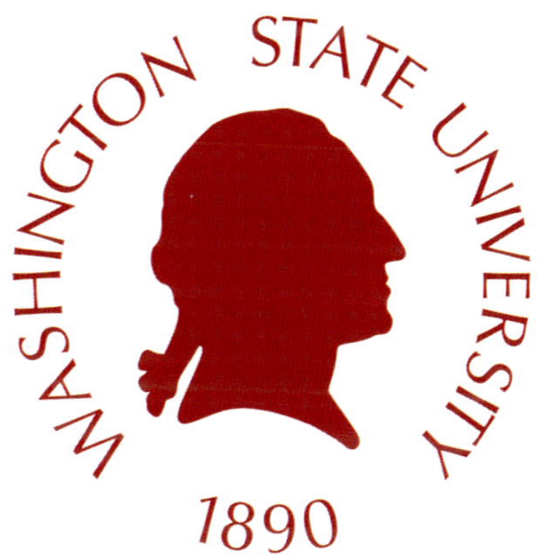

Photo Credits

1–2	Robert Hubner
3–7	Shelly Hanks
8	Robert Hubner
9	Shelly Hanks
10	Robert Hubner
11	Shelly Hanks
12–13	Jeff Lawton
14–16	Robert Hubner
17a	Shelly Hanks
17b	Robert Hubner
18	Shelly Hanks
19	Robert Hubner
20	Robert Hubner
21	Shelly Hanks
22	Henry Moore, Jr.
23	Robert Hubner
24–25	Henry Moore, Jr.
26–27	Shelly Hanks
28–29	Robert Hubner
30	Shelly Hanks
31	Robert Hubner
32a	Chris Mather
32b–33	Robert Hubner
34–35	Shelly Hanks
36–39	Shelly Hanks
40–41a	Robert Hubner
41b	Shelly Hanks
42	Dean Hare
43	Robert Hubner
44	Dean Hare
45	Shelly Hanks
46–50	Robert Hubner
51–53	Shelly Hanks
54–55	Robert Hubner
56a	John Snyder
56b	Shelly Hanks
57–59	Robert Hubner
60	Chris Mather
61a	Shelly Hanks
61b	Robert Hubner
62	John Snyder
63a	Robert Hubner
63b	Shelly Hanks
64	Robert Hubner
65–66	Shelly Hanks
67–69	Robert Hubner
70–71	Shelly Hanks
72–75	Robert Hubner
76	Shelly Hanks
77–78	Robert Hubner
79	Shelly Hanks
80	Robert Hubner
81	Yost Grube Hall Architecture
82–91	Robert Hubner
92–93	Shelly Hanks
94	Robert Hubner
95	Shelly Hanks
96–98	Robert Hubner
99–100	WSU Sports Information
101–2	Shelly Hanks
103	WSU Sports Information
104–5	Shelly Hanks
106–7	WSU Sports Information
108	Robert Hubner
109	WSU Sports Information
110a	Robert Hubner
110b	Shelly Hanks
111	Robert Hubner
112	Shelly Hanks
113	WSU Sports Information
114	Shelly Hanks
115	WSU Sports Information
116	Robert Hubner
117	Shelly Hanks
118	Courtesy WSU Spokane
119	Jeff T. Green
120	Robert Hubner
121–23	Courtesy WSU Tri-Cities
124–27	Courtesy WSU Vancouver
128–29	Robert Hubner
130	Shelly Hanks
131	Robert Hubner
132–35	Shelly Hanks
136	Robert Hubner
137–38	Shelly Hanks